Contents

Preface

Many people have contributed to the book in direct and indirect ways. The teachers and pupils at Ashton, Beechgrove and Cedars, for instance, allowed themselves to be studied and were never promised any tangible rewards for their courtesy and kindness. To them, especially the close collaborators who guided my journey into the world of the comprehensive school, I owe a particular debt of gratitude. As any author knows, there are those closer to home who also make sacrifices and indirectly contribute to the completion of the work. For this reason, and many others, **I would like to dedicate the book to my wife, Viv, to my son, Ben, to my mother, Kathleen, and to the memory of my father, Roy.** To each I owe a personal gratitude for putting me in a position to start, sustain and finish the study. Finally, I would like to thank the following editors for permission to draw on ideas I have explored in their books and journals: Peter Woods for material in *Teacher Strategies* and *Pupil Strategies* (both Croom-Helm, 1980); Len Barton in the case of discussions outlined in the *British Journal of Sociology of Education* (vol. 1, no. 3, 1980 and vol. 3, no. 3, 1982); Len Barton and Stephen Walker for material in *Social Crisis and Educational Research* (Croom-Helm, 1984); David Smetherham for material in *School Organization* (vol. 1, no. 3, 1981) and Stephen Ball for material in *Comprehensive School: a Reader* (Falmer Press).

MARTYN DENSCOMBE
Leicester, November 1984

0285232 DENSCOMBE M.   Classroom Control:
         1.86   A Sociological
         BW   Perspective.
                        7.50

371.1'624

-0. MAY 1986   COUNTY

Please renew/return this item by the last date shown.

So that your telephone call is charged at local rate, please call the numbers as set out below:

Classroom Control

Classroom Control

A Sociological Perspective

MARTYN DENSCOMBE

London
GEORGE ALLEN & UNWIN
Boston   Sydney

George Allen & Unwin (Publishers) Ltd,
40 Museum Street, London WC1A 1LU, UK

George Allen & Unwin (Publishers) Ltd,
Park Lane, Hemel Hempstead, Herts HP2 4TE, UK

Allen & Unwin, Inc.,
8 Winchester Place, Winchester, Mass. 01890, USA

George Allen & Unwin Australia Pty Ltd,
8 Napier Street, North Sydney NSW 2060, Australia

First published in 1985.

British Library Cataloguing in Publication Data
Denscombe, Martyn
   Classroom control: sociological perspective.
1. Classroom management
I. Title
371.1'024   LB3013

ISBN 0-04-371094-8
ISBN 0-04-371095-6 Pbk

Library of Congress Cataloging in Publication Data

Denscombe, Martyn.
   Classroom control.
Bibliography: p.
Includes index.
1. Classroom management.   2. Classroom environment.
I. Title.
LB3013.D467   1985   371.1'024   85–6152
ISBN 0-04-371094-8
ISBN 0-04-371095-6 (pbk.)

Set in 10 on 11 point Goudy by V & M Graphics Ltd, Aylesbury, Bucks
and printed in Great Britain
by Biddles Ltd, Guildford, Surrey

If I am to help others to gain any usable insight, I must show them the school as it really is. I must not attack the school, nor talk over-much about what ought to be, but only about what is.

Willard Waller (1932)
The Sociology of Teaching (pp. v-vi)

Introduction:
A Sociological Perspective

Classroom control may not appear on the school curriculum but people learn a great deal about it at school. In practice, they can hardly avoid getting wise to the 'ins' and 'outs' of classroom control because it is one of the most fundamental and pervasive features of school life. Teachers know it, pupils know it, the public knows it. It is not surprising, then, that plenty has been written on the subject. Some of it deals with the question of what causes some pupils to pose control difficulties (the psychological disorders or cultural/family problems suffered by the pupil) and some of it gives advice to teachers on methods for achieving classroom control (how to manage the classroom or deal with pupils in a way which minimizes the prospect of control problems). Indeed the bulk of writing on classroom control falls into these categories or an amalgam of the two. What is largely missing, however, is detailed research on the actual phenomenon of classroom control dealing with:

(1)   Why classroom control is a feature of classrooms in the first place?
(2)   What resources are available to the teacher to impose control, and by what means pupils can resist?
(3)   What social, institutional and physical features of the classroom shape the struggle for control?
(4)   Exactly what significance classroom control has for teachers in terms of their careers and their perception of their work? and, very importantly,
(5)   How classroom control is recognized as existing or not existing in the classroom by participants?

These are the kinds of questions which this book sets out to answer.

A sociology of classroom control

Since teachers spend a considerable part of their working day trying to achieve and consolidate classroom control[1], there is no shortage of informed writing on the subject[2]. What is interesting, however, is that the vast majority of such writing is based upon two important assumptions.

First, it is generally assumed that threats to the exercise of classroom control are an educational malaise – a problem for which remedies need to be sought. Second, it is generally assumed that what constitutes classroom control is really quite obvious and self-evident – the important task being to analyse and cure the problem rather than describe how it is recognized and negotiated by those involved. Both these assumption are evident in the spectrum of problems and remedies outlined in Figure I.1.

The approach of this book, though, is characteristically a *sociological* one. A sociological approach, like the others, is based on a set of key assumptions – assumptions which ought to be made explicit at the outset because they will inevitably have a bearing on the kinds of things that are seen as relevant for describing and analysing the phenomenon and, by the same token, the kinds of things that are left to one side and excluded from the picture. We need to recognize straight away, then, that by adopting a sociological approach to the area of classroom control the book tends to contrast with the mainstream of writing on the subject in the way it treats *description and analysis* of the phenomenon as its principal task rather than providing prescriptions for curing the problem. While the description and analysis will almost inevitably suggest remedies, these remedies will remain conclusions to be drawn from the study rather than its *raison d'etre*. To aid the description and analysis, the book draws on detailed *empirical research*. Evidence is taken from a variety of published studies and from ethnographic research in three comprehensive schools spanning a period of six years; two large inner-city schools in London and a community college in Leicestershire. 'Ashton'[3] in the London Borough of Brent and 'Beechgrove', an Inner London Education Authority (ILEA) school in Camden, were taken as representative of schools facing the problems of inner-city schools and, in both cases, they adopted a fairly conventional organization. 'Cedars', on the other hand, was recently built and is sited in a village outside Leicester. It was notably progressive in its organization and methods and its setting bore marked contrast with the urban sites of Ashton and Beechgrove. Between them, the three schools provide case-study material that, when used in conjunction with existing literature on classroom control, shed light on the phenomenon. It should be clear from the start, then, that the focus of attention is on *secondary* rather than primary education.

Considerable emphasis is also place on *teachers's perceptions* of classroom control. As we can see from Figure I.1, the literature contains a number of approaches to classroom control, each stressing different causes and remedies to 'the problem' and each with its particular strengths and weaknesses, but there is one facet of 'the problem' that these approaches leave largely untouched – teacher perceptions of classroom

PSYCHOPATHOLOGY	where the cause of the problem resides in the pupil and the emotional disturbance the pupil manifests.
Policy Recommendations:	special schools/units, counselling, therapy, behaviour modification.
CULTURAL MALAISE	where the root of the problem is to be found in the failings of the family or community to provide support for the exercise of authority in schools.
Policy Recommendations:	improved contact between school and community; involvement of welfare services.
PUPIL COUNTER-CULTURE	where resistance to authority in schools involves a conscious reaction against the dominant system at school.
Policy Recommendations:	incorporation of pupil counter-culture(s) into mainstream school culture; match curriculum to interests of pupils.
CRISIS OF SOCIAL CONTROL	where control problems experienced in schools are seen as symptomatic of a wider legitimation crisis and the impending disintegration of the (capitalist) social formation.
Policy Recommendations:	the radical revision of social structure.
RESOURCES	where disruption is attributed to poor facilities (buildings and equipment) and the need for increased numbers of teachers.
Policy Recommendations:	improved resources; positive discrimination.
SCHOOLING	where compulsory attendance and the hidden curriculum generate resistance in their own right.
Policy Recommendations:	deschooling.
POOR QUALITY OF TEACHERS	where control problems are attributed to teachers' lack of preparation, motivation or charisma.
Policy Recommendations:	improved selection and training of teachers.

Figure I.1   *Explanations of control problems in the classroom*

control. In this book, such perceptions are treated as a vital part of the picture and there is, therefore, a marked contrast with those analyses which have tended to assume that what constitutes 'disruption' is self-evident and which go ahead to focus attention on the causes of that kind of behaviour – causes such as psychological disturbance (Blackham, 1967; White and Charry, 1966), social background (Linton, 1966; Sugarman, 1967), organizational career (Cicourel and Kitsuse, 1963, 1968; D.H.Hargreaves, 1967; Lacey 1970), the inadequacy of teachers (Cox and Boyson 1975) and techniques of classroom management (Kounin, 1970). Such analyses attempt to specify the causes of disruptive behaviour at the expense of considering how that behaviour comes to be understood as disruptive in the first place.

Teacher perceptions, of course, cannot be considered in isolation from pupil perceptions since teachers and pupils are both parties to the interaction that gives rise to the phenomenon of classroom control. But although pupils are recognized as active participants in classroom control and are certainly not excluded from the scene, the thrust of the analysis concerns teachers more than pupils. The reason for this is that it is teachers who actually instigate classroom control in the first place. The onus is on the teachers, not the pupils, to establish and maintain control (if for no other reason because teachers receive an official mandate to control as part of their job) and it is they who tend to be the active proponents of classroom control while pupils tend to react to whatever measures are taken by teachers in their efforts to secure control of the class.

The book will also be concerned with the *social causes* of the phenomenon as the basis for explaining the incidence and nature of control 'problems' rather than, for instance, looking towards emotional disorders in the individual pupil or examining the personal capabilities of particular teachers. So, while recognizing that control problems in the classroom can owe something to the psychological state of individual pupils in the class, the perspective adopted in this book does not treat the actual psychological state as the crucial point for explaining problems of classroom control. While recognizing that problems of classroom control can be caused sometimes by the personality of particular teachers or their particular failings, again, we do not treat this as a basis for an explanation of such problems. Both factors, pupil characteristics and teacher characteristics, certainly have some bearing on the issue but if we were to focus on them we would miss perhaps the most striking aspect of the phenomenon of classroom control – its pervasiveness as a feature of classroom interaction, not limited to the presence of 'disturbed' pupils or inadequate teachers.

The 'social causes' of classroom control exist at two different levels that are usually associated with the terms 'macro' and 'micro', and this book is further selective in its emphasis on the latter, the 'micro', as its main focus of attention. The 'macro' perspective, for its part, treats classroom control as a feature of a broader *social control* and takes the line that to explain the existence and nature of classroom control we need to examine the functions it serves for the maintenance of the status quo in society. There are two politically diverse strands to this viewpoint: the conservative 'functionalist' perspective[4] and the radical 'marxian' perspective.[5] Both share the view that the role of education in advanced capitalism is not simply to instil specific skills nor even just to select and allocate individuals within the (hierarchical) social order. As well as these functions, the education system also serves to perpetuate the existing social structure by fostering a diffuse set of beliefs and experiences which both *prepares* the pupils for the work situation they are being channelled towards and *legitimizes* their allocation to particular stations in life on the basis of their educational success or failure. For both radical and conservative there is a *correspondence* between the needs of society and the nature of schooling in which classroom control plays a vital part. It is a crucial element of the 'hidden curriculum' of schooling that prepares pupils to slot into the existing order of things. Through their schooling, it is argued, pupils experience pressure to adopt attitudes involving deference to authority, acceptance of depersonalized treatment, post-ponement of immediate pleasure to achieve long-term goals, patience and tolerance of boredom, and punctuality. Pupils are, in effect, trained to meet the needs of (capitalist) industry for a passive, polite and punctual labour force through the kinds of demands they face in school under the guise of 'discipline and control'. And teachers, of course, play an important role in this subjugation of the pupils. From the marxian perspective,

> Teachers act as political agents of capital, or perform the global function of capital, through their work of control and surveillance specifically through acting as bearers of relations of political dominance over pupils; through performing police-type and bureaucratic-type activities; by controlling the schooling process; through inculcating particular norms, habits, values and attitudes in pupils; and through their role in the certification and selection processes of schooling.
>
> (Harris, 1982, p. 129)

These perspectives on the broader social functions of classroom control certainly have their value. They provide an analysis of the phenomenon which spotlights the causes and repercussions of classroom control at a societal level and this offers the prospect of a political critique of the nature and desirability of classroom control. Weighed against this, however, the macro perspective also faces two limitations. First, the theoretical premise that there is necessarily a 'correspondence' between the needs of (capitalist) society and the attitudes and values instilled in pupils through schooling is hard to match with the empirical evidence that suggests (a) that passivity is not instilled in all of the pupils all of the time (with the result that pupils actually resist classroom control despite the societal needs) and (b) that those most active in resistance are the very ones whose life or work experience is most in need of 'deference to authority', 'tolerance of boredom', and so on – in effect, the working-class pupils.

As A. Hargreaves (1982) has indicated, the main response to this lack of empirically substantiated correspondence has been to posit either a 'relative autonomy' of the education system, in which case there only needs to be a direct correspondence 'in the last instance', or to suggest that such pupil resistance is actually a genuine rejection of the dominant capitalist ideology in line with the dialectical tensions and inconsistencies we would expect to find in society (e.g. Apple, 1982; Giroux,1981).The marxists, in other words, have recognized the fact that pupil resistance to classroom control is endemic and have consequently modified the correspondence theory in a way that now acknowledges pupil resistance and treats it as a counter-hegemonic force (cf. Gramsci, 1971) – as a real and positive threat to the dominant ideology as it gets articulated in schools in the form of classroom control. As A. Hargreaves points out, though, attempts to demonstrate that pupil resistance in school constitutes a 'penetration' of the dominant ideology actually fall rather short of being convincing. This is because their interpretation of the data on pupil resistance tends to be coloured somewhat by a strong theoretical/political commitment, and their focus on what classroom control *does* in terms of social control almost inevitably leads them to concentrate on the outcomes of action rather than the intention of actors. They are, by their very nature, less attuned to the (more characteristically Weberian) task of exploring the motives and intentions of the actors. The problem here is that, whereas some pupil resistance to teacher control might well be inspired by the wish to challenge existing structural relations in society, for the most part this is patently not the case. And while some instances of teacher activity might be consciously directed towards maintaining or transforming wider structural relations, ethnographic works reveals quite unequivocally that these are the exception rather than the norm. On the vast majority of occasions, the efforts of teachers to control pupils and the resistance by pupils to those efforts are inspired by far more parochial, practical factors that operate at a routine level within the institution of the school. In most of their routine activities, teachers and pupils are influenced by immediate, proximate consideration like classroom architecture, timetables, lesson topic and so on which they do not associate with matters of ideology. So, though links might be traced between classroom activity and the wider social structure (cf.Anyon, 1981; Sharp and Green, 1975), an intentional link is hard to establish.

For this reason, *Classroom Control* concentrates on institutional factors rather than social structual factors as the context for explaining the actions of teacher and pupils in relation to classroom control. Institutional, or organizational, factors are ones recognized by those involved as shaping their actions and their influence can therefore be detected reasonably directly in the motives of the actors. Put rather bluntly it is not just the researcher who can identify the contextual variables – it is the actors themselves who can see how such factors affect their actions.

An approach drawn from *the sociology of work and organizations* is useful in this respect because it emphasizes how certain experiences and certain pressures are shared by those in any particular situation and how these can shape the attitudes and approaches of those involved. It emphasizes, for instance, how

> the school as a workplace and the classroom as a work site pose problems for the conduct of teachers: problematic situations for which they must devise strategies, more or less effective, for meeting organizational demands (from the administration), carrying out an instructional program, and coping with the regularities and irregularities of classroom events.
>
> (Dreeben, 1973, p. 462)

And it emphasizes, moreover, the way in which such problems and pressures can be peculiar to an occupation and provide, in effect, the basis for an occupationally specific view of events – a point made by Lacey when he notes that:

> To become a teacher is to become creatively involved with tasks and situations common only to teachers. It also involves being concerned with particular constraints, constraints that others do not have to subject themselves to. No other profession or occupation experiences exactly similar ones.These shared experiences and common problems give rise to a common set of interests, to certain ways of looking at the world, of interpreting the world and obtaining a world view – in short, a teacher perspective.
>
> (Lacey, 1977 p.14)

So if teachers, as they seem to, exhibit a particular anxiety about classroom control this need not imply that there is something unique about the group of people who choose to become teachers or that there is some sort of self-recruitment of types who are particularly sensitive in this direction. It is more likely to imply that the work they do has certain features which affect their thinking once they have joined the occupation and that a 'teacher perspective' results from shared experiences at work rather than predispositions derived from personality or social background.

This does not mean that the personal characteristics of the teacher are actually regarded as irrelevant to their attitudes and actions at work. Obviously, their roles in the family and community, along with their personal identity, are not left at the school gates in the morning to be picked up like a satchel at the end of the day. Nevertheless, while accepting that such personal factors have a bearing on the motivation of teachers, the perspective insists that there are shared aspects of work which cut across these with sufficient force to explain the patterns of attitudes and activities which characterize the occupation. By the same token, while emphasizing the influence of shared experiences and pressures at work, the approach does not ignore the fact that there are some major divisions within the occupation itself and that the shared aspects of teachers' experience have to exist despite the division between the primary/ secondary sector, despite the different kinds of training, despite differences of opinion about pedagogy, despite differences in subject specialisms in secondary schooling and, of course, despite the divide between men and women at various levels of the occupation. It is, perhaps, worth stressing that the approach adopted in this book does not pretend that such divisions are trivial or irrelevant and, where they are significant to the issues at hand, they are brought into discussion (cf. Deem 1978; Delamont, 1983). So, for instance, where factors like machismo have a bearing on classroom control strategies the effect for male teachers might differ from that for female and the particular division will be brought into consideration. Where men and women teachers face the same problem, the division will not be considered. The thrust of the approach, however, is to search for the influences on teacher activity and attitudes which are in large part shared.

In looking for the shared experiences at work our attention is drawn to the *social organization* of the workplace. As Lortie has argued:

> Those engaged in [the sociology of work] generally pay close attention to the characteristics of work settings and to repetitive relationships which occur there, including formal authority lines, relations of mutual

dependence, informal associations and the like. Regularities of interaction are observed and the norms controlling them analysed; we examine the interconnections between work processes and relationships with other persons. The delineation and analysis of tasks are of special importance; we inquire into the demands they make for technical and interpersonal and psychological capacities of various kinds and study the frustrations and satisfactions induced by particular task bundles.

(Lortie, 1973, p.480)

We look as well at the *physical organization* of schools and the impact this has on the way in which teachers approach their work. Here, in particular, we notice the influence of the 'closed classrooms' on teachers in secondary and even primary schools, providing a pervasive influence on the activities which go on within them. The closed classroom encapsulates features of both physical and social organization in schools which, as we will see, have far-reaching consequences for classroom control (cf. Stebbins, 1973).

In Chapters 1,2 and 3 of the book this sociological perspective is used to establish a framework for understanding the phenomenon of classroom control. Focusing in particular on teachers, it is argued that the *social context* within which they work provides a climate which shapes the task and gives a pattern to their activity. As Leacock made the point:

Teachers cannot simply interact with the children in their classrooms according to their desires and personal style. Instead, their behaviour often takes on characteristics beyond their immediate aims or intents. They must adapt their style, not only to the children, but to the institution, to the principal's requirements, to the other teachers' attitudes and to the standards according to which they will be evaluated.

(Leacock, 1969. p.202)

Their expectations about what they ought to be doing and, of course, the feasibility of achieving these aims are shaped by a context which provides pressures and opportunities, ambitions and anxieties that need to be taken into consideration. In no aspect of their work are such pressures more evident than in expectations about classroom control. Using secondary sources supplemented by data from Ashton, Beechgrove and Cedars, these pressures are examined and the picture which emerges is one in which classroom control features as central to the task of teaching. This stems from society's expectations about the work of teachers and the legacy of memories from the public's personal experiences as pupils in classrooms. This prior experience of classroom life is shared, of course, by entrants to the occupation (trainee teachers) whose expectations about the need for control and the methods of attaining it remain little altered by their experience of teacher training and are, in fact, reinforced on site by the expectations of colleagues and pupils as well as by classroom imperatives which stem from the allocation of resources in the schools and the physical and social organization of the classroom.

In all this there are three key factors which are crucial to teachers' understanding about classroom control. First there is the basic knowledge that pupils are not always willing partners to the learning process and that the work of the teacher inevitably involves a custodial element that requires an ability to control the behaviour of pupils. Quite apart from other relevant teacher skills, teachers recognize that success at their job necessarily involves *a capacity to establish and maintain classroom control.* The second factor is that in attaining classroom control, as in most aspects of their classroom work, teachers are expected to operate as individuals. The 'closed' classroom, which typifies the teaching context, carries with it both official and informal assumptions about the teacher's responsibilities which are mutually supporting to the extent that they establish and reinforce the *autonomy of the classroom teacher.* The third key factor is that *teachers have to rely heavily on man-management techniques to achieve the necessary control.* Because they operate with large groups of potentially recalcitrant pupils and because they have relatively few material or technical resources available, teachers' methods for gaining control necessarily depend on personalized authority and personal commitments. The teacher is not in a strong position to get compliance by relying on institutional authority, bureaucratic rules and procedures, or hiding behind 'imperatives of technology'.

Classroom control is an essential feature of teaching yet, as Chapters 1, 2 and 3 reveal, it is not something which can be taken for granted. Teachers certainly enter the classroom with the official authority to control but, in practice, they still have to *win* that control rather than assume it exists or simply hope to enforce it as of right. For the most part, control is something which has to be achieved, worked for and frequently re-established during the course of a working day. But, the struggle for control is not a simple one-way process. The reaction of pupils and their own attempts to exert influence on events complicate teacher's efforts at control and are the very things which make the phenomenon of classroom control so complex. Pupil's own interests in classroom proceedings, in fact, are crucial to the nature of classroom interaction concerned with control – its 'strategic' nature. Their behaviour so often serves to limit and counter the endeavours of the teacher and, in many respects, underlies the emergence of strategic action as the means of thrust and parry in the duel for classroom control. These strategies for control are explored more fully in Chapter 4 and elaborated in Chapters 5 and 6 using case -study material drawn from Ashton, Beechgrove and Cedars. From these chapters we are led to conclude that there are three broad kinds of teacher strategy aimed at classroom control: 'domination', 'classwork management' and 'co-optation'. Though differing in many overt ways, these strategies share the aims of first, reducing the classroom teacher's reliance on personal charisma as the means for gaining control, and second, minimizing the level of uncertainty which is inherent in classroom proceedings.

The use of these strategies has to recognize that control is largely negotiated with pupils who can resist and limit the official authority of the teacher by subtle counter-strategies. In the context of the closed classroom this process of negotiation is generally expected to involve only the particular class teacher and his/her group of pupils – emphasis being placed upon individual responsibility for the maintenance of control. But this emphasis on individual responsibility is just part of a broader set of assumptions about appropriate teacher activity in which the teacher is expected to retain the insularity of the classroom unit and prevent interference with the other classes (through things like noise) or interference from other teachers. Autonomy and isolation are elementary features of the culture of the closed classroom and it follows from this that pupil behaviour which threatens the autonomy of teachers or the isolation of the classroom is normally considered to be the greatest challenge to teacher control in the classroom.

All of this spells an important message for teachers. First, failure on the part of a teacher to recognize the need for classroom insularity (or failure to maintain it) has serious repercussions and can constitute a fundamental threat to the teacher's image as 'competent'. Second, given the physical and organizational insularity of classroom units, teachers' concern with classroom control cannot be limited to a state of events in the classroom but must also include a concern with the impression which permeates to outsiders about events which the outsider cannot directly witness. From the teacher's point of view, classroom control is not simply an objective condition in the classroom but an impression to be sustained to outsiders who have meagre information on which to assess the extent of control exercised behind closed doors. This is why noise (Chapter 5) and privacy (Chapter 6) have so much significance in a sociological approach which sees classroom control as a *socially constructed* phenomenon as much as an absolute state of affairs in the classroom.

A caveat is needed on these conclusions. It is stressed throughout the book that classroom control is a *context-specific* phenomenon in the sense that what passes for control in one situation may not pass for control in another. The normal context for lessons is the closed classroom and it is in this context that noise and privacy assume their importance. But alternative contexts do exist and throughout Chapters 4, 5 and 6 there is reference to fieldwork data drawn from the humanities lessons at Cedars. Because these involved team teaching in open-plan classrooms they provide a contrast with the conventional setting and are useful for emphasizing how the nature of classroom control varies in response to differing social, organizational and physical arrangements in school.

The case-study schools

The analysis of classroom control developed in this book draws quite heavily at times upon empirical data from the case-study schools of Ashton, Beechgrove and Cedars. The value of these data depends first upon a clear picture of the peculiarities of the schools so that we can gauge how far the findings are representative of schools in general and second, upon the methods used to collect the information that is subsequently used in support of the analysis.

Ashton was a co-educational comprehensive school in the London Borough of Brent. It catered for pupils between the ages of 11 and 18 years and was formed in 1967 by the amalgamation of two single-sex secondary modern schools and one coeducational grammar school. At the time of research there were about 88 staff at the school with 1,500 pupils on the roll, giving a staff–pupil ratio of 17:1. Ashton was in a London suburb that was predominately working class and which had a large, and increasingly, black population. The headmaster suggested that the pupil population was a reasonable reflection of the catchment area – an area in which there had been, in particular, a recent and significant increase in the Asian population. He estimated that the pupils were 55 per cent indigenous (in which he included English and Irish), 25 per cent Caribbean and 20 per cent Asian (mostly of Kenyan and Ugandan origin). This profile of pupils, of course, meant that the intake of non-white pupils to the school was proportionately greater than that found in the other London boroughs and, in turn, much larger than most schools in the country would experience. It was not, however, just the matter of social mix and social balance which made Ashton's intake distinctive. It was also a question of the ability range. Teachers at the school alleged that the intake did not cover the full range of ability that was needed for comprehensives to work properly and suggested that there were far too few pupils in the higher ability bracket and far too many at the lower end –

an argument actually substantiated by the test battery scores of pupils brought from their primary schools. As a result, teachers, faced a population of pupils characterized by its high proportion of 'ethnic minority' pupils, predominately working-class origins and lower than average ability.

There was a ten-form entry of approximately 270 pupils each year who, on the basis of their academic record at primary school, were placed in an academic form, a remedial form, or one of three intermediate mixed-ability forms in either of the two lower school units. The academic organization of the fourth and fifth years in the upper school continued and extended the academic segregation started in the first three years. Basically there were six courses organized into two distinct bands: the academic courses and those which provided more practical education. The tenor of the school was generally in keeping with more traditional ideas about conduct at school and there was little evidence that the move to comprehensive organization had introduced any particularly progressive (official) attitudes to things connected with discipline and control. Staff were expected, for instance, not to let the pupils leave the school at lunchtime unless the pupils were going home for lunch. Pupils were required to obtain permission to ride to school by bicycle and teachers were required to ensure that pupils met all regulations in connection with dress. As the official guidelines as Ashton stated:

> The Headmaster has the authority to send home from school any individual pupil who, in his opinion, is improperly dressed.

> The maintenance of a smart and efficient standard of dress by all pupils is very important both for the reputation of the school and neighbourhood, and for good daily organization within the school.

Girls were not to wear jewellery or heavy boots in the school, nor was anyone to carry excessive amounts of money. Personal articles and clothing were to be labelled accordingly and each pupil was to have a satchel to carry and protect his or her books.

Beechgrove, like Ashton, was a coeducational comprehensive school covering the 11-18 age range. Beechgrove, however, was in Camden and was part of the ILEA. It had been established in 1947 as part of the London plan 'of early experimental comprehensives and was a single-site school. Two older and original buildings were improved in 1949 and in 1959 a new building was added when an extensive new site became available adjacent to the existing site. During the period of research Beechgrove had approximately 1,250 pupils and 78 staff, giving it a staff-pupil ratio of 16:1. This apparently low ratio was caused partly by a falling school roll and partly by the number of specialist teaching posts created to cope with the needs of the school. The ratio, as a result, was not out of line with ILEA policy and did not imply any marked reduction in the size of most classes.

Beechgrove was quite close to central London. A large redevelopment programme in its catchment area had caused a degree of rehousing and the school experienced decreasing pupil numbers during the period of research. From a high of 1,900 it has stabilized at slightly over 1,200 as a result of the development. Although verging on a wealthy area of London, its catchment area mainly included areas of the borough which were working class with a mixture of old tenement housing and new high-rise complexes. As a result, the school population was predominately working class despite a minority from the wealthier part of the catchment area. It also had a strong multicultural element. In fact, the school was proud of this and boasted of forty different nationalities in the school with an estimated one-third of the school population being non-indigenous. Despite the variety of ethnic groups in the school, however, the major part of this group were of West Indian background.

Like Ashton, then, the school had an intake that was characterized by its relatively high proportion of non-white pupils. Also, like Ashton, it experienced an intake whose ability range was lower than might be expected for a fully comprehensive school. There was an element of creaming in the sense that the school still competed with selective grammar schools and this resulted in the proportion of higher ability pupils at the school being less than that which was actually available in the neighbourhood. Beechgrove thus ended up with an intake profile quite similar to Ashton's because it received higher than average proportions of working-class pupils, ethnic minority pupils and lower-ability pupils.

Beechgrove had an eight-form entry of about 250 pupils each year who were placed in mixed-ability groups. During the first three years there was an emphasis on retaining mixed-ability grouping though individual subject departments did exercise the right to introduce setting. Official policy at the school, indeed, while advocating mixed-ability grouping and noting its advantages for the development of the individual at his or her own pace, also contained the qualification that for certain subjects such arrangements might not be appropriate and allowed that such subjects could legitimately deviate from the norm of mixed ability. The course which a pupil took in the fourth and fifth years consisted of a core of eight compulsory subjects and a structured choice between five optional subjects. The core compulsory subjects consisted of English language, mathematics, social studies, careers, health education, religious education, physical education and music. The banding which was evident in Ashton's fourth and fifth year arrangements was not, then, reflected at Beechgrove where a common-core curriculum was a more salient feature of academic organization than courses. Remedial groups operated as distinct groups throughout the first four years providing the only direct kind of streaming but remedial teaching was available also to individual pupils on a withdrawal basis from normal timetables.

In Beechgrove, as in Ashton, there was an absence of integrated subjects or team teaching in any other than a pilot, experimental and very restricted sense. This traditionalism was reinforced by official guidelines about the conduct of pupils, guidelines which echoed the sentiments expressed at Ashton:

> Staff should insist on good manners and courtesy, and to this end ought not to allow themselves to be addressed discourteously by children, or to accept slovenliness in attitude, dress or speech. The importance of the school image should be stressed and children should be given guidance concerning their behaviour in public.
>
> (Official guidelines: Beechgrove)

Teachers were also expected to get orderly lines outside the classrooms before a lesson, one line for girls, one for boys; not to let pupils out of a classroom for frivolous reasons; not to accept verbal excuses for lateness; to check the attendance at each lesson; not to allow classes in the playground unsupervised; not to allow pupils to chew or eat in class, and to insist on homework. As with Ashton, then there was clearly an emphasis on the staff exercising a custodial control of pupils and there were few concessions to progressive educational ideas about pupil autonomy, responsibility or discretion on matters concerning either the curriculum or routine conduct in the school.

Cedars was a single-site, coeducational comprehensive school in Leicestershire. It was opened in 1969 though it had roots as a school going as far back as the eleventh century. In its new form it was an integral part of a community college and, as part of the 'Leicestershire plan', it received pupils from local high schools at the age of 14 years and covered only the 14-18 age band. During the period of research there were approximately 1,400 pupils and 82 staff at the school giving it a staff-pupil ratio of 17:1, much in line with the national average. The school drew pupils from a wide catchment area stretching from the Warwickshire border to the outskirts of Leicester with most pupils being bussed to and from the school. As a result, the rural setting of the school did not mean that the pupils were all from a rural background. As well as pupils from the surrounding villages the school took pupils from suburban working-class housing estates so that, in contrast to Ashton and Beechgrove, the intake to Cedars was characterized by a wide social mix with pupils of working- and middle-class, urban and rural backgrounds. Also in contrast was the ethnic mix of the school. Unlike Ashton and Beechgrove, there was only a small proportion of pupils at Cedars who would be classed as non-white and despite the multiracial nature of Leicester itself, the suburbs included in the catchment area of the school were not very racially mixed.

The school had an intake of 500 pupils a year with 200 pupils staying on in each of the sixth and seventh years. Like Beechgrove, there were no year-based from groups. Instead, pupils were placed in vertically organized tutor groups (each with approximately 24 pupils) who met twice a day for registration, administration and general pastoral matters. These tutor groups were split into six divisions, ten tutor groups in each, which served basically the same pastoral function as the houses at Ashton and Beechgrove.

Academic organization at the school was characterized by a strong commitment to mixed-ability grouping – a point reflected in the fact that remedial help was generally provided within the mixed-ability groups. An extra teacher would join the group to give special attention to those who warranted remedial help and there was no specific withdrawal policy at the school. There was, however, setting in particular subjects. Despite the general school policy, grouping by ability did occur in maths, physics and languages. Another striking feature of the schools organization was the relatively extensive use of team teaching in open-plan classrooms. The team teaching in open-plan classrooms occurred mainly in humanities lessons – one of the core compulsory subjects – which meant that, for their first two years at the school pupils spent one-sixth of their thirty-three lesson periods a week in open-plan classrooms being taught by teams. There was a common-core curriculum which was compulsory for all pupils during the first two years and which consisted of:

Humanities – a combined course in English and community studies, including religious education
Mathematics
Design
One science subject
Physical education/drama

In addition to these, all pupils had courses in education and careers guidance. There were, as well, options in languages, humanities, sciences, design and commerce – twenty-eight in all and each pupil normally chose three.

There was a strong emphasis on pastoral care at the school combined with a general school policy geared towards personal as well as intellectual growth in the pupil. As stated in the school prospectus, the aim of the school was to treat the pupils (or students as they were called at Cedars) as young adults and to expect them to respond in similar fashion. Personal qualities such as curiosity, perseverance and self-discipline, argued the principal, were to be regarded as just as vital as the three Rs and the aim of the school, in consequence, was to foster all these qualities. As a result, the ethos of Cedars bore a marked contrast with that of Ashton and Beechgrove. At Cedars there was a conscious effort to generate an atmosphere of collaboration between teachers and pupils and to minimize overt expressions of the teachers' authority. Pupils, for example, were encouraged to refer to teachers by their first name and there were noticeably fewer rules and directives governing the routine conduct of pupils. The pupils were given more leeway in terms of dress, jewellery, and so on, and, as the principal stressed, the emphasis was placed squarely on the self-discipline and responsibility of pupils as adult contributors to the school community.

Fieldwork research

Fieldwork at Ashton, Beechgrove and Cedars involved *protracted observation* in classrooms, *interviews with teachers* and the use of *official guidelines*. Documents in the form of pamphlets or brochures aimed at the public, headmasters' reports to the governors, and official directives to staff concerning approved courses of action/channels of communication/expected standards for pupil behaviour, effectively constituted *official statements about school organization and school policy*. Such official guidelines at Ashton, Beechgrove and Cedars provided a useful ally for research because not only did they give some instant picture of the formal policy and organization of the schools, but also they were available as a source of information that did not depend on the openness or honesty of particular individuals. They existed as an objective statement about the school. This did not mean that such official guidelines actually depicted reality. While they provided information on matters of formal organization, almost inevitably they left the analysis of routine, *informal* practices rather unexplored. This was not to say that formal rules and procedures had no influence on practical, everyday approaches to the job – they certainly did. The picture they presented, however, was partial and incomplete as an account of everyday activity because they did not explain the way members of the organization interpreted the rules and procedures and the way they could neglect or bend the rules. Any formal picture of the school, therefore, needed to be complemented by a picture of the way members *interpreted* the formal structure. To do this it was necessary to undertake protracted observation in classrooms and to interview teachers to get to grips with their perspective on things.

Observation of lessons, naturally required the approval of the teachers involved. The relevant teachers were approached (often through an introduction by a teacher who had already co-operated with the research) and asked for permission to sit in on their lessons, to observe and make field-notes. The purpose of the research was outlined in a broad sense though the issue of classroom control as such was not broached until the interview later on. The request was generally received favourably, probably due to the presence in Ashton, Beechgrove and Cedars of a regular supply of student teachers. An association between the role of researcher and that of student teacher was a useful one to foster. It eased teacher anxiety about being evaluated in some sense and allowed questions to be asked without implied criticism. It put the teacher in the position of expert and giver of information; researcher in the position of learner and receiver of knowledge. My intention was to adopt a passive back-seat role to avoid, as far as possible, disturbing the naturalness of the setting. In the course of observation, however, it was sometimes necessary to become involved in the proceedings of the class. Teachers occasionally asked me for a second opinion on a classroom topic or actively involved me in the classroom activity to the extent of persuading me to teach the class (or some other class). This was not considered to be desirable practice as it tended to identify the researcher as teacher, possibly closing channels of information from pupils in the class (cf. D.H. Hargreaves, 1967). As the research developed, however, it became more pertinent to gain the trust of the teachers and, though not encouraged, expediency determined that such involvement was occasionally necessary. Observation of lessons was protracted in the sense that the process of observing continued throughout the whole period of research and, also, in the sense that any particular teacher was observed on a number of occasions. As a rule of thumb, there would be a minimum of five observations of the lessons before any formal kind of interview with the teacher about his/her approach to the work and understanding of the situation.

Informal discussion with teachers, whether in the staffroom or elsewhere, provided an indispensable source of information. Its limitation in terms of research, however, was that it rarely, if ever, lent itself to any systematic control or rigorous recording. Useful snippets of information arose in the course of conversation but the very informality of the situation in which they arose precluded the possibility of tape recording them or openly taking notes. In a sense, the information gleaned from such discussions was not for the record which meant that, on ethical as well as practical grounds, it could not be cited as evidence. In this respect there was an obvious need to devise a method that provided an accurate, permanent and detailed record of what was said with a context in which research was acknowledged to be in progress. An example of this would be the tape recording of interaction during lessons. As it happened this was not employed as a research method during the research at Ashton, Beechgrove and Cedars for two reasons. First, the tape recording would reproduce only the *audible* (verbal) aspects of interaction in a classroom and, of that, it would reproduce only fragments. It could produce, for instance, an accurate record of the verbal interaction instigated by the teacher with selected pupils or it could reproduce verbal interaction between selected pupils. It would not, however, reproduce the totality of verbal interaction in the classroom. (The number of microphones and operatives necessary to render this possible would prohibit the normal operation of the classroom.) Second, and a more immediate practical basis, permission to tape record classes in progress was not forthcoming from the relevant authorities, thus barring any further advance along those lines. The realistic alternative was to tape record interviews with staff and to use these as a complement to the protracted observations. That is why, after observing a teacher at work for a least five lessons, he/she was invited to explain the approach adopted and discuss specific aspects of the school or events witnessed in class. Only three teachers declined such interviews.

With due care being taken to avoid the fob-off type of answer, *interviews* reveal the way the respondents interpret, bend or ignore the formal rules and point to the set of assumptions, rarely explicit in official guidelines, that are actually vital to their routine activity in the organization (Denscombe, 1983). In the event, to foster these products of the interview situation, the interviews conducted at Ashton, Beechgrove and Cedars were as unstructured as possible. Certainly there were some themes emerging in the research which served as a guide to the general direction of responses but teachers were given much leeway in the substance and direction of their answers. One strategy that proved very useful was to simply refer back to an incident that had occurred during one of the lessons that had been observed. Teachers usually took this as a signal to reinterpret (that is, redescribe) what had happened and then to justify the course of action they had adopted. There was another advantage to this ploy. It kept the discussion firmly grounded at a practical level and reminded the teacher that events under discussion were jointly witnessed. It was, then, difficult for teachers to present an image of their work widely at variance with what they actually did and it also prevented the prospect of a high-level abstract discussion of education principles that could be kept remote from the reality of everyday tasks and practices.

The interviews, conducted along these lines, seldom ran dry and were usually quite lengthy (45 - 60 minutes). The presence of the tape recorder occasionally caused some initial hesitancy but the vast majority of the teachers displayed considerable enthusiasm for the interview when approached in the manner described and soon appeared to talk at ease despite the presence of the tape recorder.

The kinds of lessons observed and the kinds of teachers interviewed might be expected to have a bearing on the findings of the research. The criteria for selecting specific lessons and teachers, therefore, formed a vital part of the overall research strategy deserving particular attention in the account of research methods. The first point to be made in this context is that there was no discernible interference in the choice of lessons/teachers by those in authority at any of the three schools. The selection was left as a matter of negotiation between the researcher and individual members of staff and, in view of the extensive co-operation of the teachers, this allowed the choice to be based on research criteria rather than opportunities limited by restricted permission from school authorities or the co-operation of particular teachers. The initial research criterion governing the selection of lessons and teachers was that they should be drawn from subjects like social studies, English, history, religious knowledge and humanities. There were four reasons for this:

(1)   The teaching of such classes usually occurs in a classroom, as opposed to laboratory or metalwork-shop. Interaction in such lessons would not, therefore, be affected by special or abnormal physical factors of the environment.

(2)   Within these subject areas the pedagogic 'awareness' of staff might be expected to be more articulate than in other areas, possibly promoting the more progressive teaching styles that are controversial in terms of classroom control (cf. Keddie,1971, pp.135-65).

(3)   The researcher's association with this field could act to minimize the doubts or suspicions of the staff, who might be more willing to recognize the researcher as a prospective colleague.

(4)   In the early stages it was felt that some knowledge about the *content* of the lessons might provide useful insights to the situation.

Selection of lessons and teachers from within these subjects was neither random nor arbitrary. It was, instead, based on Glaser and Strauss's idea of 'theoretical sampling', that is

> The process of data collection for generating theory whereby the analyst jointly collects, codes and analyses his data and decides what data to collect next and where to find them, in order to develop his theory as it emerges. This process of data collection is *controlled* by the emerging theory.

> (Glaser and Strauss, 1967, p.45)

In practice, this meant that during the course of the fieldwork certain issues connected with classroom control came to attention through interviews or observation and these issues provided clues for the future direction of research which would be investigated only where the selection of cases involved a fair degree of flexibility. So, for instance, when the interviews with teachers at Ashton and Beechgrove began to indicate a link between classroom noise and teachers' perceptions of classroom control, special efforts were made to investigate those situations where the issue of noise might be expected to take on an added significance. Music teachers and language teachers were thus deliberately incorporated in the research in order to follow up this lead.

The result of using this kind of approach, of course, is that the researcher is obliged to adapt his selection of cases to the ongoing development of the study in a fashion that requires a flexibility which Glaser and Strauss[6] see as disturbing to those who look for tests of preformed hypothesis incorporating a definite statement at the start of the fieldwork about the amount of, and kind of, persons involved in the study because, as they point out, 'the sociologist trying to *discover* theory cannot state at the outset of his research how many groups he will sample during the entire study.' (Glaser and Strauss, 1967, p. 61, emphasis added). It was, then, inappropriate to identify a sample of teachers to be studied at the outset of the research. To have specified, for instance, that half the teachers should be interviewed, controlling for age, sex, experience subject and seniority, might have proved inflexible enough to prevent the follow-up of leads gathered along the way.

The final profile of teachers interviewed, nontheless, was substantial in number and provided what Glaser and Strauss describe as a 'theoretical saturation' – a point where, in the researcher's estimation, he cannot add to or refine the analysis through the collection of additional data. Approximately a third of the staff at Ashton and a third of the staff at Beechgrove, after having been observed in their lessons on a number of occasions, were formally interviewed during a period of four years (see Table I.1)

Table I.1   *Teachers formally interviewed:** Ashton and Beechgrove

	Ashton	Beechgrove
Heads of building:	3	—†
Heads of house:	8	8
Heads of subject:	13	7
Subject teachers:	16	12

*Teachers interviewed in their capacity as heads of house have not been included in their subject teacher capacity unless specifically reinterviewed.
†No such position at Beechgrove.

At Cedars, the humanities lessons were observed over a period of two years. Interviews were conducted with two assistant principals and the head of the humanities faculty as well as senior pastoral staff (i.e. that is two division heads and two deputy division heads). Eleven of the twenty-seven staff teaching on the humanities course were also interviewed after the observation of their lessons. After the first year of observation and interviews, a pilot questionnaire was distributed to sixty pupils which sought their opinions on the humanities situation. An open-ended format was employed. On the basis of the comments and observations of pupils a further limited-option questionnaire was administered as part of the humanities course unit which dealt with social research. This latter questionnaire included further space for wide-ranging comment and was answered by over 200 of the pupils. It served as the basis for further discussion with pupils on the topic as well as analysis of the relationship between pupil attitudes and aspects of classroom experience.

Notes

1   Delamont (1983) estimates that at least one-quarter of teacher talk in classrooms is directed quite explicitly towards discipline and control as opposed to the lesson content *per se.*
2   See, for example, Curwin and Mendler (1980), Docking (1980), Eggen *et al.* (1979), Francis (1975), Galloway *et al.* (1982), Gillham (1981), Gnagey (1975, 1981), Haigh (1979), Jones-Davies and Cave (1976), Laslett (1977b), Lowenstein (1972, 1975), Marland (1975), Millman *et al.* (1981), O'Leary and O'Leary (1977), Saunders (1979), Sloane (1976), Tattum (1982).
3   The names 'Ashton', 'Beechgrove', and 'Cedars' are pseudonyms.
4   See, for instance, Davis and Moore (1945), Durkeim (1925, 1956), D. H. Hargreaves (1982), Parsons (1959), Turner (1971).
5   Examples here are Althusser (1971), Bourdieu (1977), Bowles and Gintis (1976), Willis (1977), Young (1971).

6 Glaser and Strauss emphasize this relationship between the theoretical orientations of research and the data itself when writing about 'grounded theory'. As they put it, 'Generating a theory from data means that most hypotheses and concepts not only come from the data, but are systematically worked out in relation to the data during the course of the research. *Generating a theory involves a process of research*' (1967, p. 6).

1
The Problem of Classroom Control

Schoolteachers operate *in loco parentis*. Their rights and duties are taken to be the same as that of a parent to his/her child and, in this sense, the law sanctions the exercise of discipline within tolerable bounds (Barrell, 1975). Indeed, in some respects such as matters of pupil safety, it places upon the teachers a clear obligation to restrain aspects of pupil behaviour and control their behaviour 'as any parent might expect to do'. For example, as a result of the Health and Safety at Work Act 1974, classrooms, laboratories, workshops, corridors, playgrounds and even official outside visits have come under the auspices of safety legislation, and action could be taken against a teacher if an accident could be attributed to negligence in exercising control. Clearly then, the law places upon the teacher an obligation to control the pupils in his/her charge and provides what can be seen as an *official mandate* for control. As Stenhouse puts it,

> The teacher is sent into the classroom with a legitimate power and authority, vested in him by society through legislation and through custom. This authority carries with it a responsibility to exercise some control over the life of the class.
>
> (Stenhouse, 1967, p.47)

The exercise of this control, like other aspects of teachers' work, receives a good deal of scrutiny by the public. One reason for this is that during their time as pupils, members of the public will have built up considerable first-hand experience of the situation within which teachers work, and perhaps feel as a consequence that they are privy to the demands facing teachers and pupils. This familiarity with school life puts the public in a position to express opinions and preferences about schooling and comment on the performance of teachers in a way that they would not feel justified in doing with most other occupations. The public *knows* something about teaching and can, therefore, judge the work of teachers more easily than that of bank-clerks, quantity surveyors, accountants or computer programmers. The public's knowledge, as teachers will be quick to point out, is likely to be highly selective and usually well out-of-date but this does little to detract from the rather unique position in which teachers find themselves.

The result is that teachers find themselves more exposed to public debate and political controversy than most other occupations. This has been particularly evident in the educational debates of recent years where the quality of teachers and the nature of their teaching have been subject to a series of public interrogations. The reorganization of secondary education proposed in Circular 10/65, for instance, sparked off an increased intensity of debate about matters like the organization of schools, the methods used in schools and the proficiency of the teachers involved in the system, and the Black Papers, the Bullock Report and Mr Callaghan's 'Great Debate on Education ' have all invited a detailed and public scrutiny of the work of teachers.

From such public debates it seems clear that on matters of schooling and education there are three major areas of concern in the public's mind. First, there is the question of literacy, numeracy and general standards of academic attainment. Second, there is a public concern with the relevance of education for meeting the demands of today's technology and commercial needs. Third, the public is anxious about the ability and willingness of school teachers to control their classes and get what is loosely called 'discipline' in lessons. Gallup polls in the United States have shown that parents there regard it as the biggest problem facing schools (Curwin and Mendler, 1980) and in Britain, as well, a public concern with discipline in schools continues to rival questions about curriculum and falling standards of education for top spot in the anxiety ratings. In the case of Britain, there have been persistent allegations of declining standards of discipline and control, especially in the comprehensive schools. These allegations have come mainly from the more right-wing press, politicians and teachers for whom the levels of violence, vandalism and indiscipline in the schools bear testimony not only to a general social decay but also to a specific malaise associated with teaching. This line of thinking was clearly evident in the series of Black Papers (Cox and Dyson, 1969-70; Cox and Boyson, 1975, 1977) in which progressive teaching methods and poor quality teaching were 'held responsible for an alleged decline in general standards and basic skills, for a lack of social discipline and the incongruence between the worlds of school and of work' (Centre for Contemporary Cultural Studies, CCCS, 1981, p. 212). Time and again the tabloids and right-wing press have fanned the flames of the controversy with alarmist reports of violence, vandalism and truancy of crisis proportions and, as the contributors to *Unpopular Education* discovered when analysing the coverage of educational matters by the *Daily Mirror* and the *Daily Mail* between 1975 and 1977,

> What was presented as 'debate' was in effect a monologue concentrating on items concerning teachers' lack of professional competence or the negative aspects of pupil behaviour.
> Central to the reporting were pictures of the current state of British schooling. Images of incompetence, slovenly, subversive or just trendy teachers who had failed to teach or control the indisciplined pupils in their charge became too familiar to need elaboration.
>
> (CCCS,1981, pp. 210-11)

Recent reporting by the *Daily Mail* would suggest that things are much the same, with violence, vandalism and arson continuing to capture the headlines (see Figure 1.1)

Such reporting is based, in part at least, on the premise that the newspaper is expressing public opinion as well as informing it and as the CCCS writers comment about the period of their study:

> There were confident assertions that 'millions of parents are desperately worried about the education that their children are receiving' (*Daily Mail* 27.4.76) and that 'parents' throughout the country are becoming increasingly frustrated by the lack of discipline and low standards of state schools (*Daily Mail* 18.1.75)
>
> (CCCS,1981, p.214)

Whether as a cause or a consequence of press reporting there does appear to be some substance to these claims. Wilson (1981), for example, found that 99 per cent of the parents he interviewed felt that discipline was not adequately enforced in schools and the image of schools held by the parents in his study was one in which teachers were becoming bullied and intimidated by their teenage pupils.

The teaching profession itself has not been immune to the idea that classroom control is a major contemporary problem. Part of the policy of the National Association of Schoolmasters and Union of Women Teachers (NAS/UWT) over the last decade, for instance, has been to expose what it regards as the very real crisis of control in schools and to draw attention to 'the facts' about violence, vandalism and truancy in schools (Comber and Whitfield, 1979; Lowenstein, 1972, 1975). Her Majesty's Inspectorate of Schools (HMI) have added their professional voice to the growing chorus. As they concluded in their report, *The New*

Daily Mail, Thursday, June 2, 1983

Detention rebel 'attacked his teacher with a brick'

A YOUNG teacher was savagely beaten in a revenge attack by a 13-year-old boy he kept in detention, a court heard yesterday.

Daily Mail, July 1, 1983

Schoolboy detained for attack on master

A SCHOOLBOY who attacked a maths teacher after he kept him behind for misbehaviour was ordered yesterday to be detained for two years during Her Majesty's Pleasure.

David Christian, 13, who smashed a brick into the face of Mr Alistair Phillip, after lying in wait with his older brother, was said in reports to be potentially 'very dangerous'.

Daily Mail, March 29, 1984

Destruction after school 'punks' are sent home

Rioting pupil hits pregnant teacher on head with a brick

A PREGNANT teacher was hit on the head with a brick hurled through a window as children went on the rampage at a school.

The rioting pupils threw bottles at staff, smashed desks and yelled abuse. The ringleaders then tried to organise a full-scale strike and at one stage about 150 children blocked traffic on the main road outside until they were dispersed by police.

The scenes of near anarchy happened at Mexborough comprehensive school in South Yorkshire after two pupils were sent home for turning up in punk clothing and spiked haircuts.

Daily Mail, December 16, 1982

The growing menace of petrol bomb pupils

A GROWING number of pupils are hitting back at authority by trying to burn down their schools, according to a new report.

Lack of achievement in the classroom is thought to be one of the reasons behind an alarming increase in the number of school fires.

In its annual report the Fire Protection Association reports more than 2,000 blazes, of which a third were probably started deliberately. The 34 biggest caused £13·8 million worth of damage.

Daily Mail, Monday, November 22, 1982

AS CITY PLANS TO BAN CANE...

77 attacks on teachers in a year

TEACHERS in a city which plans to outlaw the cane, today reveal frightening details of violence in their classrooms.

In a single year a group of staff in schools in Leeds have been physically attacked 73 times by pupils — and four times by parents.

Daily Mail, Monday, May 30, 1983

Teacher quits after pupils rampage

CHANTING, swearing children on the rampage have driven a teacher from his job.

Staff returning to a school after lunch on Friday had to run a gauntlet of about 60 senior pupils, who were hissing, jeering, chanting obscenities, and some of whom tried to spray teachers with lacquer.

The pupils' siege was the last straw for Mr Allan Steven, £8,600-a-year head of the drama department at Malbank comprehensive school in Nantwich, Cheshire.

He says he will never teach in a State school again.

And he claims he has seen other teachers forced to turn to tranquillisers because of the stress of coping with school 'bullies'.

In his letter of resignation, Mr Steven, a 31-year-old bachelor says: 'Distasteful verbal abuse in and out of school is well established. How soon before it turns to a case of serious physical assault?'

Trouble began on Friday when some senior children gathered in the town square a few hundred yards from the school.

The headmaster, Mr Herbert Rowsell, had told senior pupils not to attend school on Friday, the last day of term.

But shortly before one o'clock on the day the children moved from the town centre to the school.

'It was obvious their actions were orchestrated,' said Mr Steven at his home in Lancashire Road, Crewe, yesterday. 'Girls appeared to be playing a major part and the behaviour around the school grounds got out of hand.

'The pupils were chanting insults at staff as, they returned from lunch to teach the first, second, third and fourth forms.

'There were attempts to spray teachers with lacquer and although none was physically assaulted there was a great deal of intimidation.

The headmaster of the 1,100-pupil school was not available for comment yesterday.

Figure 1.1   A bad impression.

Teacher in the School (HMI, 1982b) one-quarter of the new teachers they observed were not adequately prepared for the job when they entered the profession. Some of the lack of preparation concerned the level of proficiency in the subject specialism and some of it the match between the subject qualification and the kind of job the new entrant first took up in school. Significantly, though, much of the criticism concerned the preparation of newcomers to deal with matters of classroom organization, management and control. There are clear indications that HMI would like to see more attention given to such skills in the content of initial teacher training (HMI, 1982a) because where new teachers struggle in class it frequently appears to be due to a lack of control (HMI, 1982b). Summarizing the nature of the least successful lessons they had witnessed, HMI point out that the

> Characteristics most commonly associated with lessons of low quality included ... poor relationships and class control, particularly in the secondary schools, where occasionally these seriously inhibited the teaching and rendered meaningless any comment on other aspects.
> (HMI, 1982b, p.23)

The rapid growth of 'special' schools and units for maladjusted pupils in recent years might also been seen as an acknowledgement on the part of the teaching profession that there is a real, and worsening, problem of control in schools. As an HMI report noted, 'The widespread provision of units for disruptive pupils is a relatively recent phenomenon, the bulk of them having been established in or since 1974' (HMI, 1978, p.41). By 1977, sixty-nine of the ninety-six local education authorities had special schools or units mainly catering for pupils of secondary school age (72.1 per cent). The total provision in England at that time consisted of some 3,962 places in 239 schools/units. Such special schools and units, as it happens, were never intended to deal solely with problems of discipline and control arising from particularly disruptive pupils. They were intended to cover a number of psychological disorders contained under the umbrella term 'maladjustment' ranging from nervous disorders, habit disorders, organic disorders, psychotic behaviour and specific educational difficulties as well as behaviour disorders (Laslett, 1977b, pp.48-9). But as Dawson (1980, p.13) found from his survey, pupils with 'conduct disorders' (that is socially unacceptable behaviour such as aggression, destructiveness, stealing, lying, truanting and so on) formed about 76 per cent of pupils in these schools. It is with some justification, then, that special schools and units have come to be regarded as 'sin bins' where particularly disruptive pupils get sent away from the normal classroom. Their rapid growth during the 1970s might be seen, on the surface at least, as symptomatic of an increasing problem of control.

A crisis of control?

The picture of classroom control presented so far is clearly one of the declining standards of discipline and a developing crisis of control in schools. But this is not the whole picture because we need to weigh against this impression a number of research findings which suggest instead that a far more cautious and qualified position is justified (Docking, 1980; Galloway et al., 1982; Jones-Davies and Cave, 1976; Laslett, 1977a). Historical evidence, for example, casts doubt on the idea that the control problem is anything new to schools (Grace, 1978; Humphries,1981; Swift, 1971) and, as Galloway et al. conclude:

> The evidence does not suggest that schools today are any closer to anarchy, than they were in the 1920's and 1930's ... The limited available evidence lends no support to the notion of a large increase in the number of pupils presenting problems, or in the severity of the problems they present.
>
> (Galloway et al., 1982, pp.11, ix)

Humphries, emphasizing the point, produced evidence of severe disruption in schools during the period 1889-1939 specifically to

> challenge the popular stereotype and academic orthodoxy that portrays pupils in the pre-1939 period as disciplined, conformist and submissive to the school authority [and to] expose this misleading stereotype by tracing the extensive nature of pupil opposition to provided schools.
>
> (Humphries, 1981, p.28)

Swift (1971) points out that, in the United States, control difficulties have an even longer history. As far back as 1837 the records show that 10 per cent of Massachusetts' schools were broken up by rebellious pupils. This kind of information should make us wary about getting caught up in any hysterical response to a 'new crisis' of classroom control. It does not prove that things have always been the same but it does warn us against a blind acceptance of the common sense truth that control problems are worse than they used to be.

The second reason for caution concerns the evidence of violence. If, for the purposes of the present discussion, we turn a blind eye to corporal punishment as a form of institutionalized violence administered by teachers on pupils (and since 111 of Britain's 125 local education authorities still permit corporal punishment this is quite a significant narrowing of the whole issue) then it seems that violence in schools is actually quite rare. Mills (1976), for example, on the basis of extensive research on 13–16 year old pupils in the Midlands, found that the chances of a teacher being actually assaulted were very low and that within the area studied there appeared to be a hard-core of only about 3 per cent of this age-range who could be identified as 'seriously disruptive children'. Even Lowenstein's (1972) inquiry for the NAS in which it was claimed that 'the amount of varied violence occurring both in secondary and primary schools [was] much larger than might have been anticipated from the occasional press report' (p.25) did not actually uncover a picture of extensive violence in schools. Of the 1,065 questionnaires returned by NAS representatives in secondary schools (from 4,800 sent out), 443 reported 'no real problem of violence' in their schools. Of the 622 who reported the existence of violence in their schools, only 66 said it was frequent. Furthermore, the *kinds* of violence reported were not always matters as serious as assaults on teachers or other pupils. There were many more reports of violence against property than of violence against the person.

My own fieldwork in Ashton, Beechgrove and Cedars served to reinforce the idea that physical violence aimed at teachers by pupils is relatively rare. Certainly, there were some incidents that matched the atrocity stories to be found in sections of the press. One, in particular, was horrific. During fieldwork at Beechgrove a teacher was stabbed in the back with a chisel. She suffered a punctured lung and did not return to teaching when she eventually recovered. Fortunately, this incident was the only very serious piece of violence against a teacher or pupil that occurred. There were probably a number of milder assaults on teachers during the period of research and certainly at Beechgrove a male chemistry teacher, quite small in stature, even developed something of a reputation for getting assaulted by pupils. On two separate occasions I actually witnessed during fieldwork he was punched repeatedly on the chest and had abuse shouted at him by pupils who seemed to have completely lost their temper. Interestingly, on neither occasion did the boy (a different one each time) hit the teacher in the face, stomach or elsewhere that would have caused real injury and the attacks were actually, consciously or otherwise, controlled and limited in their viciousness. The teacher was left standing and, before the pupil could be constrained by other teachers, was warning the boy,'Your're in a lot of trouble already doing this. I'd stop now if I were you before you go too far.'

Gauging from the fieldwork, though, assaults even of this milder variety were not common events and it became quite clear at least from interviews with the staff that violence, or the threat of violence , was not a major source of anxiety for them. Approximately a third of the staff at Ashton and a third of the staff at Beechgrove were formally interviewed, in each case after their lessons had been observed on a number of occasions. Apart from the incidents involving the chemistry teacher at Beechgrove, at no time during the classroom observation was a teacher molested, assaulted or threatened with violence and in none of the sixty-seven formal interviews did a teacher suggest that the threat of violence affected his or her routine work. When the subject of violence in classrooms was broached during the interviews the general theme of the responses was that violence certainly *might* happen but it could generally be avoided unless the pupil concerned was 'psychopathic'. In fact the spirit of the responses was captured by the comments of the language teacher at Beechgrove whose lessons were interrupted by the attacks on the chemistry teacher next door:

> You see, there are some kids who really ought not to be here because they're emotionally unbalanced. There's not a lot you can do about them is there? I mean if they're in the school and you're stuck with them, if they're going to do something dreadful like with Miss—— who got stabbed, well ... you can't do much to prevent it. But I think you'll find most of the teachers here would argue that when there's trouble it's usually the case that the teacher can sense when something's brewing and can usually manage to calm the situation before the kid goes over the top – you know, get them out of the room or something. But then there are some teachers who just seem to aggravate the stroppy kids and then don't know how to ... kind of back down or defuse the situation.

The teachers I observed and interviewed, while they were aware of a slight risk of being assaulted, were actually more concerned with the mundane forms of control problem they had to deal with day in, day out, as a normal and predictable part of their job. It was in effect, disruptive behaviour rather than violent behaviour which they saw as the basic problem of classroom control.[1] The reason for this was not that physical assaults were regarded in their own right as trivial but that they occurred quite rarely in comparison with the less extreme forms of disruption. This point emerged also from the research of Lawrence *et al.*(1977) in a London comprehensive school where they tried to gauge the extent of, and nature of, disruptive behaviour during two one-week periods; the first in November 1976, the second in February 1977. Thirty-six of the teachers were asked to write special reports on disruptive incidents and these reports were subsequently followed up by interviews to clarify the nature of the event. During the two weeks, 101 incidents were reported by teachers of which only 9 could be categorized as 'very serious'. Lawrence *et al.* admit to some surprise about this since in their definition of 'disruptive behaviour' as 'behaviour which seriously interferes with the running of the school (pp.6,11) they originally had in mind the more extreme cases of disruption like 'physical attacks' and the 'malicious destruction of property'. As it became evident, the teachers were more keen to focus on boisterousness and minor infringements of rules since these were the prevalent form of control problems they experienced. Disruptive behaviour, from the teacher's point of view, seemed to include 'ordinary misbehaviour in the classroom, playground, corridors etc.' and was not restricted to the more severe incidents of assaults and vandalism in school (contra Lawrence *et al.*, 1983, p.82). This is a feature of teachers' understanding of the control problem which needs to be emphasized. From their point of view, control problems are not restricted to the explosive instances that occur occasionally: the serious incidents involving violence or extreme verbal abuse. *What troubles teachers more are the less extreme challenges to their authority* – indiscipline, such as lack of co-operation or attention during lessons, dumb insolence, noisiness in class, cheeky comments to teachers, larking about and 'having a laugh'.

Even on this score, though, it does not appear that teachers are facing an acute problem akin to a 'crisis'. Indiscipline is certainly a *common* problem facing teachers (and one that clearly becomes worse depending on the particular motivation of the pupils) but the great majority of teachers work in schools where it would not appear to be a *desperate* problem. As the HMI (1979) conclude, having investigated 384 secondary schools, it was in only 6 per cent of cases that indiscipline could be seen as a 'considerable problem' and in fewer than 1 per cent of the schools that it was a 'serious problem'. Similarly, Dierenfield (1982), surveying the opinions of 465 comprehensive school teachers in 41 local education authorities, found that none felt disruption in their school to be 'totally out of hand' and only 3.6 per cent regarded it as a 'severe situation'. The majority (67.8 per cent) felt it to be a 'problem but one with which it is possible to cope'. Indeed , Dierenfield argues from his research that:

> The most important conclusion to be drawn from the data ... is that the people most directly concerned with disruptive behaviour in comprehensive schools, the teachers and heads, are convinced that classroom discipline is a serious, but not critical problem. ... Teachers and heads in comprehensive schools look upon classroom disruption as a serious problem but believe it can be handled by emphasising several standard procedures available to every school.

Disruptive behaviour in class: teacher and pupil expectations

Defined in this way, the 'problem' of classroom control has certain interesting characteristics. Perhaps the first thing to note is that it is not only the teachers who regard disruptive behaviour in class as a problem; pupils see it as a problem too, even those who actually resist being controlled in classroom (cf Marsh *et al.*,1978; Willis, 1977). The reason for this is because, across a variety of schools and pupils, it is evident that pupils *expect* teachers to be able to exercise control over classes.[2] As we see at a later stage, being a 'soft' teacher is a heinous sin so far as most pupils are concerned and a teacher who shows weakness tends to be seen as 'fair game' because the 'good teacher', from the pupils' point of view, must be both willing and able to obtain classroom control. There is, in other words, an expectation of control in classrooms that comes not just from the public nor just from colleagues in the profession but from the pupils themselves as well. But this does not mean that pupils will always be supportive of teachers' efforts to establish classroom control. Without defying the laws of logic, pupils can dislike being controlled and, where possible, take active steps to undermine the teachers' efforts to obtain control, yet, at the same time, they can (and generally do) expect teachers to overcome such resistance and reserve respect for those teachers who can impose order on the situation even against the resistance they themselves might put up.

The extent to which pupils resist teacher efforts to get control varies widely, of course, from school to school, classroom to classroom, depending on the particular circumstances. Put rather crudely, some pupils are more of a 'control problem' than others – both in the opinion of the staff and by their own admission. Pupils of a particular age, for instance, are notoriously more difficult to handle than others. It is amongst the 13–15 year olds that resentment and resistance to control become most evident. Without suggesting for a moment that younger and older pubils acquiesce to control without a struggle or that they can be disregarded as sources of indiscipline, the 13–15 year olds pose greater problems because of the stage of emotional, physical and social development that accompanies 'adolescence'. The 13–15 year olds have certain experiences and aspirations which make the whole issue of control more sensitive than at other stages. Their dignity is particularly vulnerable (Davies, 1978; D. H. Hargreaves, 1982) and their relationships with peers frequently take precedence over school concerns (Furlong, 1976; Lomax, 1978). And, given the economic climate of the 1980s, the prospect of long-term unemployment facing so many of this age group can only serve to cause added anxieties and frustrations as it becomes an imminent reality. Without an incentive to strive for examination success the potential for disruptive behaviour in class obviously swells.

As well as the age factor, it is generally held that boys are more disruptive in class than girls. This reputation is not without foundation in the sense that research evidence points to the fact that boys are more often told off in class and that boys tend to be more boisterous and noisy during lessons (Corrigan, 1979; Spender, 1980; Standworth, 1983). This picture of a clear disparity between boys and girls as a control problem, however, should not lead unquestionably toward the conclusion that disruptive behaviour is exclusively the province of boys. Research show quite clearly that girls are not completely passive during lessons and certainly cannot be ignored as instigators of control problems in their own right (Bird, 1980; Furlong, 1976; Lomax, 1978; Meyenn, 1980). Fuller (1983) for instance, on the basis of her research at 'Torville', a comprehensive school in the London Borough of Brent, found 'no support for the view that girls are massively more approved by teachers nor that being troublesome in educationally relevant ways is the prerogative of boys' (p. 170). Also Davies (1978, 1979) argues that, in practice, girls can end up posing more of a problem to teachers than boys. Although she found that boys received far more canings and detentions than girls at 'Gladstone High' – a comprehensive in the Midlands of England – she stresses that this reflected the type of disruptive behaviour rather than its extent and that 'any idea first of all that girls are more conformist than boys is given little support by either teachers of pupils' (Davies, 1979, p. 60). In essence the punishments reflected the 'masculine' forms of overt resistance used by the boys compared with the more 'reserved' resistance of the girls, plus the fact that girls got away with a lot more deviant activity than the boys and were dealt with more leniently.

The difference in style of resistance was recognized by teachers and pupils alike at Gladstone High but, for the teachers, the difference had interesting repercussions. As they saw it, 'Girls were initially quieter, perhaps, and more conscientious; but having transgressed some rule, they were less amenable to discipline. Struggles were longer drawn out, and fought with different weapons' (Davies, 1979, p. 60). This made it more difficult to deal with the girls. Quite apart from the special problems (especially for male teachers) of using forms of constraint or deterrence, the difficulty of disciplining girls reflected the girls' more sullen style of resistance. As a result, over two-thirds of the teachers at Gladstone High actually preferred teaching the boys partly because they saw them as better contributors to the lessons but also, and rather ironically, because they found boys *easier* to control. 'Boys did not take offence, were not malicious, bitchy, vicious, catty, surly, resentful' (p. 65) according to the staff.

Teachers' preference for teaching boys has been discovered elsewhere (Spender, 1982; Stanworth, 1983). Because of their more extrovert and attention-demanding behaviour in class, boys become known to the teacher more quickly, and it seems in any case that both male and female teachers feel more attached to the boys in their classes even where the girls have a better academic record. This raises an interesting point. On the basis of the evidence available it appears that, though boys tend to use more rowdy forms of disruptive behaviour and figure more prominently in the rogues gallery of punishments, this does not necessarily mean that boys are seen as more difficult to handle nor does it mean that teachers prefer to teach girls. On the contrary, it seems that girls are just as nonconformist as boys but use forms of resistance to teacher control that teachers find more difficult to deal with. Certainly, this was the kind of conclusion reached by Fuller (1982, 1983) on the basis of her research at 'Torville'. The girls she studied frequently 'had an instrumental orientation to education, believing that it could offer them something useful (paper qualifications) in their longer term efforts to obtain a measure of control over their lives' (Fuller, 1983, p. 177). This was particularly the case for the girls from ethnic minority backgrounds for whom educational qualifications offered some hope of increased control over their lives in the face of discrimination both as women and as members of ethnic minority groups. For the 'black' girls (of West Indian origin or descent) some educational success meant the prospect of a slightly better job and a route to a better wage. For the Asian girls, educational attainment meant slightly more control over the choice of husband along with higher status in the eyes of relatives 'back home' in the Indian subcontinent. But this did *not* mean that the black pupils were well behaved or easy to control. They seemed, instead, to walk a tightrope that allowed them to distance themselves from the teachers, the lesson and other pupils yet, at the same time, avoid falling foul of system.

In terms of classroom behaviour, the black girls gave all the appearance of being disaffected. Along with many pupils they viewed school as 'boring', 'trivial', 'childish'; their intolerance of the daily routines and their criticisms of much that went on inside the school were marked. They displayed a nicely judged [indifference] for most aspects of the good pupil role; *eschewing behaviour which would bring them into serious conflict with teachers, the girls were nevertheless frequently involved in activities which irritated or exasperated the staff.*

(Fuller, 1982, p. 91, emphasis added)

This leads us on to another factor commonly associated with pupil resistance to classroom control: ethnic in racial origins. As Tomlinson (1983) points out in her authoritative review of research findings up to 1982, it is actually those of West Indian origin or descent ('black') who have been regarded by teachers as a particular source of difficulty in the classroom. Unlike the 'Asian' pupils who have a reputation for being diligent, well-behaved, intelligent and committed to the work ethic, black pupils tend to be negatively stereotyped. Black girls, in particular, have a reputation for being disruptive in class and hard to control – a reputation that can possibly draw support from the research of Cochrane (1979) and Herman (1972). In fact, compared with white pupils and compared with Asian pupils, black pupils, girls and boys, are seen by teachers as more disruptive and generally less favourably disposed towards their educational experience (Bagley, 1976; Coard, 1971; Cochrane, 1979; Haynes, 1971; Herman 1972). Townsend and Brittan (1972) found in their survey of teacher attitudes to ethnic minority education that there was a 'high degree of consensus' that West Indian pupils posed particular discipline and control problems. West Indian pupils were stereotyped, somewhat self-contradictorily, as both 'lazy/passive/withdrawn' *and* 'boisterous/aggressive/disruptive'. Also from the research of Rutter *et al.* (1974) and Bagley (1975) covering 2,000 10 year olds in a London borough (350 of whom had West Indian origins) it was evident that teachers regarded West Indian pupils as more troublesome than others. According to the teachers, 19 per cent of English pupils had 'behaviour disorders' compared with 41 per cent of West Indian pupils. As Bagley (1979), p.76) reports, 'West Indian children according to the observations of their teachers, showed a particularly marked prevalence of behaviour of the rebellious and aggressive type'.

The interesting discovery of Bagley, Rutter and colleagues, however, is that many West Indian pupils deemed by teachers to have behavioural problem in schools behaved quite normally at home. In fact, the proportion of West Indian pupils exhibiting disturbed behaviour both at school *and* at home was actually lower than that of English pupils (17.5 per cent compared with 25 per cent). The conclusion was that the prevalence of West Indian pupils causing control problems at schools could be explained by their particular experience of schooling rather than any inherent disruptiveness in the pupils themselves. The evidence here is that West Indian pupils tend to suffer low self-esteem in ethnically mixed school situations (Bagley, Mallick and Verma, 1978), that there is sometimes a contrast between the liberal regime of many contemporary comprehensives and the authoritarianism characteristic of the West Indian family (Miller,1970) and that West Indian pupils are becoming increasingly aware that schooling 'serves them badly' (Bagley,1979). As the Rampton Report (Department of Education and Science (DES), 1981) confirmed, there are good grounds for this last point because West Indian pupils continue to underachieve educationally relative to white and Asian pupils largely through an 'unintentional racism' on the part of teachers which channels them away from educational success.[3] Cochrane (1979) makes the point, though, that the level of disruptiveness he found amongst West Indian pupils was less damaging than that identified by Rutter *et al.* in 1974 and that the image of West Indian pupils as particularly disruptive might be something of a legacy from the 1960s when there were special problems of 'settling into' the British education system faced by West Indian immigrants. During the 1970s the situation has eased, he suggests, as both West Indians and whites, pupils and teachers, have begun to accommodate to the reality of the multi-ethnic classroom.

A caveat

A cautionary note is needed at this point. Conclusions about the extent of violence and disruption in schools and about the potential of certain pupils such as adolescents, girls and blacks to engage in disruptive behaviour must be seen as somewhat tentative. One reason for this is that new evidence is emerging and new situations are developing which invite a constant review of existing 'truths'. We have already seen how some orthodoxies about girls and classroom control have been challenged by the findings of Davies and Fuller; conventional wisdoms about blacks and schooling have also come under fire recently. Jeffcoate (1984), for instance, questions the idea that black pupils in the 1980s any longer have a particularly negative self-image and both M. J. Taylor (1981) and Troyna (1984) have argued that the research evidence generally used in support of the belief that black pupils underachieve is actually far from conclusive.

Another reason that the conclusions should remain tentative, is that they involve generalizations which obviously mask a highly complex reality in which individual pupils and individual teachers interact to produce situations that, to some extent at least, have a certain uniqueness about them. Personalities, personal 'careers' and identities, specific reactions to specific subjects, and so on, combine to make simple generalizations at best a partial account of the situation.

Added to these reservations, we should note that research on control is particularly difficult in view of the nature of the event being studied and it would be naive to treat the available research evidence as conclusive or to ignore the fact that it often faces methodological problems which limit the reliability of its findings. We need to recognize that the measurement of control problems in schools is very much affected by the ways in which incidents are defined, identified and recorded, and that events connected with control do not readily lend themselves to objective or unequivocal analysis because they generally involve subjective interpretation and personal discretion rather than precise, absolute matters of fact (D. H. Hargreaves *et al.*, 1975; Stebbins, 1970). In the case of assaults on teachers, for instance, while teachers might claim to have been the victim of an assault they might not be prepared to make a formal complaint or prosecute the pupil(s) involved. The example of the chemistry teacher at Beechgrove illustrates the point. The boys were reported to their heads of house but this did not lead to any kind of official complaint against either boy for assault. In consequence, the two assaults would not have appeared in the official statistics for attacks on teachers because neither the teacher himself nor the other teachers immediately involved chose to pursue the matter any further. In effect, the incidents were *treated* as cases of particularly disruptive behaviour but not as assault. The degree of the assault will obviously have a bearing on this and the matter is further complicated because the term 'assault' itself covers the whole range of violence from vicious attacks that cause serious injury to milder forms of physical contact that leave no real damage. The crucial point is, though, that where statistics on assault are restricted to those that teachers are prepared to follow up in such a way (for example, ILEA figures) then clearly the official figures will understate the situation.

Equally, if not more important, are the limitations inherent in the use of questionnaires as the means for gathering data on control problems in schools. Questionnaire surveys [4] depend either on reports by local authorities or on reports from teachers about their own experiences of the problem and such 'self-reporting' causes two kinds of difficulty. First, as Docking (1980,p.8) indicates, surveys of this kind cannot control for variations in teacher perceptions of, and attitudes towards, violent or disruptive behaviour and cannot, therefore, provide any objective index of trends in the incidence of such behaviour. Second, 'self-reporting' assumes that teachers are *willing* to reveal the extent of control problems they face. Yet as Comber and Whitfield conclude from their survey, 'Perhaps the most significant impression of all is [the reticence] of most teachers to admitting any disciplinary problems and the stigma attached to not being able to keep order' (Comber and Whitfield,1979,p.10). The implications of this, of course, are that estimates based on teachers' reports will be prone to *under*estimating the extent of the actual control problems in schools because teachers themselves might not wish to admit to such problems.

Complications such as these, while they do not entirely invalidate the survey estimates of control problems, suggest the need for a method of inquiry about classroom control which does not rely just on teachers' self-reports. In particular, it suggests the need for some in-depth fieldwork to complement the survey/self-report type of research and to check just how far the survey/self-report conclusions can be substantiated *in the practice* of control in schools.[5] For this reason, the investigation of control in this study does not embark on a wide-ranging survey leading to the production of statistical data but, instead, rests heavily on qualitative/interpretive studies of school settings. Whenever possible this involves *ethnographic* data which aid the understanding of the phenomenon of classroom control not by bombarding the reader with figures but by investigating the *meaning* of classroom control for teachers and pupils involved in specific settings. Secondary source material is used from a variety of studies, particularly in Chapters 2, 3 and 4, where it is drawn upon quite extensively in order to provide a framework for analysis and to 'set the scene'. The subsequent Chapters 5 and 6, rely more exclusively on primary source fieldwork data drawn from Ashton, Beechgrove and Cedars. But, even though the balance of primary and secondary source material changes, the concern remains the same: to explain the participants' perceptions and experiences of classroom control and the way these are, on the one hand, shaped by the organization of the school and, on the other, shape interaction in the classroom, corridors and playgrounds.

Notes

1 On this point we can adopt Lowenstein's (1975) distinction between 'violence', which he defines as 'fairly vicious attacks on other pupils or members of the school staff', and 'disruptive behaviour' in which he includes 'any behaviour short of physical violence which interferes with the teaching process and/or upsets the normal running of the school'.

2 See, for example, Davies (1978), Delamont (1983), Docking (1980), Furlong (1976), Gannaway (1976), D. H. Hargreaves (1982), Marsh *et al.* (1978), Nash (1976), Woods (1979).

3 Though as Fuller (1980), Troyna and Smith (1983), Jeffcoate (1984) and Troyna (1984) have argued, the notion of 'West Indian underachievement' is one that needs to be treated with considerable caution as emerging evidence points to social class factors rather than cultural traits associated with the West Indian home as the causal agent concerned with underachievement.

4 Examples of this approach are Association of Education Committees (1975), Comber and Whitfield (1979), Dierenfield (1982), Lowenstein (1972, 1975), Mills (1976), Pack (1977). Notable alternatives to a dependence on questionnaire responses can be found in D. H.Hargreaves *et al.* (1975), Galloway *et al.* (1982), Lawrence *et al.* (1977). Anecdotal accounts of the issue exist, for example, in Francis (1975) and Haigh (1979).

5   The work of Lawrence *et al.* (1977, 1983) provides a good example of how research on incidents of disruptive behaviour can use self-reports by teachers in conjunction with interviews to provide a more detailed picture of the incidents, the motives of those involved and the context in which the incidents occurred.

2
Teacher Training

Underlying contemporary debates about the causes and extent of control problems in school there is some consensus that responsibility for control ultimately rest squarely on the shoulders of the classroom teacher. Teachers appreciate this as much as the public and politicians. But this fact tells us little about why classroom control is considered to be such a vital part of the job, nor does it explain *how* control is recognized, established and challenged by those involved. Without the answers to such questions our knowledge of the phenomenon of classroom control has to remain at best sketchy, at worst crude. For this reason, this chapter and the next start to explore the reasons why classroom control is regarded as so central to the life of classrooms and what meaning it holds particularly for those charged with establishing control – the teachers.

This chapter starts from the premise that, since classroom control is a basic part of a teacher's duties, clear guidance on what it is and how to get it might expect to be found in the professional training which teachers undergo in their passage from novice to fully fledged teacher. Certainly, there are a number of books aimed at helping teachers on this score.[1] The evidence suggests, however, that when it comes to solid, practical help in the classroom the guidance is rather dilute and indirect. Neither during their experience at college nor at their initiation in school do newcomers receive coaching about classroom control to anything like the extent that is necessary to ensure their survival in the classroom. As we shall see, the result of this situation is that newcomers are thrown back on to their earlier experience of classroom life as pupils in an attempt to cope with the tense situation into which they find themselves thrust, and end up giving little credence to the principles of teaching that were presented during their college training. Their success indeed, seems to depend far more on a rather tacit set of assumptions that are based on first-hand classroom experience both as a pupil and as member of staff – what can be called a 'Hidden Pedagogy'. This, rather than the principles for teaching laid out in 'traditional' or 'progressive' pedagogies, appears to be the basis of survival, and its significance rests in no small part on the assumptions it makes about classroom control.

Teacher training and attitudes towards classroom control

In the case of teaching the link between training and the way experienced teachers operate in the classroom is not at all straightforward. One of the main reasons for this is that, within the world of teaching, there is no single approach to the job which is universally accepted as the right approach and there is actually a level of controversy and disagreement within the profession which complicates matters by confronting newcomers with an element of choice, discretion and interpretation of their role. This means that the passage from novice to qualified teacher involves more than simply learning a set of standard procedures because, from the moment they enter the occupation, newcomers become embroiled in a debate between two contrasting versions of what the teacher ought to be doing – the 'traditional ' and 'progressive' pedagogies.

In a sense it is obviously too simplistic to suggest that approaches to teaching are really to be split into just two types that correspond exactly with traditional and progressive pedagogies and there is sufficient empirical evidence for us to be sure that, in practice, styles of teaching are a complicated amalgam of ideas and methods that are unlikely to fit neatly into any set of formal principles about teaching (cf. N. Bennett, 1976; Galton,1980). Yet, having said this, the broad distinction between traditional and progressive pedagogies serves a useful purpose by putting into relief alternative visions of the teacher's role and it is perhaps mainly for this reason that the dichotomy has become firmly embedded in discussions about the role of the teachers.

With traditional pedagogies, the teacher is regarded as the instigator and director of all that passes for learning during a lesson. Worthwhile knowledge is the preserve of the teacher until he/she dispenses it to the class and, from this perspective, there is considerable emphasis on the teacher's strong control over what is to be learned, at what pace and in what order. This strong academic control is generally coupled with an element of what has been called 'social Darwinism'. The pupils here are seen as having a rather low capacity for social responsibility and as exhibiting in pronounced form a fundamental intractabililty inherent in human nature. As a result, the teacher's role is very much involved with curbing antisocial behaviour in pupils and great emphasis is placed on the teacher's ability to control a class.

Contrasting with this vision, the progressive pedagogies promote a teaching role which is far less obviously authoritarian. Pupils' knowledge is respected in its own right and teachers are encouraged to use the pupils' existing knowledge and interests as a means for discovering new things. In this case the teacher's role is seen as that of a facilitator or catalyst whose function is to mobilize the pupils' inherent inquisitiveness. The control element is played down. Control, it is argued, can be reduced in significance as part of the teacher's role if pupils are encouraged to become interested and involved in the learning process and are therefore less in need of cajoling or forcing into the lesson structure. Pupils' compliance, in this view, derives from the teaching while for the traditional pedagogy control precedes the teaching.

In practice, though, the newcomers are not faced with an entirely free choice between such alternative views of the work because when they start their training they are generally exposed to progressive rather than traditional pedagogies. Education professors are well known for promoting ideas about the job which are generally far more 'progressive' in nature than the ideas and practices of those at the chalk-face and, as a result, trainees tend to exhibit an orientation to teaching which is correspondingly progressive. This progressive orientation, however, is rather short-lived because it appears from the available evidence that the ideas and practices promoted by education professors actually fail to achieve much of a long-term impact on the thinking of recruits and that there is, in some ways, a 'discontinuity' between programmes of training and the later classroom activity of teachers. Repeatedly, researchers have been led to the conclusion that, whatever the short-term impact of college courses, experienced teachers appear to bear few of the hallmarks of their professional training.[2] They develop an attitude of what Hoy (1968, p.314) refers to as 'impersonality', pessimism and 'watchful distrust' and, as Morrison and McIntyre confirm,

> When the educational opinions of ... teachers are examined over the whole period of training and initial teaching it is clear that changes during training in the direction of increased naturalism, radicalism, tendermindedness are to varying degrees being reversed after a single year of teaching.
>
> (Morrison and McIntyre, 1967, p.162)

There is an apparent shift from progressive to traditional pedagogy and, in essence, a change in attitude on the part of new recruits

(1) away from warm, child-centred, humanistic, progressive and 'open' approaches, and
(2) towards cold, bureaucratic, traditional approaches with a 'custodial' pupil control ideology.

Changes is attitude towards classroom control are, of course, crucial to this general change of direction. As Hoy, amongst others, has demonstrated, despite the attempts of college tutors to promote a permissive approach to pupil control and discipline, teaching practice and the probationary year witness a distinct shift to a more 'custodial' pupil control ideology and to a generally more authoritarian approach. The new teachers he studied showed a quite dramatic change in attitude which meant that, despite what they were taught during training,

> after two years of teaching experience, 87 per cent of the elementary teachers and 82 per cent of the secondary teachers described their school as one in which 'good teaching and good classroom control tend to be equated'.
>
> (Hoy, 1969, p.262)

In this respect, perhaps more than any other, despite the great variety of training establishments,[3] the one thing the training programmes have in common is their apparent inability to instil any lasting influence.

But what causes the newcomers to change their attitudes so sharply when they leave their college? It could be, as writers like Hoy have suggested, that the change is simply a response to the new set of demands facing the recruit when he/she starts in the classroom. While at college these demands centre largely on satisfying tutors in terms of predominantly academic criteria and this puts some pressure on the trainee to express views more or less in line with the (relatively progressive) thinking of college tutors.[4] What is expressed during training, in other words, is shaped to a large extent by the ethos and demands of life in the college setting where theoretical/academic considerations are important. But, when faced with the particular demands of teaching practice or the initial year of teaching, orders of priority are likely to change and the changing attitudes might merely reflect the new demands of the particular circumstances in which they are operating. This point, though, has led some recent writers to be suspicious about the extent to which the attitudes-as-expressed can be treated as an authentic representation of the internalized views of the student teacher or probationer – particularly in the light of the rapid and dramatic reversal of these attitudes (Hanson and Herrington, 1976; Lacey, 1977; Mardle and Walker, 1980; Shipman, 1966, 1967). These writers argue that attitudes-as-expressed need to be understood not necessarily as a genuine response to the situation but possibly as a 'front' disguising other more internalized attitudes which the trainee or new teacher feels it would be unwise to express under the prevailing circumstances. So while trainees might *appear*, for the purposes of success on the courses, to have adopted a progressive stance, they might just as easily remain detached from this position and secretly hold other views about the nature of teaching.

Such a 'strategic fraud' on the part of trainees would imply, of course, that in many basic respects, the attitudes of trainees could remain unaffected by the content of training courses, a point brought home to Petty and Hogben in their research. On the basis of their findings they argue that,

> Students [can] employ 'impression management' to insulate themselves from college influence and to retain attitudes they entered with, attitudes more akin to those found in schools than those the training institutions would like to transmit.
>
> (Petty and Hogben, 1980, p.51)

As they go on to suggest, this prospect is due in large part to the relatively weak socializing impact of the training establishments. Unlike other professions such as medicine and law where considerably more attention is devoted to instilling new 'professional' attitudes, for teachers the training rigours are relatively mild and ineffective (Dreeben, 1970; Lortie, 1968). As a result, the vision of their work with which newcomers emerge after training is not necessarily one moulded by the period at college, but can depend on beliefs and expectations about the work which existed prior to, and independent of, what went on at college. The initial predispositions of those entering the occupation, in other words, have every chance of surviving the period of training to emerge as strong as ever in the attitudes and expectations of fully fledged teachers. Certainly, Petty and Hogben's findings led them to conclude just this because they discovered that teachers, probationers and trainee teachers viewed the job of teaching in basically the same way as a sample of students who had had no contact with the world of schools since they themselves had been there as pupils. Training it seemed, had done little to alter the teachers' or trainees' conceptions of the task.

The power of these prior expectations, and their ability to survive despite the efforts of college tutors, owes much to the ingrained nature of those expectations. Trainees, after all, have sat in classrooms and watched teachers at work for some thirteen years before starting their training and during this period it is reasonable to assume that they developed some pretty firm beliefs about what was good teaching and what was bad. So, by the time they enter college, *trainee teachers like most other members of the public have an ingrained conception of what the job is all about as a result of their protracted experience as pupils in classrooms* (Hanson and Herrington, 1976; Lortie, 1969, 1975; Maddox, 1968; Mardle and Walker, 1979). This means that even as trainees they are not really total newcomers to the world of teaching. They do not have to struggle to fathom out the job since their previous experience would appear to be quite sufficient to inform them about the nature of the demands they face and the things they are expected to achieve. Their primary concern, indeed, is not to discover what the job is all about but to find out how to accomplish it.

For trainees and probationers, then, the main anxiety tends to revolve around developing the skills that will enable them to put into practice what they already know to be the demands of the job. This, as Petty and Hogben's research revealed, would explain the trainee teachers' preference for the practical side of training. In their words:

> The orientation shown by the respondents was essentially practical and task-oriented, and reflects the common complaint by teacher educators that students have little interest in the wider ramifications of their jobs: the sociological, psychological, philosophical and political implications and consequences of what they do. Again, this finding is consistent with Lortie's assertion that education students, having been socialized for teaching by their experiences as pupils, and thus believing they know teaching, are more concerned with learning practical skills than theory which may bear upon those skills.
>
> (Petty and Hogben, 1980, pp. 55-6)

In this respect the situation of new teachers can be likened to that of someone starting driving lessons. New drivers have probably already observed what driving is all about as passengers but during driving lessons the problem they face is how to achieve the various manoeuvres they know to be necessary. Their anxiety is not about what is to be done but about the practical skills which will allow them to accomplish their goals – and protracted study of the Highway Code is of limited value for this purpose. The Highway Code will not furnish the learner with the skills of steering, changing gear, three-point turns or hill starts yet it is these which are the kinds of practical concerns which rightly capture the attention of the beginner.

In the same way, it is easy to predict that new teachers will worry about their abilities at the practical side of the job and therefore look favourably on the opportunity to practise the skills in class. That is why teaching practice is seen as the most important part of the training programme. For the same reason, we can see why training programmes which appear to be weighted towards theory raise anxieties on the part of the trainees about the amount of practical experience they can get (Morrison and McIntyre,1969).

Socialization on site

The newcomers' anxiety about the practical skills of the job, as Dreeben points out, is compounded by the fact that,

> Unlike medical training institutions, institutions that train teachers do not provide anything approaching a system of supervised apprenticeship; thus many new teachers start their first job green – and then go it alone. ... Immediately following graduation (or even before), students embark on the first job, one entailing full classroom responsibilities, ecologically isolated from experienced colleagues, but subject to sporadic supervision from school administration, supervision that even if helpful cannot be based on prolonged observation. Hence the portrait of the beginning teacher: cut-off from the sources of knowledge underlying his work, isolated from colleagues and superiors, left alone to figure out the job – discover, correct or repeat his own errors – through his own experience.
>
> (Dreeben,1970, pp. 64,128-9)

Given the same responsibility in the classroom as senior staff, their problem is not only that they are pretty 'green' but that, right from the start, they are left very much to their own devices, as Lortie (1968) puts it, 'to sink or swim'. They actually receive remarkably little direction on the mechanics of coping with a classroom full of pupils and what guidance they do receive tends to be around broad patterns of acceptability rather than specific details of practice because, as Edgar has argued:

> Teaching differs from the professions in the relatively small amount of colleague interaction if affords newcomers. Isolated in individual classrooms, experienced colleagues have little time to 'socialize' the new teacher into the 'teacher subculture' other than in terms of broad 'general acceptability'.
>
> (Edgar, 1974, p. 246)

This process in which newcomers are assimilated [5] into the existing regime does not normally need to be oppressive because the new teachers are generally anxious to win the approval of the established staff and are prepared to slot in with their approach rather than cling to ideas gathered from training or elsewhere (cf.Hanson and Herrington, 1976; Leacock, 1969; McPherson,1972). It is the rare exception indeed who stands out against established practices during his/her first years in the profession. When we consider, too that pupils exert considerable pressure on newcomers and experienced alike to fit in with established conventions, in particular the need to assert control,[6] it is not surprising that if the newcomer is conscious of any inconsistency between approaches suggested at college and those advocated by colleagues, it is the ideas of senior school colleagues which carry the day. Just as Hanson's (1975) research revealed:

> The contrast between [the need for control] and the radical rhetoric at college creates no great tensions for most students. What matters most to them is what is seen to matter most to senior colleagues.

In practice, then, it tends to be the *ability* of newcomers to establish control, rather than their willingness, which proves to be the main stumbling block. This point was illustrated by Mr Evans, a senior teacher at Ashton's upper school who had official responsibility for overseeing the performance of new teachers in the school. In his experience 'performance' generally boiled down to 'control' and, during an interview, he recalled several cases of newcomers who had struggled because their classroom control was not good enough. As he saw it, *all* teachers suffered occasionally from difficult pupils and awkward classes but new teachers had to work especially hard at establishing a reputation for good control.

> But some can't and, just rarely, some don't want to. In most cases, with a school like Ashton, it comes as quite a shock to the system to have to face a class of [lower band] kids. Most of the probationers are pretty level-headed, though, and use their common sense. They soon adapt and sort of tone down their high-flown theory they've just learnt at college and concentrate more on control. Well ... they have to just to survive. I help to an extent – usually a word in their ear if I feel they're not putting enough emphasis on control. More usually it's kind of counselling while the probationers go through the trauma of adjusting to reality ... the real world of teaching as it is in Ashton.

On another occasion Mr Evans described his anxiety over Miss McCready, a geography teacher on her probationary year. She had spoken to Mr Evans on two or three occasions about leaving the job. Mr Evans was convinced that she was potentially a good teacher and that, if she could 'stick it through the early stages', she would survive and flourish. What worried Mr Evans was that, in the last instance, there was little he could actually do to help. Certainly he could encourage her and console her when things were bad. He could also suggest certain general ways of improving the situation. But his advice and counselling, as he saw it, could have little direct effect on the classroom situation since he could not engage in coaching practical skills without joining her lessons and effectively broadcasting her 'failure' to pupils and colleagues alike.

Miss McCready was one of only three teachers who declined to be observed or interviewed. She said that, because she was new to the job, there was little she could say that would be enlightening and little to see by way of 'good practice' in her lessons because she was still learning the ropes. In the staffroom she avoided discussion of work-related matters except with colleagues with whom she worked closely. At the end of her probationary year she left the job and, as later word of mouth indicated, had quit teaching altogether.

The question posed by this is whether Miss McCready would have fared better had she been initiated in a less isolated manner. At Cedars, for example, new humanities teachers could expect to spend a good proportion of their time (usually one-third to one-half) as part of teams teaching in open-plan classrooms. Here they had the chance to witness experienced teachers at work and to operate under the protective wing of senior colleagues whose very presence in the same room could do much to alleviate initial control problems. Certainly the probationers observed at Cedars were appreciative of the help this gave them and it was an advantage to the team teaching arrangements which was openly discussed by both the experienced teachers and probationers.

In general, the newcomers said that they received implicit support, occasionally direct support, from the more experienced members of the team and this made their initial teaching experience less fraught with tension and anxiety. This support could be observed in the way experienced team members reacted when they were joined by a trainee or probationer. On one occasion, for instance, when a team that had been observed over five double periods was joined by a student teacher who replaced one of the regulars, the lesson started with an uncharacteristic outburst from one of the regulars demanding work and 'no mucking about this lesson'. The other team regular went on to operate with his group behind a partition, while the 'task-master' worked alongside the student teacher. Though they worked with separate sets of pupils his presence and occasional admonishments to his own set seemed to have a ripple effect on the student's set of pupils. When the situation was discussed later, the regular team member said that his actions were consciously those of the 'team heavy'. As most of the humanities staff recognized, it generally fell to one of the team members to become the 'team heavy' who took the burden of responsibility for control in the group. As this particular member of staff put it:

> One person often gets to be the 'team heavy' – an uneasy role. The role will be more of a responsibility for the experienced teacher – and it's good for the less experienced who get sheltered a bit.

By 'coming on heavy' he felt he could show the student how to 'make your presence felt' and 'get things moving' while at the same time, giving the student a chance to settle down and get some confidence. The student appreciated these motives and said she felt that

> as an inexperienced teacher, it's a great help to be alongside more ex- perienced colleagues, especially in a course which makes heavy demands.

Two of the staff in their probationary year, however, expressed some reservations about being cosseted by the system. Both had come to the school on their only teaching practice (being postgraduates) and spent most of their timetable with humanities lessons. Both were subsequently appointed to their first posts in the department. At the start of their probationary year they were slightly worried that their experience of 'solo' teaching was slight and that they were not well prepared for the more individualized approaches of the conventional classroom. They also reflected upon the embarrassment that team teaching could cause trainees. As one of the probationers, Miss Robinson, put it:

> You have to weigh the good against the bad. I mean, the best side of [team teaching] for me was that I was never so much worried about discipline ... more about how good my lesson preparation was if the other staff were going to hear it. *That* caused me sleepless nights. Then back at [the postgraduate education department] I was really a bit surprised at the horror stories that the other students had. I don't mean I never worried about control but the others seemed to talk about it as being everything ... and bugger the lesson content. ... Now *I've* got the jitters a bit because I've not had to really face a long spell with a particular class up till now. ... and another side of it is this. When you start off in team – er, the team situation – all your mistakes are visible not just to the kids but to the colleagues as well. God knows how I got the job when I think of some of the things I did when I started last year on T.P. – and that they all saw. At least I suppose they saw them. I felt I wished the floor would swallow me up sometimes. There was no chance of making your mistakes in private and keeping quiet about them.

The situation at Cedars, it ought to be stressed, was not common and for the vast majority of teachers there is no opportunity to choose between shared and individual modes of induction. For them it is a case of necessity that they go solo straight away and draw on a fund of common sense to help them survive initial encounters.

Classroom experience and the 'Hidden Pedagogy'

There seems to be an inherent continuity in approaches to the work, handed on from generation to generation of teachers and remarkably impervious to changes in educational theory. As we have seen, this is because the crucial factor in shaping teachers' understanding of their work is *classroom experience*. As pupils, before they ever enter the world of professional teaching, and later as trainees and probationers, it is through this medium that they come into contact with the kinds of ideas and practices which are vital to the job.

Both kinds of experiences expose the teacher to the culture of the classroom – to a system of beliefs and expectations about appropriate behaviour which carries with it some demand for conformity from those who participate in the class. And both kinds of experiences expose the participants to certain pressures which have to be understood and met if the participants are to operate successfully in the classroom. For the pupils, as it is well known, this means coming to terms with the 'hidden curriculum' (Jackson,1968; Snyder,1971). Informally, they learn about such things as the need for tolerance and patience, and how to cope with the frustrations of classroom life. Through harsh experience they learn what frame of mind they need to adopt, what deceptions and what strategies, if they are to survive in the classroom. Most of all, they learn about the vast difference in power that exists between teachers and pupils. To survive in classrooms, in other words, pupils learn to deal with a covert set of hoops and hurdles. But what is generally overlooked is that teachers also face a set of pressures arising from the informal organization of the classroom. They, too, need to conform with an unwritten set of assumptions about their conduct if they are to survive and flourish – assumptions that do not stem directly from either the formal organization of the school or the principles of teaching outlined in formal pedagogies. These assumptions, on the contrary, stem from the culture of the classroom and they provide the teacher with a set of aims and methods for use in class which, as a parallel to the 'hidden curriculum', we can call a 'Hidden Pedagogy'. At the heart of this Hidden Pedagogy is the need for teachers to establish classroom control. As Haigh has noted,

Control the class, then *teach* the class is a common theme passed on from one teaching generation to another, with the accompanying notion that the teacher who cannot control never gets to the point of being able to teach.

(Haigh,1979, p.7)

It means that no matter how brilliant in their subject, teachers who are unwilling or unable to establish control of the classroom are doomed to failure and will always be seen as poor teachers. And it states quite categorically the order of precedent which the two aspects of the job deserve, with control being not simply a desirable complement to teacher skills but an absolute imperative without which there can be no progress in the task. As Marland (1975, p.4) has made the point, 'a teacher must face up the fact that "controlling" is part of his task, and if he fails in that he will fail in much else'. This was the crucial issue facing Miss McCready at Ashton. As a history teacher, with twenty-two years teaching experience commented on her plight, the training establishments were largely to blame for not preparing the likes of Miss McCready for the basic realities of successfull teaching.

> They come out of college with all these bright ideas – these marvellous ideas – and yet, when they find they're in the classroom situation they try and put these ideas over before establishing their own classroom discipline. And so many of them find that they're failures ... and, you know, a lot of them give up very easily.
>
> You know, they don't seem to teach them in colleges now it's discipline first – you can put over your subject afterwards. You have to establish your rapport with the child ... the children in the classroom. They'll know where they are with you. You'll know where you are with them. And then you can start from square one – but you have to have control first. You cannot go wading in with kids flying all over the place.

Obviously, this facet of the Hidden Pedagogy is not hidden from teachers. Nor is it necessarily hidden from pupils because they are a part of the setting that gives rise to the Hidden Pedagogy. The Hidden Pedagogy is, however, 'hidden' in the sense that it contrasts with the explicit principles and formulae for teaching that exist in the traditional or progressive pedagogies. The Hidden Pedagogy, for its part, is an *implicit set of assumptions about the aims of teaching and methods of achieving them* which, whilst certainly understood and practised by teachers, rarely becomes articulated into something with the status of a theory of teaching. It is a common-sense knowledge of the job that underpins successful teaching but one which is not usually given much credence in philosophical or theoretical considerations of the job. This common-sense knowledge, as we have seen, *exists prior to, and independent of, formal pedagogies*. Although in many respects it is similar to the traditional pedagogies, especially in terms of classroom control, it comes from a very different source – classroom experience. It is not learnt in the college lecture theatre but the school classroom and because *it tends to be learnt on site through classroom experience* it is, in this sense markedly different from formal pedagogies. For the same reason, it also differs from Bernstein's (1977) concept of 'Invisible Pedagogy'. The Invisible Pedagogy as used by Bernstein differs basically because it refers specifically to the pre-school and infant stages of teaching and it stems from the organic solidarity of the 'new middle class' in which the relevant teachers are located. The Hidden Pedagogy, in contrast, stems from school organization and permeates primary and secondary level of teaching. It derives from classroom experience rather than social class experience and emphasizes the classroom context as the salient factor in shaping teachers' attitudes and activity at work. Finally, as the previous comment would suggest, the Hidden Pedagogy is *a practical response to the prevailing classroom circumstances*. Prevailing classroom circumstances play a vital role for the Hidden Pedagogy especially when it comes to explaining classroom control in the contemporary school because they are treated as independent variables rather than dependent variables. Unlike formal pedagogies which stress the way teachers can *create* the circumstances that best suit the required approach the emphasis is clearly on the way teachers *react* to situations which they did not initiate. It reflects the real world of the classroom where teachers find so much of their time is spent responding to situations rather than creating them and where the dominant features of classroom life are frequently preordained. The Hidden Pedagogy is a response to these circumstances. It is a set of aims and methods of teaching which stem from practical imperatives in the classroom and, unless these imperatives are altered, it will tend to persist despite changes in pedagogic theory espoused at training establishements or elsewhere.

As a basis of teaching, the 'Hidden Pedogogy' contains wisdom about survival in class and guidelines that differentiate practical competence as a teacher from practical incompetence. Fundamental to this is the belief that classroom control is the prime duty of the teacher and that classroom control is an absolutely necessary prerequisite for successful teaching. The centrality of classroom control to the work of teachers, then, does not depend upon the acceptance by teachers of some sort of theoretically supported pedagogy which locates classroom control amongst a variety of related aims and methods. The centrality of classroom control, in reality, reflects partly the way ideas held by the public and enshrined in legal precedent can permeate into the thinking of those who embark on teacher training courses, partly the legacy of classroom practices witnessed and experienced by entrants to the profession during the thirteen or so years when they themselves were pupils, partly the failure of teacher training courses to destroy the trainees' lay or common-sense assumptions about the job, and partly the socializing effect of senior colleagues who tend to reinforce the expectations about control most new teachers bring to their first job. When these factors are combined, it is little wonder that any formal pedagogy that espouses less emphasis on classroom control, no matter how logical or justified its argument in its own right, is likely to be resisted. It flies in the face of what 'everyone knows' about the job of teaching.

Having identified in the Hidden Pedagogy a source of continuity in attitudes about classroom control, we need to be wary about treating it as some static, monolithic force dictating to teachers the aims and methods it is reasonable for them to adopt. For two reasons, indeed, the Hidden Pedagogy ought not to be seen in this light. First, whereas formal pedagogies strive for logical consistency in the ideas and beliefs they put forward, the Hidden Pedagogy as we have argued, is a pragmatic response to a variety of classroom pressures and strives for practical usefulness more than anything else . Coherence and logical consistency, therefore, are not top of its lists of priorities. It is likely to contain certain contradictory ideas. It can adopt ideas associated with traditional pedagogies and it can adopt ideas associated with progressive pedagogies but the rationale for their inclusion has little to do with the development of a logically related set of ideas and practices. Their inclusion, instead, depends on their ability to cope with the practical problems confronting the the teacher in the classroom.

The second reason the Hidden Pedagogy should not be seen as a static, monolithic force is because it is *context specific*. Because the Hidden Pedagogy is related to classroom conditions, if these conditions change so will the Hidden Pedagogy. What we have argued so far is that teachers face some characteristic problems and that these exist despite some more obvious differences surrounding the organization of lessons. That does not mean that such problems are immutable or that alternatives are out of the question, Alternatives in the form of 'free schooling' pose radically different problems for teachers, especially in terms of the teachers' control function and, according to this reasoning, can expect to generate a different Hidden Pedagogy (cf.Swidler,1979). Even within more mainstream schools, team teaching and open-plan classrooms can pose basically new problems that promote a different Hidden Pedagogy and, to a lesser extent, so will those lessons that occur outside the normal kind of classroom. Games lessons, drama, art classes and lessons that take place in laboratories all contain circumstances liable to cause a slight variation in the Hidden Pedagogy pertaining to those specific kinds of lesson.

Conclusion

It appears that neither teacher training nor the induction of newcomers on site does much to alter perceptions about the classroom control originally brought to the occupation. Teacher training has a limited influence because of its relatively weak socializing effect and the ability of trainees to put up a 'front' disguising and protecting deeper-felt views of the job. And at school, during teaching practice and the probationary year, the socialization of the newcomer is usually of a general nature and, in any case, such pressure as exists tends to confirm and reinforce expectations already held by the newcomer. So there is a good chance that teachers, even when fully fledged, hold certain views about the job which match their assumptions before they entered the occupation.

Classroom experience is crucial to this deep-rooted continuity in ideas and practices: it is classroom experience that shapes the Hidden Pedagogy. But what *is* the experience of classroom life which affects generation after generation of pupils and teachers, and what features of schooling can we identify that have remained stable over a number of generations and which are so general that they are experienced across the spectrum of schools in the educational system? If we are to probe the phenomenon of classroom control further these are questions that must be answered.

The answers, as we see in the next chapter, emerge from a consideration of the way schools are organized. School organization involves certain arrangements which are so common and fundamental to our perception of the normal school that their effects are all too easily overlooked or regarded as immutable facts of life. However, close investigation reveals that we can hardly afford to overlook the basics because it is these basics that account for the continuity of the Hidden Pedagogy: they have survived changes in curriculum and formal pedagogy, and permeate most types of schooling.

The pressures and opportunities experienced by teachers and pupils are shaped in large part by these basics of school organization and, in particular, we will concentrate on the effects of the closed classroom arrangements that are prevalent in contemporary schools. But to emphasize the point that aspects of school organization like the closed classroom are not immutable facts of life, we will also look at case-study material drawn from Cedars to consider how classroom experience can be radically altered by changes in organization – in this instance the adoption of team teaching in open-plan classes instead of the conventional closed classroom.

Notes

1 See, for instance, Curwin and Mendler (1980), Docking (1980), Gnagey (1975,1981), Marland (1975), Robertson (1981) and Saunders (1979).

2 Notable contributions to this argument come from Butcher (1965), Dreeben (1970), Hanson and Herrington (1976), Hoy (1967, 1968, 1969, 1974), Hoy and Rees (1977), Kuhlman and Hoy (1974), Lacey (1977), Lortie (1968, 1969, 1975), McNamara (1981), McIntyre and Morrison (1967), Morrison and McIntyre (1967), J.K. Taylor and Dale (1971), Williams (1963),Willower et al. (1973), Wiseman and Start (1965).

3 As Lacey (1977) amongst others, has argued, there are a variety of routes towards qualification as a teacher and this multiple-type entry does much to make teaching a divided profession – split by subject specialisms, by the type of institution for training, by the final qualification, and by the distinction between primary and secondary teachers.

4 Ironically, as Mardle and Walker (1980) argue, the colleges retain a highly traditionalist hidden curriculum even if the content of the work espouses progressive alternatives. Student success *demands* a certain traditionalism in this respect.

5 The socialization of new teachers is dealt with in some more detail by Coulter and Taft(1973), Hanson and Herrington (1976), Lacey (1977), Lortie (1968, 1975) and Willower (1969).

6 The socializing effect of pupil on teachers has been examined for instance by Delamont (1983), Hanson and Herrington (1976) and Nash (1976), and the pupil's expectation of strong control is explicit in Corrigan (1979) and in Docking's (1980) review of the relevant literature.

3

School Organization

Schools tend to be large, crowded places. Though there are a number of primary and rural schools with just a few teachers and fewer than fifty pupils, the norm is much larger particularly in the case of secondary schools (see Table 3.1) and this generates certain problems characteristic of large organizations. As large organizations, schools first need to achieve goals and *meet objectives set by the environment* in which they exist. They need to be responsive to the social, political and economic demands that dictate whether they survive or fail. Second, they need to co-ordinate the activities of their personnel in a manner which is effective for achieving these goals within the constraints of the available resources. Such co-ordination of activities normally involves a *formal organizational structure* in which duties are specified through rules and procedures, where responsibility and accountability is established through a hierarchy of authority, and where resources like materials, personnel and time get distributed in a rational manner. Third, there is a need to *motivate members to comply with the formal structure*. Without a tolerable level of compliance the formal blueprint for activities becomes irrelevant and useless, and this is why large organizations tend to build in to their structure a blend of incentives, rewards and sanctions designed to persuade the members to operate within lines set by the formal structure. But to point to such aspects of organization which schools share in common with other large organizations is not to imply that schools are simply the same as all other large organizations. This would miss the fact that, in terms of their goals, their structure and motivation of their members, schools have certain features which give them a distinctive character (cf. King, 1983). What it does do, instead, is to suggest a perspective for investigating the effects of schools on their members – a perspective which might reveal something about the character of control problems and how they have their genesis in the ways schools, as a particular kind of organization, try to cope with

Table 3.1   *School size based on pupil numbers: England, January 1983*

Type of school	Number of pupils							
	1–50	51–200	201–400	401–800	801–1,200	1,201–1,500	1,500	Total
Primary	1,905	10,503	6,723	472	1	—	—	19,604
Middle deemed primary	1	147	533	76	—	—	—	757
Middle deemed secondary	—	33	286	326	3	—	—	648
Secondary	1	43	206	1,401	1,550	486	218	3,905
Total	1,907	10,726	7,748	2,275	1,554	486	218	24,914
Total Pupils	65,387	1,410,495	2,096,588	1,298,087	1,519,335	644,293	364,717	7,398,902
% of pupils	(0·89%)	(19·06%)	(28·34%)	(17·54%)	(20·53%)	(8·7%)	(4·93%)	

Source: DES, Schools Statistics Dept, May 1984

co-ordinating many staff and pupils towards given goals using limited resources.

School goals

Paisey (1981) argues that an important hallmark of schools as organizations is the degree of uncertainty surrounding their goals. There is no one agreed educational goal nor is there agreement on the political purpose of education. Teachers, pupils, parents, politicians and governors bring to bear a variety of perspectives and values which ensure that schools operate with goals that are complex, shifting and frequently disputed from within their own membership.

This absence of any single, agreed educational goal has repercussions in terms of classroom control. It means that classroom control can have no universally accepted role to play in the achievement of educational goals, with different members being able to interpret the role in different ways. As we saw in Chapter 2, traditional and progressive pedagogies provide very different visions of the role of the teacher and few signs exist of any consensus emerging from the competing paradigms. There are, in other words, no absolute bench-marks offered by educational theory against which teacher activity, pupil behaviour or school results can be measured.

But to make matters even more complicated, schools have to contend with a vast range of environmental factors that have a direct bearing on what the members themselves see it as possible to achieve. Quite distinct from ideal goals – goals that educational theory might suggest are desirable – there are material and social factors affecting each individual school which account for differing *perceptions* of the kinds of goals it is feasible to pursue. For instance, where schools draw on deprived, inner-city areas – materially and culturally ill-disposed towards the kind of experience offered at school – schools can develop expectations which elevate the significance of classroom control and relegate the significance of instruction and learning. Schools can become permeated by a *'low achievement orientation'*. This low achievement orientation results from mutually reinforcing expectations held by teachers and pupils where teachers, looking at factors like the social class, ethnic mix and material environment of the school, come to hold low expectations about the pupils' academic performance while the pupils, reflecting such expectations and bringing relatively low academic aspirations from their social background, combine to provide a school ethos in which academic attainment gets written off as irrelevant. At the same time, the task of getting classroom control takes on added proportion and added significance for the routine daily life of classrooms; so much so that, at the extreme, lessons can become all about classroom control and precious little to do with inculcating knowledge. This happens in the 'sink' schools, the ghetto schools, the rough inner-city schools where survival for the teacher means being able to impose a semblance of order in class in a situation where pupils have a low tolerance for having discipline imposed on them and little respect for the authority of the teacher. In these situations, control can become so important that it actually seems to become the be-all and end-all of teaching, a point which Kohl noticed when recounting his experience of teaching in a ghetto school in New York. As he writes:

The [administrative] demands were as frequent as they were senseless. Yet they were insignificant when compared with the pressure to fulfil the functions considered most essential to a teacher's success – controlling the children. The entire staff at the school was obsessed by 'control'.

(Kohl, 1970, pp.12–13)

More than a trace of this was evident at Ashton and Beechgrove where the staff felt that they suffered rather badly as a result of the catchment areas. Ashton being in the London Borough of Brent and Beechgrove being in the London Borough of Camden, the teachers at both schools argued, with some justification (Denscombe,1977) that their intake of pupils posed special difficulties which exacerbated problems of control and hindered the prospects of concentrating on the inculcation of curricular knowledge – 'teaching proper'. The pupils did not reflect the full range of abilities and were particularly under-represented at the the top end of the range: there was a large ethnic mix in the schools; and there was predominance of pupils from working-class backgrounds. As a result, the staff at both the schools were not optimistic about the possibility of concentrating on 'teaching proper' and held modest expectations about the academic potential of their pupils. This low expectation, it is fair to point out, did not appear to be based on elitism or prejudice on the part of the staff but was a product of the teachers' understanding of their pupils' social background and the way this provided the pupils with limited academic aspirations. Reinforced by their classroom experience, this low expectation led the staff at Ashton and Beechgrove to stress that, under the circumstances in which *they* worked, the control aspect of their job assumed particular significance and occupied much of their time. As a social studies teacher as Ashton commented:

> I think the main problem is that we have got a group of kids whose sort of natural intelligence is being masked by their social background and inability of communicating with the teachers – an inability to cope with this kind of structure of class that we have got. So they get bored and become behaviour problems. And this, you know, snowballs into the fifth year when there are behaviour problems for everybody, you know. We just struggle with the control, control, control, all the time. And that's what it's all about then, you see, getting control.

Schools with 'control' goals are not necessarily the norm, of course, but what the situation of sink, ghetto, 'problem' schools illustrates is the variety of goals that can coexist where goals are shaped by theoretical preferences and practical considerations in the absence of any universally accepted or unilaterally imposed goal covering all schools.

Accountability

The variety and complexity of goals in education does not prevent individuals from having fairly coherent conceptions of what they would like to see achieved and how they would pursue their goals. Head teachers, in particular, wield considerable influence in this respect and normally have the power to implement their vision via their control over the organizational structure of their school. Burgess (1983) demonstrates this point in his ethnography of a Midlands comprehensive school in England. He shows how the head, Mr Goddard, had a definite conception of the school's purpose and maps the ways in which Mr Goddard sought to impose this vision through the school organization. As with most schools, Mr Goddard was aided by the formal articles of government of the school which stipulated that 'The head teacher shall control the internal organization, management and discipline of the school'.

Limits to the power of head teachers are set by the accountability of schools to the community. Though head teachers in Britain, the USA and Australia have considerable autonomy in the way they organize their schools and the educational goals they set for staff and pupils they cannot entirely ignore the pressure put to bear by central government, quangos, local education authorities, school governors, the media or parents, each of which has an interest in the school's activity and can, through certain channels, exert pressure to operate in a given manner. These pressures, especially those arising from the local community's involvement, are admittedly greater in the USA than in Britain (Banks, 1976; Dreeben,1970) but, even in the British context, obligations founded in the Education Act, 1944 (England and Wales) provide a basis for some accountability of head teachers to the community and hence allow the public some control, however oblique, on the policies of schools. Through school governors, a body of representatives not only of teachers but also of the local authority, political parties, parents and 'lay' personnel, the public has some assurance that the interests of the community are being served by the school. The school governors have powers which include the appointment and dismissal of the school's head teacher, the determination of the general direction of the school (including conduct and curriculum) in consultation with the head teacher, participation in the appointment, dismissal or suspension of teachers, and the monitoring of all proposals and reports affecting the school. They are, therefore, in a position to affect the ethos of the school and even to have some broad influence on matters like the curriculum and school discipline through their authority over the head teacher of the school. It may not prove to be a direct interference but it certainly sets bounds to the liberty of the head teacher to run his/her school in defiance of public wishes.

The parameters to the head teacher's autonomy seem to be set only by broad, possibly vague, ideas about the effectiveness and acceptability of the school's work, and perhaps Reynolds and Sullivan capture the point when they argue that

the individual school has wide latitude in its choice of strategies, providing only that the end result of the use of a particular strategy is successful social control of the pupils.

(Reynolds and Sullivan, 1979, p.49)

This still leaves considerable discretion open to head teachers in the kinds of goals they seek to achieve and the way they organize their schools – a point well illustrated in the US context by Metz's (1978) study. She provides detailed ethnographic material showing differences between two schools in the same school district in California. Despite being in the same school district, having a very similar student intake, balanced by race and class as a result of deliberate policy and the shared catchment area, Metz notes how the two schools were markedly different in their ethos and their output. 'Hamilton' stressed student initiative and good teacher–pupil relations rather than academic performance and had an open, democratic style of organization. It was normally quite a noisy place with plenty of distractions and disturbances in the classrooms and corridors. The students, for their part, were mainly 'responsible' and 'creative'. By contrast, 'Chauncey' emphasized a more traditional approach focusing on academic performance rather than pastoral welfare and having a firm, centralized administrative structure. The school was generally orderly and quiet with passive, if 'uncommitted', learners.

Metz points out that the 'Canton' school district in which the schools were located contained a particularly challenging and sceptical body of students including militant working-class blacks and radical middle-class whites. Hamilton's head had set out to win over these disaffected students and to incorporate them into the school. He appeared to succeed in this but the price to pay was the stress and turmoil engendered in school life. Chauncey's head had tried to tackle the matter of alienated students 'head-on' by trading off a 'residual awe' of teacher authority. The result was a far more orderly existence but one which systematically 'failed to engage the skeptical students'.

School ethos

Such emphasis on the importance of each school's organization, of course, goes against the grain of a certain orthodoxy in the sociology of education which stresses the impact of the home, family and social class as determining factors on school performance. It stresses, instead, the role of individual schools and, especially, the ability of individual head teachers to influence the ethos and organization of 'their' school in a way that has a definite impact on the kinds of pupils produced by the school.

Support for this position has come from research by Rutter *et al.*(1979) which captured the attention of the media when it was published because it seemed to confirm what common sense had always suggested – that some schools are better than others and that the relative success or failure of a school owes much to the way the school is organized. Rutter and his colleagues drew this conclusion from a comparison of pupils at twelve inner London comprehensive schools in which they measured standards of behaviour, academic achievement and attendance at the school. Their findings, they argue, show that the 'ethos' of a school has a definite impact on the behaviour and academic performance of its pupils. This 'ethos' results from certain facets of the school organization such as the types of rewards and punishments used in the school, the relative emphasis placed on academic or pastoral matters, the nature of teacher actions in classrooms (that is, the extent to which such actions are directed to individuals or the whole class), the extent of surveillance exercised by senior staff over things like the syllabus and homework, the nature of pupil responsibilities and participation in the school, and the degree of stability in both teaching and friendship groups. Quite separate from things like the size of school, the age of the buildings and the quality of the facilities available, these organizational factors are seen as providing a climate in the school which is more or less conducive to good behaviour and academic performance. Specifically they suggest that pupils performed better in those schools in their study which adopted an 'academic' ethos – where academic matters were emphasized, where homework was incorporated into the work-plan, where there was a well co-ordinated curriculum and where the teachers had high expectations of their pupils.

A similar kind of message is to be found in the research of Reynolds and Sullivan (1979). They report on research in eight secondary modern schools in South Wales, schools which they distinguish in terms of those that tended to us 'coercive' strategies and those that tended to use 'incorporative' strategies, that is those that stressed power and authority as the basis for control compared with those that encouraged participation by both pupils and parents, and which emphasized the interpersonal nature of education. Like Rutter *et al.*, Reynolds and Sullivan argue that a different school ethos has an effect on the success of a school. They found that the schools that tended to use 'incorporative' approaches showed a higher academic success rate, half the delinquency rate, and attendance rates that were 6 – 7 per cent better than at the 'coercive' schools. Since all eight schools were located in the same local authority and took pupils from a similar working-class area, they feel confident that the *cause* of the observed differences between the output of the schools can be attributed to the nature of the organization (coercive/incorporative) and that 'schools do make a difference'.

Rules and procedures: the formal specification of conduct

The first and most obvious way in which the school organization can be structured to achieve specific goals and create a specific ethos is through general policy statements and through particular school rules designed to implement that policy. In practice, schools almost invariably have some written statement covering the aims of the school and the ethos it hopes to provide. Sometimes these are geared towards the conduct of pupils. As Burgess reports from Bishop McGregor school, there were ten general school rules instigated by the head which were explicitly aimed at the pupils. The last two of these, incidentally, were quite interesting in the way they left little doubt about the position of pupils in the authority structure of the school: 'All [pupils] are to refrain from prohibited practices', and 'All instructions from teachers and other adults are to be obeyed'(p.45).

Other rules are designed for teachers to follow, acting like procedures or guidelines. At Ashton and Beechgrove, for example, new staff arriving at the schools were given folders containing guidance on most aspects of their work explaining the broad policies of the school and the way the school operated. These folders, in effect, provided more than just a description of how things actually operated because they also included *official guidelines* on the attitudes and approaches that teachers in the school were expected to adopt towards various facets of the job. At Ashton, for instance, the official guidelines included the following recommendations specifically relating to pupil discipline and classroom control:

If any pupil is persistently unduly mischievous or lazy and the individual teacher is unable to correct this, the matter should be reported to the Head of House, who should then deal with the pupil.

Isolated cases of anti-social behaviour may occasionally blow up in a classroom and threaten to disrupt a lesson. If an emotional outburst seems imminent, it may seem advisable to remove the pupil from the classroom. Such a pupil must *not* be stood outside the classroom door.

Outside the classroom, it is the duty of every member of staff immediately to deal with any cases of unruly or silly behaviour they may observe.

Pupils should be given to understand that they sit where the teacher wants them to sit: it is desirable that they should have a regular place. Do not allow any furniture to be moved without your express permission. Do not allow pupils to open other pupils' desks.

Except where a class is to use its own room, pupils should not enter a room before the arrival of the teacher. Pupils who are waiting should always be seated on a bench in the corridor. Do not permit standing round a doorway. It is preferable and more useful if teachers who are waiting for classes wait in the corridor and exercise general supervision meanwhile.

Before beginning dismissal procedure at the end of a lesson check the floor for litter and have each pupil clear his own area before moving. Check that the desk and chairs are tidily arranged so that the room will have an orderly appearance for the next class.

Have all the class on their feet and in lines before instructing them to go. Do not keep back any pupil or allow yourself to be manoeuvred into delaying a pupil. Try at all times to convey the importance of punctuality.

Pupils are not permitted freely to visit toilets during lesson time and a first request should be refused on principle. Subsequent requests should not produce an easy permit either.

Pupils should not be sent back to another room to retrieve a forgotten item. Do everything you can to discourage the incidence of individuals moving from one room to another during lesson time for trivial or avoidable reasons.

Given a secure, well defined framework and pattern of behaviour the great majority of pupils will produce good work and conduct. Constant praise and encouragement should be dispensed, and recognisable co-operation from the pupil should be rewarded.

Official guidelines such as these are common enough in schools and tantamount to *formal rules* governing the work of teachers and conduct of pupils in the school. They are an attempt to exercise control over activity in order to gain some uniformity of operation and to help in the achievement of an officially designated goal. As the study of organizations in general tells us, these are likely to become more prominent in large schools because the larger the school the greater the need for formal rules and procedures to control the activities of its personnel. As the feasibility of personal control fades, more bureaucratic methods are required to coordinate the workings of the various members and more formalized procedures are need for allocating responsibilities, time, resources and personnel within the school (Anderson,1968).

In reality, however, the impact of formal, bureaucratic rules and policies on the conduct of teachers and pupils is fairly limited and, as a control mechanism, they turn out to be fairly weak. One reason for this, as Delamont (1983, p.39) points out, is because 'no set of formal policies, however detailed, can cover all everyday occurrences, and specific events inevitably have to be negotiated'. Another related reason for the weakness concerns the nature of classroom life: specifically, the *uniqueness* of pupils in the class, and the *uncertainty* surrounding events and situations. The uniqueness of pupils baulks the influence of formal rules and prescriptions for teacher behaviour because such rules would require teachers to operate in a uniform fashion toward pupils in classroom situations which vary widely and are, in a sense, unique and ever changing. As Dreeben argues,

> the diversity of pupils in classroom and the range of differences in interest and capacity they present, make carrying out the main instructional activities according to rules exceedingly difficult because rules work best in more standardized setting.
>
> (Dreeben, 1970, p. 47)

The uncertainty surrounding events arises because the pupils in the classroom are not passive recipients of commands by teachers and their reactions can be unpredictable even to the most experienced of teachers. Within the classroom there are highly complex set of personal relationships between the teacher and individual pupils/groups and, of course, between the pupils themselves. The extent to which the teacher can predict, let alone control, events in classrooms puts a logical limit to the possibility of planning the lesson and rationally moulding events according to pre-established, formal guidelines. Because the events that arise are frequently 'out of their hands', teachers actually spend much of their time *reacting* to events.

The uncertainty of classroom events figures prominently in teachers' accounts of their work. It means, for them, that their activity in classrooms is frequently a response to situations they had neither planned nor predicted and that, whatever reaction they make, it cannot always be made on the basis of considered deliberation. Almost inevitably there will be an element of spontaneity and even guesswork about it because there is little time to delay or investigate matters prior to decisive action. As Jackson has observed, because the 'good' teacher realizes that reactions need to have some immediate impact on the situation, frequently the teacher 'must be content with doing not what he *knows* is right, but what he *thinks* or *feels* is the most appropriate action in a particular situation. In short, he must play it by ear' (Jackson, 1968, p.167). Smith and Geoffrey

(1968) similarly identify the need for instantaneous decision-making and 'situational thinking' as imperative to the routine activity of teaching. Teachers, they argue, have little opportunity to reflect before taking action and have little opportunity to take courses of action designed to achieve distant educational goals. The pressures of classroom life oblige teachers to operate with short-term, 'proximate' concerns geared towards coping with immediate problems that arise in the classroom.

Informal rules

The extent to which teachers and pupils can be bound by formal rules and policies is limited, in effect, by the situational exigencies of the classroom and the way these make it unrealistic to operate on the basis of rigid rules and policies designed for general purposes. But this does not mean that rules are irrelevant for classroom behaviour. In their study *Deviance in Classrooms*, D.H.Hargreaves et al. (1975) note that rules exist in schools in different levels and in different forms. Their research in two northern comprehensive schools makes it clear that, though formal 'school rules' normally exist, they are supplemented by a variety of informal rules.

In one sense these informal rules are much more localized than general school rules. They operate in particular classrooms, at particular times and with particular people: they are 'context specific'. So, for example, rules about the amount of noise which is permissible will depend on the kind of lesson being taught, on the teacher in charge, on the kinds of pupils, on the phase of the lesson, and on the time of day/week/term. Even then, these rules can be altered, suspended or renegotiated depending on the circumstances. Occasionally, this can cause problems – as in the case of a history teacher at Beechgrove. During one of her lessons on a Tuesday afternoon she was having difficulty with a group of four girls who were persistently noisy and would not attend to the lesson. The girls were disrupting the other pupils through their talking and the teacher, though obviously aware of the disruption, made no strong effort to stop the pupils. To the observer there seemed little out of the ordinary about the episode and my field-notes simply noted who was involved and what kind of disruption they caused. Yet after the lesson the teacher made a point of confiding how awful she felt about what had happened. Apparently one of the girls was in the teacher's tutor group and the teacher knew that there were special problems connected with the girl's home life at the time. In view of these severe domestic problems the teacher said that she deliberately 'soft-pedaled' and avoided 'reading the riot act' to the pupil. As she explained later during an interview:

Normally I'm pretty strong on discipline and control and I wouldn't have tolerated the disturbance. After a few polite requests for quiet and concentration I would have to put a stop to it. I sort of throw a fit and act up a bit angry. But with 'Jean' in the group I couldn't, could I? – I mean not with knowing about her problems and how this might affect her. So on this occasion I had to break my rules about behaviour in class ... sort of, just for the sake of the one child. And it gets so annoying because really there was no excuse for the other three girls and it was certainly interfering with the rest of the class. But what can you do? I mean, if you're going to be sensitive to the needs of particular pupils. I'll have to have a word in quiet with her during the tutor group meeting tomorrow and tackle it that way.

In the eyes of this teacher, circumstances dictated a relaxation of the usual classroom rules governing pupil behaviour. As she interpreted the situation it called for a change of approach in response to the change in the context.

Informal rules are not only context specific, they are also characteristically *'personal'*. They are personal in the sense that they can differ from teacher to teacher and, perhaps more importantly, they are personal in the sense of being negotiated by the parties to the interaction (Delamont, 1983). Rules are not simply imposed by teachers on pupils but are the end-product of a subtle bargaining procedure between teachers and pupils in which disagreement and resistance need to be overcome. As Delamont emphasizes:

> The classroom relationship of teacher and pupils is ... a joint act – a relationship that works, and is about doing work. The interaction needs to be understood as the daily 'give and take' between teacher and pupils. The process is one of *negotiation* – an on-going process by which everyday realities of the classroom are constantly defined and redefined.
> (Delamont, 1983, p. 28)

This 'symbolic interactionist' perspective on classroom behaviour, the way it is negotiated and the significance it has for the participants, is at the heart of the analysis of classroom control presented in subsequent chapters.

Authority and autonomy: control and the closed classroom

The uniqueness of pupils and uncertainty of events in classrooms, in fact, does more than just limit the applicability of formal rules. For the teachers at least it also limits the extent to which it is possible to make them accountable to outsiders. Teachers develop specialized and particularized knowledge of the pupils in their classes so that their decisions, geared as they are to the specific circumstances of the class, cannot be held accountable to those outsiders (including colleagues) who are excluded from the particularized knowledge. As Eggleston has argued:

> No authority outside the individual classroom can possibly make many of the decisions now required of the teacher because no external authority can have access to the evidence on which they must be based.
> (Eggleston, 1979, p. 2)

Lortie (1969) and Bidwell (1965) have indicated that this unique nature of classes, and the power over decisions which it affords the classroom teacher, has been a highly significant factor in the ability of teachers to promote the image of the teacher as a 'professional'. Lortie, in particular, emphasizes the point that aspirations to professional autonomy are characteristic of teachers' attitudes about their work and that teachers value highly the autonomy which their work affords. But this autonomy, as he argues, cannot be traced back to the power of the occupational group as a 'profession' to demand independence in the exercise of their work from 'lay' outsiders. As we have seen, teachers do suffer interference to some extent from their accountability to the public via school governors and the local authority and, especially in the United States, teachers are not accorded a status which allows or justifies the level of autonomy to which they lay claim. Neither in terms of a professional association nor in terms of controlled entry and training can teachers align themselves with the classic professions like law and medicine and claim the autonomy accorded practitioners in these occupations. Indeed few of the traits normally associated with the professions are fully evident in the case of teachers (Wilensky, 1964). As employees working in large organizations with little *de jure* basis for professional autonomy, the strength of these aspirations might seem hard to explain but, as Lortie and Bidwell both argue, we have only to look at the immediate work situation to begin to understand why it is that teachers value autonomy and regard it as a rightful part of their job. Bidwell, for his part, points to the 'functional and temporal differentiation' which characterizes the job. Because the work splits teachers into separate classrooms and segregates them during lesson periods, a sense of autonomy is built into the everyday practices of teachers. Because their work is organized in concurrent lessons – each teacher being responsible for separate portions of work involving subject matter not familiar to most colleagues – teachers are rarely in a position to observe let alone supervise or control, the activity of colleagues. (Dreeben,1970; Hanson and Herrington,1976; McPherson,1972).

The reason for this lies *within* the school organization. As Bidwell (1965) has emphasized, schools are characterized by what he calls a 'structural looseness' in their organization and it is specifically this looseness that allows the members of the organization a reasonable degree of freedom from constraints imposed by the formal structure, rules and procedures, and which fosters teachers' aspirations to professional status and autonomy. The crucial factor in the 'structural looseness' according to Bidwell is the existence of the 'closed classroom'. In terms of spatial arrangements the closed classroom has the effect of physically isolating lessons from one another. The four walls separate teaching units in a most concrete fashion. But as Lortie indicates:

> The self-contained classroom ... is more than a physical reality, for it refers as well to a social system, a set of recurrent and more or less permanent social relationships. Under this arrangement the teacher is separated from immediate supervision, and intrusion into his private domain is prevented by a set of understandings subscribed to by administrative officers and teacher colleagues. A set of norms exist which act to buttress the ecological separation:
>
> (1)   the teacher should be free from the interference of other adults while teaching,
> (2)   teachers should be considered and treated as equals, and
> (3)   teachers should act in a non-intervening but friendly manner towards one another.
>
> (Lortie, 1964, pp. 274-5)

Interestingly, the norms of the closed classroom are to be found in different cultural settings. Warren's (1973) research, for instance, demonstrates quite clearly that in both the United States and Germany the effect of the closed classroom is to provide something of a 'sanctuary' for teachers, limiting their accountability to outside bodies for what goes on within the classroom. As he puts it:

> while a teacher's public behaviour is the object of continuing and effective cultural surveillance, his classroom behaviour is relatively immune to control processes generated either within or outside the formal structure and operation of the school.
>
> (Warren, 1973, p. 291)

This is not to imply that the closed classroom provides an impregnable sanctuary because:

Legal sanctions establish teachers' responsibility for the physical safety and well-being of pupils under their supervision [and] ideological pressures from the community affect the teacher's use of curricular materials. Irresponsible classroom management provokes administrative intervention, and collegial sanctions may operate to constrain classroom behaviour. Furthermore, the pupils themselves constitute a socio-cultural force to which teachers must respond.

(ibid, p. 291)

But it *does* mean that what goes on in classrooms is more or less protected from direct surveillance, supervision and direction from colleagues or administrators so that, though rules and regulations may exist at a general level, their application in the classroom is very much open to the discretion of individual members of staff according to the specific circumstances as they perceive them. In effect, it provides a setting which enhances the possibility of aspiring to professionalism by isolating teachers from one another and obliging them to operate as individuals with a minimal amount of supervsion. In Lortie's words, it

supplies teachers with the personal and spontaneous choice which they would have if they possessed the privileges granted those high-prestige, fee taking professions ... It acts to limit the influence of the formal and bureaucratic order which, on paper, is the structure [of the school].

(Lortie, 1964, p.279)

The closed classroom, then, serves a vital role in the school organization because, not only does it generate aspirations to professional autonomy amongst teachers, at the same time is also satisfies those aspirations. It provides a situation which largely overcomes an inherent strain between, on the one hand, the *bureaucratic* demands from administration and external authorities who aspire to accountability, routinization and uniformity of output, and on the other, the demands for *autonomy* from teachers for whom the idiosyncratic, intractable and even incorrigible nature of unit-inputs (pupils) requires flexibility of method and assessment, and a particularized knowledge not available to outsiders.

The mutually reinforcing effects of the closed classroom and teacher aspirations for autonomy over affairs in their own classrooms have a fundamental influence on the nature of classroom control in schools. In the first place, it puts the burden of achieving control squarely on the shoulders of individual teachers. Despite the rhetoric of head teachers about control being the responsibility of all the teachers – a collective effort – the material circumstances tend to dictate otherwise. During lesson time, at least, teachers are left to their own devices to make what they can of the situation. The second repercussion of the closed classroom is that the process of negotiating classroom control normally takes place between *individual* teachers and the specific cohort of pupils in the class. And what is agreed with one class might not count with another. In other words, in terms of both the formal delegation of authority and the informal negotiation of rules, a dependence on the closed classroom makes classroom control a very 'personal' phenomenon. As we shall see in Chapter 4, there are a variety of forms of control that can be deemed 'personal' (cf. Swidler, 1979), but at present the key thing to note is that formal rules and authority structures contained in the school are of less significance for classroom control than the ground rules for behaviour negotiated informally between individual teachers and their pupils.

The allocation of resources: materials and personnel

The highly individualized responsibility for control and personal basis for negotiating control are factors reinforced by the technology of teaching which means that the vast investment in education is characterized by a heavy expenditure in areas like wages and buildings and a relatively small allocation to equipment and consumables. As Table 3.2 demonstrates, in England and Wales salaries for teaching and non-teaching staff in the financial year 1979–80 accounted for over 60 per cent of the gross recurrent expenditure of local education authorities whilst items like books and equipment together accounted for only 3·3 per cent. It is not surprising, therefore, that most schools suffer a chronic shortage of equipment and materials and, as teachers would be quick to point out, this puts considerable burdens on them in their efforts to put across their subject.

Table 3.2   *Educational expenditure, England and Wales, 1979–80*

Teachers' salaries	49·0%
Non-teaching staff salaries (inc. administration and maintenance)	13·1%
Premises and fixed plant	10·2%
Books and equipment	3·3%
Other educational expenditure	6·9%
Fees awards and allowances	9·2%
School meals and allowances	9·2%

Sources: DES, Statistics of Education, vol. 5, 1982

The problem of equipment and materials, however, is not simply one of ageing textbooks and worn out workcards. There is, quite apart from this, a rather more fundamental way in which the available equipment and materials influence the teachers' approach to their work. This is the fact that, in the age of space exploration and the microchip, the classroom remains strikingly bereft of technologically sophisticated equipment. Normally, the only things a teacher can rely upon being available in the classroom are the desks and the chairs, the blackboard, textbooks, paper and pens of various description – all rather cheap and primitive in terms of today's technology. In the last couple of decades, it is true, there has been a drive towards greater use of audio-visual aids but the point is not without poignancy for the currrent practice of teaching because, although things like television, films, records, tape recorders, pocket calculators, overhead projectors, slide viewers, and a host of other slightly more up-to-date resources – even micro computers – have become available in schools, their use in the classroom is still the exception rather than the rule.

There is, of course, one very obvious reason why the use of such audio-visual aids and relatively high technology has remained the exception rather than the basis for routine teaching. Externally imposed *financial constraints* limit the amount of such equipment that can be bought by schools. But less obvious, perhaps, is the fact that the availability of the equipment for use in lessons is limited further, so far as individual teachers are concerned, by a variety of practical problems they face when trying to make use of the equipment. Shared facilities need to be booked in advance and are not always available when needed; technician support might be lacking; new skills and retraining might be required. Looked at in this light, it is easy to see why teachers might prefer to retain a dependence on books and paper, chalk and blackboard, textbooks and lectures. In a sense, they have little alternative because they work in a situation that limits their options in this respect. The circumstances dictate that they have to operate with a rather rudimentary technology, only occasionally enjoying (restricted) access to high technology equipment and audio-visual aids. Westbury (1973) argues that this can have significant repercussions for the practice of teaching. Most importantly as he points out, low technology and limited equipment tend to foster a reliance on the available *personal* resources as the means for managing the class; that is, teachers' charisma and the development of personal relationships with the pupils. Under the circumstances, 'managing' the classroom will have relatively little to do with the allocation and co-ordination of technical resources and must have much to do with the allocation of personal resources (teacher time and effort). Particularly in terms of classroom control, the limited and low-level technology available in classrooms effectively precludes the possibility of the teachers abdicating a central, personal position in control and obliges him/her to use personal, rather than technical, means for controlling the class. The teacher is not actually in a position to use technology as a means for either gaining control or justifying his/her demand for obedience simply because to hide behind 'technological imperatives' requires a suitable technology in the first place.

Clientele: the pupils

The *interpersonal* nature of the classroom technology is a feature of classroom life that is reinforced by the number of pupils facing the teacher during lessons. The average *pupil*–teacher *ratio* in England stands at 16.5:1 for maintained secondary schools and 22.3:1 for maintained primary schools (1983 figures: DES Statistical Bulletin 6/84, April 1984). Such averages, of course, disguise considerable variations between local education authorities in the primary sector from 25:1(Thameside) to 18.4:1 (Brent and Newcastle upon Tyne) and, in the secondary sector, from 18.5:1 (Bradford) to 13.3:1 (Brent) (DES Statistical Bulletin 2/82, 1982). More importantly, perhaps, such ratios also tend to underestimate the actual *size of classes*. In 1983 the average size of class in English maintained primary schools stood at 25:1. Secondary schools in the maintained sector had an average class size of 21:1, with over half of all classes having 21 or more pupils in them (DES Statistical Bulletin 6/84, April 1984). Such figures for secondary schools include sixth-form classes for the 16 plus age band for whom the average class size was 10.4 in 1983 and, as Table 3.3 shows, the actual size of classes tends to be much higher than pupil–teacher ratios alone would suggest. But even these figures shroud the extent to which teachers face large classes. Other DES figures, for instance, show that the proportion of pupils in classes with over 30 pupils is much greater than the overall pupil–teacher ratio or average class size might suggest (see Table 3.4).

Table 3.3   *Average class sizes for selected subjects and age-groups*

	Yr 1	Yr 2	Yr 3	Yr 4	Yr 5
English	25·6	26·3	26·3	24·2	24·5
Maths	25·7	26·1	26·2	24·5	24·1
Chemistry	27·0	27·3	27·1	21·6	20·7
French	27·4	27·9	27·8	21·7	20·7
History	27·0	27·5	27·1	22·3	21·8

Source: Derived from DES Statistical Bulletin (5/82) March 1982

Table 3.4 *Proportion of pupils in classes of over 30*

PRIMARY SCHOOLS:

proportion of pupils in classes of over 30 %			%		%
Birmingham	47·9	Hampshire	38·3	Cambs	32·8
Bolton	43·6	Dorest	37·8	Coventry	32·7
Somerset	43·5	Northumberland	37·4	Warks	32·6
Avon	42·4	Bucks	37·1	Leeds	32·6
Sutton	42·3	Cornwall	36·9	Tameside	32·4
Hereford/Worcs	41·7	Gloucs	35·5	Devon	32·2
Kent	40·6	Oxford	35·3	Berkshire	32·1
Oldham	39·5	Kingston	35·2	Cheshire	31·8
Lincs	39·3	Trafford	35·0	Dudley	31·6
Redbridge	39·0	W. Sussex	34·0	Solihull	30·9
Bexley	38·4	Kirklees	33·7	Essex	30·7
Lancs	38·4	St Helens	33·5	Herts	30·6
		Wiltshire	33·5	Wigan	30·5
		Bury	32·8	Derbyshire	30·2

Secondary Schools:

proportion of pupils in classes of over 30 %			%		%
Sutton	26·5	Leeds	19·5	Rotherham	16·8
Merton	24·0	Dorset	19·4	E. Sussex	16·1
Somerset	24·0	Birmingham	19·4	Bury	15·9
Oldham	22·9	Bradford	19·3	Sefton	15.9
Bolton	22·2	St Helens	19·3	Solihull	15·9
Hereford/Worcs	22·1	Lancs	19·0	Cornwall	15·6
Liverpool	21·8	Derbyshire	18·6	N. Yorks	15·5
Enfield	21·5	Kingston	18·5	Warks	15·4
W. Sussex	21·5	Cheshire	18·5	Oxford	15·3
Wakefield	21·0	Glous	17·9	Bromley	15·0
Northumberland	20·7	Devon	17·8	Manchester	15·0
I. of Wight	20·2	Cambs	17·7	Durham	14·8
		Kirklees	17·5	Humberside	14.7
		Staffs	17·3	Hampshire	14·6

Source: Guardian, 22 May 1984

Dealing with large groups, teachers have to develop strategies which, though personal in the sense of relying on interaction between teacher and class, become depersonalized in the extent to which they are geared to the individual pupil. With all the goodwill in the world, as they point out, it is difficult to react to pupils as unique individuals with distinct personal biographies and needs because, given the large number of pupils with whom the teacher interacts in different classes, the teacher cannot always be familiar with the detailed circumstances of particular pupils. Added to this, the imperatives of group-management in the classroom require spontaneous action and immediate results covering the conduct of the whole class and rarely afford the prospect of reflection and deliberation on the course of action best suited to the personal needs of a specific pupil. So, as a result, the teacher is obliged to devote considerable energy to matters of 'man-management' and to basic problems of organizing large groups of people.

It is not only the number of pupils per class which puts pressure on teachers to adopt a man-management function, *the nature* of the pupils also is significant on this point. Different kinds of pupils give rise to different kinds of problems and these, in turn, lead to different kinds of treatment. Teachers are highly attuned to the diversity between kinds of pupils and are quick to adapt their style to what they perceive as the the requirements of the particular pupils being dealt with at the time. Under the circumstances, of course, they can hardly afford to be insensitive to the variety of pupils they get in the class since the pupils are, in effect, the 'clientele'. As Gray has made the point:

> Since the teaching relationship has much of the counselling relationship in it, 'client' would seem to be a useful term to describe the pupil–teacher relationship, particularly since it implies a degree of professionalism in the relationship.
>
> (Gray, 1979, p.38)

Unlike most clients, however, pupils are not free to opt out of the relationship if it does not meet their perceived needs. Like prisoners, involuntary mental patients and, to some extent, military personnel their membership is compulsory in the sense that it is not a voluntary act that can be reversed at will.

The *obligatory attendance of pupils*, perhaps more than any other single factor, provokes the possibility of an unwilling participation by pupils in school affairs. As Dreeben points out, the fact that there is compulsory attendance at school means that

> most classrooms are bound to contain some pupils who would rather be elsewhere and who express that desire through disruptive activities. [And] in any classroom of twenty-five or more pupils it is likely that at least one brings with him symptoms of psychological disturbance sufficient to upset the proceedings.
>
> (Dreeben,1970,p.95)

But, as any teacher will be quick to point out, in practice, some classes are decidedly more difficult to control than others. The reasons for this are, by now, fairly well known. It is because pupils undergo a selection process in which they are segregated according to variables like age, sex, social class, ability and religion that the group who finally appear as a class before the teacher are likely to share many vital characteristics – including, of course, a general disposition to schoolwork and classroom discipline. On the one hand, it can produce the kind of clientele in a class who are academically ambitious and prepared, in the main, to accede to the wishes of the teacher while, on the other, it can generate 'pockets of resistance'. But, in either case, teachers are all too conscious of the fact that control problems are not spread evenly between all classes and are definitely concentrated in particular schools, in particular years and in particular subjects.

Segregation exists in the first place because the education system tends to be stratified by age. Pupils, in the vast majority of cases, are parcelled into age-groups according to their year and month of birth and this 'year' basis for organizing schools clearly serves to present teachers with classes who are less diverse than so-called 'vertically grouped' classes where pupils of different ages are mixed together for instruction. In fact, it goes a long way to establishing an element of homogeneity within classes. This is not to deny that some primary schools have integrated pupils of different ages within one class. In small rural schools this has always been a necessity. In some larger primary schools it has been adopted for conscious pedagogic reasons. In secondary schools and the majority of primary schools, however, classes are normally based on single-year groupings. This age factor is often taken for granted or seen as an immutable feature of the education system but, on the matter of classroom control, its influence cannot be ignored. Certain 'years' are notoriously worse to handle than others with severe control problems normally being more prevalent in particular years such as the second to fifth forms in secondary school than elsewhere.

The characteristics of the class are also affected by the catchment area of the school and methods of selective entry to the school both of which help to bring pupils of a similar kind into the school. Initially the location of the school will a have an effect of the kind of pupil who joins, segregating urban from rural and, to a large extent, giving intakes which draw on characteristically working-class catchment areas or characteristically middle-class catchment areas. This segregation by social class is evident all the more because of the co-existence of fee-paying schools alongside the system of local authority education, with the fee-paying schools predominantly getting pupils from the wealthier and more educationally ambitious backgrounds. In a similar fashion, single-sex schools and religious denominational schools have an entry policy which presents the teacher in the classroom with a group of pupils whose backgrounds and expectations are likely to have a distinctive, common character.

The nature of the clientele is further influence by selection based on ability. D.H. Hargreaves (1967) has demonstrated this in terms of the secondary modern school, Lacey (1970) in terms of the grammar school. But even in the comprehensive school, selection by ability continues to exist. Streaming, setting and banding persist as forms of segregation-by-ability and selection to GCE/CSE groups in the fourth and fifth year of comprehensives does much the same thing in the sense of providing classes whose educational proclivities tend to be of a kind.

The effect of this on classroom control is shown in Ball's (1981) ethnography of 'Beachside', a comprehensive school on the south coast of England. In the early stages of Ball's research at the school a system of 'banding' was in in operation in which pupils were segregated into three broad ability groupings. Control problems were concentrated in the middle band – not the lower band as one might expect because the lower band were placed in smaller classes, often with specialist remedial help and were treated with a high degree of pity and sympathy by the teachers who regarded them as 'unfortunates'. The middle band, by contrast, were seen as troublesome, lazy and noisy, and in some classes teachers are reported to have ceased to struggle to get them to work in lessons because the control problems were so great. The middle band, in which the working class were over-represented compared with the top band, were absent from school nearly twice as often as the top stream , received ten times more detentions, completed one-third as much homework and were generally more alienated from the school.

Aware of the social effects of such banding, the staff at Beachside introduced a mixed-ability organization to replace the banding. They abandoned banding, Ball recalls, explicitly because they were worried about its effect on discipline. The move appeared to have been successful because the new organization led to improved attendance, less frequent disruption of lessons and two-thirds reduction in the rate of detentions. Ball points out, however, that there was opposition to the introduction of mixed-ability organization which centred around the teaching of maths, French and science, and that pressure from these quarters led to the retention of setting for these subjects. A similar situation was to be found at Ashton, Beechgrove and even Cedars where, despite official policies which favoured mixed-ability grouping, certain subjects were taught in 'sets'. At Ashton and Beechgrove it was maths, French and English; at Cedars, despite its explicitly progressive ethos, maths and physics were taught in sets. Such subjects would seem to present a special case.

The question of whether certain subjects do not lend themselves to mixed-ability grouping was taxing the minds of the French department at Ashton, as one incident vividly demonstrated. I was conducting an interview with the junior member of the French staff – a probationer – in an empty staffroom. The teacher drew attention to the controversy within the department about the need to introduce setting for the subject. He was opposed to the move and felt that the introduction of setting in French after the first year at Ashton had been a betrayal of the principle of comprehensive education. During this criticism of his department, especially his head of department, two other members of the French staff came into the staffroom and began to discuss the issues in a three way debate. Tempers began to rise, even more so when the head of department joined the discussions after he came into the staffroom at break. The tape recorder was switched off early in the three way debate – it seemed prudent – but the interview had obviously touched a raw nerve and sparked off a heated exchange of views which left me in an embarrassing position. The head of French left at the end of break asking to see me first thing the next day. At this meeting, rather than any allegations of being an agent provocateur, he set about 'putting me in the picture' and explaining why the department, under his guidance, had found it necessary to introduce sets from the second year. Basically his argument was a practical one:

You see, with the comprehensive set-up came the idea that there should be mixed-ability teaching. That is, doing away with streaming and doing away with any sort of selection, where you just pile them all together regardless of ability. And, quite honestly, as far as I can see over the years, it has just not worked. I mean I think the current Fifth Year exam results have shown that ... which have been appalling ... um ... because the mixed-ability arrangements need ... maybe they would succeed – given a great deal of time and organization on the part of the staff, and secondly, given the most appropriate teaching materials. Now you see it is awfully difficult to find teaching materials suitable for the slow learner in French. When I say slow learner I mean average to slow learner. I mean there's lots of excellent material suitable for the brighter pupils, the grammar-school type children, but relatively little for your remedials, or for your slow learners ... very little. So, it means that the teacher has an extra burden there to cope with even finding materials before he can even start teaching. *And, of course, if you don't have adequate materials or very satisfactory materials then it means the ... er ... discipline problems arise you know, because you need a fairly strong personality to cope with ... to interest ... the majority of the children we have at the best of time.*

Possibly his main objection to mixed-ability organization is revealed in the comment that 'if you don't have ... satisfactory materials, then it means that ... discipline problems arise'. As it is argued further in Chapter 4, opposition to mixed-ability grouping from the 'academic' subjects like maths, French and sciences owes much to its perceived threat to classroom control – contrary to other subjects for whom mixed-ability grouping provides something of a remedy to control problems. In the case of the 'academic' subjects, mixed-ability grouping could potentially jeopardize classroom control by frustrating teachers' efforts to keep *all* pupils interested in the work and by inviting the possibility of pupils who are bored because the work is too simple or frustrated because the work is too hard. As the head of French at Ashton saw it, the only hope under these circumstances rested with 'a fairly strong personality'.

The open classroom

So far, the explanation of classroom control has reflected the experience of teachers and pupils operating in the closed classroom. This is because the closed classroom is the prevalent kind of classroom organization. Only 2.2 per cent of secondary school classes and only 3.3 per cent of primary school classes in the UK are taught by two or more teachers (DES Statistical Bulletin 3/83, March 1983). But it is not the only social and physical context in which the phenomenon of classroom control arises. Other arrangements currently exist, albeit to a limited extent, which might reasonably be expected to put different kinds of pressures on the teachers and pupils and offer different opportunities to them in connection with classroom control. There is good reason, then to look at a situation that offers a contrast with the closed classroom and this is where a closer scrutiny of humanities lessons at Cedars is useful.

Cedars, remember, had a reputation for being progressive both in its own right and by virtue of being part of the internationally famous 'Leicestershire Plan' (Bernbaum,1972; Rogers,1971). As Hannan (1978) argued on the basis of previous research at the school, in many respects it aspired to 'open schooling'. Such open schooling differs from more traditional approaches in a number of crucial ways. Specifically, open schooling

(1)   attempts to develop non-authoritarian relationships between teachers and pupils;
(2)   minimizes divisive forms of social groupings based on intelligence, social class, sex, age and so on;
(3)   integrates subject boundaries;
(4)   moves towards a more active involvement of pupils in the

content and pacing of their schoolwork, with the teachers adopting the role of 'catalyst' to learning rather than director of learning.

It was in the humanities lessons at Cedars that the principles of open schooling received their fullest expression. Here, more than anywhere else in the school, there was a concerted effort to breakdown social divisions and subject boundaries, and adopt kinds of classroom organization that allowed pupils greater control over the content and pacing of their work. There was a strong emphasis on resource-based methods of individualized learning. Apart from 'lead lessons' where the whole class was taught together by one or more of the team members, generally for the purpose of introducing a new topic, most of the pupils' time was devoted to individualized styles of learning with the teacher operating as facilitator rather than instructor. The pupils were, in fact, encouraged to adopt a self-motivated and self-discipline approach to their work and were given a degree of freedom to move about the open-plan unit, to discuss the work amongst themselves and to sit where they chose. In line with school policy, humanities used mixed-ability grouping. But there were two other facets of the lessons which made them unique even at Cedars; their integration of subject disciplines and their use of team teaching in open-plan classrooms. The integration of subject disciplines arose from the combination of two subjects – English and community studies – under the aegis of humanities lessons. Both could be taken to CSE or GCE O level, but for the most part, were taught within the same syllabus. The lessons were normally taught by teams of three teachers operating with about sixty pupils in an open-plan area.

The result was a situation that appeared to offer a marked contrast with conventional ideas about teaching because, at least on the surface, the circumstances seemed to demand[1]:

(1)   giving up a subject specialist identity in favour of a multidisciplinary one; that is, becoming a humanities teacher rather than an English teacher, history teacher or social studies teacher;

(2)   giving up claims to autonomy about how the class is run in favour of group decisions made in team planning and classroom activity;

(3)   losing the privacy of conventional classrooms and being directly observed at work by colleagues;

(4)   forfeiting the right to use formal authority relations as the basis for asserting control.

This had some significant repercussions. In the first place, the team organization required some adaption on the part of the teachers because it cut at the roots of conventional teaching by demanding a *corporate approach* to the work. Those involved had to foresake autonomy in order to abide by team decisions and team practices. Secondly, in the open-plan setting, the presence of more than one teacher meant that teachers became *observable* to colleagues. In quite dramatic contrast to the closed classroom situation, teachers could watch how colleagues operated and see the success or failure of approaches other than their own. This, it was argued, could be beneficial since teachers, no matter how experienced, stood to learn from observing others in action.

The fact that the individual was also the subject of observation, however, did not escape the notice of staff. Some acknowledge that this developed a self-awareness that could prove beneficial to their teaching style. In the words of one teacher, 'team teaching is like a regular dose of in-service training. It gives me a chance to see myself as others see me. This prevents "tin-goddery".' More commonly, though, this observability was seen in a threatening light. It reinforced the challenge to teacher autonomy which already existed through the need for corporate decision-making, this time by making visible to colleagues the styles and strategies used by individual members of the team. Their methods and their competence became exposed to others because the absence of the four walls of the conventional classroom allowed others to observe directly (and evaluate) their work.

Shared responsibility for control

Working on the principle that responsibilities were to be shared, the humanities teachers were faced with a situation that, in some ways, could prove to be a great bonus for control. Shared responsibility helped, for instance, in the way the presence of more than one teacher in the classroom allowed any individual teacher to leave the classroom for periods of time during lesson to collect additional materials without having to worry about the supervision of his/her pupils. It was quite normal for teachers to leave the classroom during the humanities lessons, usually to go to the store room to collect resources requested by pupils and it was not uncommon, indeed, to find only one of the team in the open-plan area.

The presence of other teachers in the vicinity also meant that there was instant support for any one teacher in the case of a confrontation with a pupil. Rare as any such case may be, the advantage of team-teaching in this sense was the ever-ready mutual support to control of the classroom it provided. There were obvious benefits for probationary teachers in this respect and, in fact, for any newcomer to the team including teachers covering for an absent team member because these people received an instant and automatic back-up control. Because the regular team members were within view, they were less prone to being played-up and did not have to face the practical problems of being able to name particular pupils or negotiate afresh a whole set of ground rules for behaviour. Newcomers could, as it were, slot into existing arrangements.

Sharing responsibility for control had other advantages as well. It reduced the likelihood of the kind of control problems that arise simply from a clash of personalities between a teacher and a pupil. In the team-taught lesson, control was no longer dependent on a relationship between pupils and one teacher but on relationships with all the teachers in the team. Some teachers in the team saw this as actually something of a problem because they felt it was difficult enough for many pupils to establish a relationship with one teacher and they saw the need for multiple relationships as a source of unnecessary complications. Most teachers, however, including those who expressed this reservation, also acknowledged the potential advantage of depending on relationships with three members of staff – that it defused some problems that might otherwise erupt from relationships between individual teachers and individual pupils. By diffusing the relationships a potential source of control problems was defused. Added to this, team support for control could operate to the advantage of even regular team members if it meant that teachers with better control could support less capable teachers by dealing with particularly difficult pupils. This would prevent the difficult pupils from causing the kind of control problems they might otherwise have done and reduce the amount of disruption experienced in the class by allowing the best equipped teacher to exercise control. Potentially, at least, the result could be to raise the general level of classroom control above the aggregate for three individual teachers working separately by taking the standard of the best of the team as the baseline for control of the class.

The overall effect of spreading responsibility for control across the team would, on the basis of these points, suggest that team control was an advantage. The mutual support for control, however, was not without its drawbacks, as the humanities teachers were quick to point out. On the issue of support for probationers, for example, some of the probationary teachers, while acknowledging the benefits of mutual support, also made the point that any mistakes they made were inevitably brought to the attention of team colleagues. They suggested that although they might suffer additional problems of control working alone in the closed classroom, at least their problems, efforts and mistakes in this setting were hidden from other teachers and not publicly exposed.

The fact that control was shared could also lead to problems of identifying where responsibility for control was ultimately to lie. It was possible for individual team members to abdicate responsibility for control and consquently for the level of control in the team to fall to the 'lowest common denominator'. The teachers frequently made the point that shared responsibility could just as easily cover up the effects of the best teacher as the worst and, in practice, *reduce* the level of control. So team support could work in two ways. On the one hand it could diffuse and defuse problems but, on the other, it could compound them by creating some confusion over responsibility for control and allowing individuals in the team to retreat from the task of exercising control.

The difficulty of pinpointing responsibility for control in teams also led to difficulties for pupils. Not only did the team situation oblige them to relate to three members of staff, but also it caused an uncertainty on occasion about whose instructions to follow. It would be unfair to emphasize this 'confusion' too much because, in practice, it was not common. Where it did arise it generally took one of two forms. It was either in connection with work where pupils seemed confused about when work was due in. One teacher might ask for work for a different date than the others. Or, the 'confusion' was engineered by pupils as a counter-strategy to control. Their professed confusion about aspects of events in the classrooms could be used, in effect, to play off teachers against one another. On a hot summer's day, for example, three pupils in the humanities lesson sat on the grass outside the ground-floor classroom. One of the team, seeing this, asked why they were not inside the classroom and was told that one of the other teachers had given them permission to go outside. It was not clear if this was true or not but it caused other pupils, currently inside the classroom to ask why they too could not go outside. More pupils began to drift outside as the 'rumour' spread that 'one of the teachers' had said it was all right to be outside. It was not until an opportunity arose for the three teachers to consult and work out that no one had actually given the go-ahead that the situation was clarified – but by this time half the pupils were sitting outside. Prudence seemed to prevail at this point and, rather than risk a direct confrontation and the adoption of a clear authoritarian stance, the team agreed that pupils would go outside – on the proviso that they worked. The shared responsibility for control, here, was exploited by the pupils by fabricating a confusion and trading on the fact that the team members themselves did not wish to contradict one another openly.

Individualism, autonomy and the open classroom
The nature of classroom control and the strategies devised to achieve it in the humanities lessons did not, in fact, constitute a pure or full expression of the principles associated with the open classroom. Particularly in terms of the way the teachers understood the situation and the way they operated in class, there were remnants of aspirations more suited to the Hidden Pedagogy of the closed classroom. Hidden Pedagogies, as we have

argued, are more than just a reflection of personal preference and are fostered by the material conditions surrounding the teaching situation. At Cedars, then the fact the the humanities teams adopted practices apparently inappropriate for the open classroom ought not to be seen as simply a personal hesitancy to go along with open classroom principles – it needs to be explained in terms of the conditions which affected the teachers in the classroom. Here it was evident the the particular Hidden Pedagogy for operating in the humanities lessons owed a great deal to the way in which the school itself amalgamated the open classroom within an otherwise more conventional arrangement for classroom organization. The school, in effect, was *partially reorganized* to accommodate the special ethos of humanities lessons.

In the first place, staff taught on the humanities course for only a proportion of their timetable complementing it by specialist teaching on courses such as social studies, geography, history, literature, German, French, human ecology, communications, religion, English, economics and sociology; courses which were more discipline-oriented and more individualistically taught and prepared. Sixteen of the humanities staff spend twelve periods a week in the team situation (out of the twenty-seven period timetable), fourteen spent six periods a week, and two spent eighteen periods a week in teams.[2] Added to this, teachers were still essentially English teachers, social science teachers, history teachers and so on, co-opted to the interdisciplinary humanities lessons, and they were always treated as individuals for timetabling purposes rather than members of a team.

This partial reorganization put the teachers in the rather awkward position of having to operate in two kinds of situation, each carrying a set of specific expectations about how to approach the job. Under these circumstances it was hardly surprising that the team members should be tempted to incorporate some practices from their conventional teaching experience into the humanities lessons as a way of coping with the diversity of demands produced by the two kinds of situation, and there was practical pressure on teachers to amalgamate the espoused principles of open education with the autonomy and authority relations suited to the conventional situation.

Such an amalgamation occurred in the first instance in the *selection of team members*. When considering which teachers were to work together in teams, the humanities staff acknowledged that, in principle, a degree of co-operation and collaboration between teachers was a good thing because it had the potential to stimulate new approaches to the work through cross-fertilization of ideas in terms of planning the syllabus, sharing new ideas and generally being exposed to the thinking and activities of other team members. But they were also anxious to ensure that, before all this, there was a level of compatibility amongst the members of each team that allowed them to operate a reasonable level of harmony. It was seen as important that the composition of the teams avoided personality clashes, achieved a balance of more extroverted with more quiet teachers, and brought together those with similar attitudes and approaches to working in the humanities lessons. Experience had taught the humanities staff that, as they put it, certain teams 'clicked' while others did not and that some teachers worked better together than others.

The conscious effort to constitute teams with compatible members, however, can unwittingly produce a situation of stagnation simply because members already agree on subject matter and approach (cf.Martin,1975). Where there is high degree of agreement within the team, decisions have a dual status. They are at once a collective effort – the outcome of group interaction – yet at the same time they correspond with the wishes of the individual teacher so allowing the individual teacher to retain autonomy by proceeding as he/she sees fit in terms of planning and instruction. Compromise with the corporate decision, with its implications for teacher autonomy, is consequently excluded as a practical problem because the team decision, in effect, becomes little more than a *joint statement of individual preferences.* The search for compatible group members,then, served to reduce tension not only in terms of personal and pedagogic antipathies but also by reassuring the individual teacher of retaining autonomy within and despite the team organization. It can, for this reason, be seen as a strategy for coping with this desire for teacher autonomy within the team teaching situation.

The amalagamation of closed classroom practices into the open classroom was also evident in the extent to which there was a separation of pupils into *three subgroups within the class*, each with one teacher taking charge. It was, in fact, normal for the team members to identify a group of pupils for whom they were responsible – 'my lot', as opposed to ' the others'. The desks were placed in a manner which accorded with a division of the unit into three working groups and, although the staff moved freely amongst the other groups when necessary and there was a lack of territoriality associated with 'closed classrooms', there was identifiable teacher–pupil groupings which constituted a move away from a totally 'open' situation in which any teachers were responsible for any pupil in the whole unit.

These subgroups in the humanities classes were based on the pupils for whom a particular teacher was responsible in terms of the assessment of work and, on this point, the impact of the partial reorganization of the school on the teachers' approach to humanities teaching became very obvious. In terms of responsibility for coursework *assessment*, teachers were clearly expected to take individual responsibility for marking the work of particular pupils. This individualized responsiblity, it is true, was not total because there were systematic attempts at cross-moderating work during the school year but basically within the team teaching of humanities responsibililty for assessment remained individualized. There were obviously good reasons for this. The time, and hence resources, necessary for teachers to engage in collaborative marking for all work submitted would be excessive and the use of individualized assessment, in fact, would currently seem to be the only viable arrangement in terms of financial constraints and teacher work-loads. None the less, the persistance of individualized responsibility for assessment had a fundamental impact. It not only reduced corporate responsibility for assessment *per se*, it also *provided the rational and justification for separating the large team* units into the three distinct *subgroupings*. It provided the basis for identifying 'my lot' from 'the others'.

The opportunity to capitalize on this separation of responsibilities was enhanced by two physical aspects of the open-plan classrooms within which humanities lessons occurred. In the first place, the rooms had a structure which neatly suggested three distinct areas each of equal size and corresponding with the normal size of a conventional classroom (see Figure 3.1). The *architecture* of the place, as it were, automatically presented the idea of breaking down the long, narrow open-plan areas into three square areas. The fact that each of the three areas was actually designated with a separate room number reinforced the conception that the open areas were simply three conventional units joined together by having the walls removed. In a way, it was an official reminder of the hegemony of the conventional closed classroom and a thinly disguised invitation from the formal organization to treat the open-plan area as a combination of three normal classrooms rather than as an indivisible unit. The rooms also lent themselves to individualized approaches because in each open-plan area one of the three segments could be separated from the rest using a *movable partition*. These partitions could be, and were, used to separate one area of the class from the rest.

A number of things about the situation, however, led to the conclusion that, though the humanities staff used strategies that appeared to go against the spirit of open education, these did not constitute a complete shunning of the open classroom ideal. It is worth emphasizing, for instance, that the partitions were generally left open enough to allow movement of individuals between the sections; generally a gap of about 18 inches was left. Also the teacher/group units were not entirely cohesive because some pupils chose to move outside the group and were allowed to

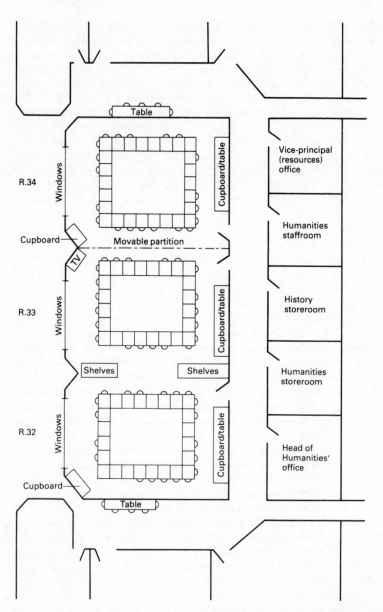

Figure 3.1 *Open-plan classroom at Cedars; typical arrangement.*

sit in another area of the open-plan classroom. Consequently there was some movement between groups by the teachers to attend to a pupil for whom they had assessment responsibility who had been allowed to sit with another group. Also there was still a level of observability of colleagues completely alien to those normally working in closed classroom settings, with even those who preferred to operate behind the partitions becoming observable, and observing, colleagues during the normal course of the lessons. Importantly, lead lessons were regularly employed in which all pupils in the unit came together for the purposes of instruction, and these lead lessons were really the epitome of the team ethos in terms of the classroom situation. It is vital, in fact, to recognize the element of 'openness' which pervaded the units. Staff (and to some extent, pupils) freely moved within colleagues' areas, interacting as a matter of course during lessons, and felt no inhibitions about entering units unannounced and unapologetic. In no sense should it be construed, then, that the teachers operating with 'their lot' during the course of a normal lesson constituted merely closed-classroom-teaching-without-the-walls because not only were they reasonably observable, but also the taboos on entering the action-zone of colleagues operating within these open-plan units were almost entirely absent. The situation in humanities remained very different from the conventional closed classroom. What *was* evident in the lessons, however, was the sensitivity of the staff to matters of autonomy, individualism and privacy which seemed to owe more than a little to their experience of closed classroom teaching and the fact that on certain key issues the school organization remained wedded to the individualistic model of teachers' work.

Conclusion

The point emphasized by the studies of Rutter *et al.*, Reynolds and Sullivan, and Metz is that despite forms of accountablity to the public, it is possible for a variety of school organizations to coexist. More than this, such differences in school organization can actually go some way towards explaining why schools vary in their academic results, their rates of truancy, and – significantly in this context – their level of control problems arid delinquency. Schools are not seen simply as the passive recipients of pupils whose academic capacities and disruptive potential is determined by factors outside school in the social environment but are seen as active agents in the production of particular kinds of pupil behaviour.

The idea that individual schools can generate their own levels of control problem through their form of organization is an important one to recognize, but a degree of caution is needed about claims that specific aspects of school organization have a direct association with matters of control. As D.H. Hargreaves (1981) argues, there are some methodological problems with Reynolds and Sullivan's and Rutter *et al.*'s attempts to isolate the organizational factors that cause control problems and there is a lack of precision in defining and measuring such factors. There is also some doubt about the comparability of the schools on which the conclusions are based. In the case of Reynolds and Sullivan, for instance, we are told that 'the social homogeneity of the area means that the secondary schools are receiving similar pupils at intake' (p.50) and that this justifies the conclusion that observed differences can be attributed to the schools themselves – not the social environment. The fact that 'the intake to the coercive schools includes a higher proportion of children from the valley's council estates' (p.52) is not treated as a significant difference in terms of the catchment areas or pupil intakes to the schools. As Acton (1980) has argued in connection with Rutter *et al.*'s research, even if we overlook the methodological problems, their conclusions do not actually deny the broader effects of social environments and social class on the performance of pupils at school, nor the determining effects of these social factors on the life-chances of pupils in terms of the labour market once they leave school. It would seem prudent, then, to recognize that while the ethos and organization of particular schools can have a differential influence on matters of control, the precise nature of that influence is not altogether clear because it is difficult to isolate such factors from the effects of social class and social environment on the performance of pupils. This, of course, casts doubts on the prospects of identifying types of school organization as 'good' or 'bad', 'better' or 'worse' because the output of individual schools cannot be compared except where inputs (pupils) are the same and, equally, where the aims of each school are held to be identical. But 'goals', as we saw, offered no bench-mark for comparisons between schools because they varied so widely. There is, however, another way of approaching the whole issue of the way schools generate or reduce control problems. Rather than focus on the differences between schools within the same social environment and educational system we can look instead at those aspects of schools which are more universal and which literally produce common features of schooling. This would draw us to look at features of school organization that are shared by most, if not all, schools in the system and to ask what effect they can have on the nature of classroom control. The overall picture which emerges from this organizational perspective is one in which the closed classroom, coupled with a non-voluntary clientele and poor pupil–staff ratios, provides certain fundamental facts of life about classrooms. Principally, *it heightens the personal responsibility of the teacher for what goes on in his/her class.* First, because the work primarily involves the management of people (not materials) and because teachers are expected to organize, manage and control pupils using unsophisticated technology, there is little opportunity for them to bureaucratize the process or to hide behind a facade of technological imperatives. Whatever methods are used they are inevitably 'up-front' and visible in the highly personal authority of the teacher. Second, the school organization actually delegates responsibility for the management of classrooms at a very individual level thus emphasizing, in another sense, the essentially personal basis of classroom control in today's schools. Third, the informal rules of conduct basic to matters of classroom control are negotiated at a personal level between individual teachers and the pupils. In all these ways the school organization tends to promote the vision of classroom control as the province of personal qualities, personal perceptions and personal negotiations between teacher and pupils rather than a product of abstract formal rules or technological necessity. Yet, as the humanities lessons at Cedars demonstrate, this is not an immutable law of classroom life but a result of specific form of school organization – the closed classroom. Though relatively rare, other circumstance like team teaching in open-plan classrooms must not be ignored because they can evoke a different set of demands, opportunities and imperatives. It is vital to recognize, in other words, that *classroom control is a context-specific phenomenon* and that the school organization is the most significant factor shaping the immediate context.

Notes

1 These points about team teaching are drawn from Chamberlain (1969), H. Davis (1966), Forward (1971), Freeman (1969), Lortie (1964), Lovell (1967), Polos (1965), and Shaplin (1964).

2 Even this experience of team teaching was not entirely shared with the same teachers and the same pupils. Those who spent twelve or eighteen periods a week in the team situation did so with two and three groups respectively so that, in practice, the extent to which any particular group of teachers and pupils met together was limited to the particular six periods which pupils had allotted to the humanities course. Where teachers were involved with more than one group of pupils they did not constitute part of the same team of teachers but were part of a different team specifically convened for that group.

4

Classroom Strategies

Methods for gaining control are subject to legal constraint in some respects because the law not only provides teachers with a mandate for control by placing them *in loco parentis* but also obliges teachers to operate within the general laws concerning assault, theft, discrimination and moral standards. As B. Bennett and Martin (1980) point out, despite being delegated the rights of a parent over the pupils, teachers still have to work within certain other parameters set by the law when trying to establish and maintain control. This is the case particularly in their use of

(1) *Corporal punishment*, where the teacher must avoid allegations of assault, actual bodily harm and indecency, and also observe LEA regulations governing the administration of corporal punishment. Following the judgment of the European Court of Human Rights on 25 February 1982 in the case of Campbell and Cosand, parental consent will also become a factor in law which limits the use of corporal punishment on pupils.

(2) *Confiscation of pupil property*, where the Theft Act 1968 makes no explicit exception for teachers and thus requires that confiscated articles must never be kept, used or destroyed by the teacher. Even offensive or dangerous articles must be returned via the pupil's parents or, if serious enough, handed over to the police.

(3) *Detention of pupils*, where, though having the legal right to detain pupils, teachers need to observe LEA regulations which usually specify the maximum period for which a pupil can be detained and the period of notice that needs to be given.

(4) *Social and physical contact*, where legislation again makes no exception for the particular circumstances of teachers and requires, therefore, that teachers avoid any social or physical contact, however intended, which might be construed as improper. Their dealings with pupils have to be beyond moral/legal reproach or suspicion of indecency because gross

moral turpitude is a ground for dismissal in its own right quite apart from any prosecution which could be involved.

(5) *Discriminatory practices*, where the exercise of classroom control must avoid discrimination in terms of a pupil's sex or race in a way that would contravene the Sex Discrimination Act 1975 or the Race Relations Act 1976.

Other than these constraints, however, the law gives no specific guidance on how control may be obtained. It simply acts as an ultimate sanction reflecting social norms relating to assault, theft, discrimination and standards of decency. It gives the teacher some official authority and responsibility and it provides limits to the methods which teachers can employ to establish control but it does not specifically give teachers rights in the classroom other than these. So pupils who are indolent, cheeky or generally disruptive in class cannot be prosecuted for the attitude – it is simply up to the teachers to use whatever methods they can to establish control. This is where the notion of 'strategies' comes in.

Strategic action for classroom control

In recent years the idea of analysing classroom activities in terms of their strategic qualities is one that has grown in popularity amongst ethnographers, particularly where the activities in question are concerned with classroom control (Delamont, 1983; Hammersley, 1980, 1983; A. Hargreaves, 1979; Pollard, 1982; Woods, 1980a, 1980b). Principally this is because classroom research by ethnographers has revealed a marked similarity between the nature of teacher and pupil activity connected with control and the properties of action associated with the term 'strategy'.

To start with, control activity and strategic activity are both *intentional* activity in the sense that they involve consciously held motives stemming from participants' perceptions of the situation. So, for example, when trying to understand something like 'pupil misbehaviour in class' the focus of attention will be on the rational, purposeful aspects of the behaviour which are geared to achieving specific aims. Robertson (1981) follows this line when he analyses the behaviour of pupils which threatens the classroom control of teachers. The five main causes of disruptive behaviour which he identifies in his book he classifies as

(1) *Immediate pay-offs.* Here the motive is simple and uncomplicated. If a pupil talks it is because he/she has something to say that will not wait. If he/she runs in the corridor it is because there is a hurry. The act itself is quite acceptable, but it is done at the wrong

time, in the wrong context, so far as the teacher is concerned.

(2)   *Attention-seeking devices.* The purpose of disruptive behaviour can be to put the pupil in the limelight and keep the pupil as the centre of attraction – noticed by teachers and pupils, accepted by peers.

(3)   *Excitement.* In an effort to alleviate the frustration and boredom of life in classrooms, pupils can search for excitement by interfering with the progress of lessons and causing episodes that break the tedium of normal classroom routine.

(4)   *Malicious teasing.* By purposely provoking a confrontation with a teacher or subjecting the teacher to subtle forms of ridicule, pupils can gain excitement and prestige in the eyes of their peers. This brinkmanship, if operated successfully, can elevate the status of the pupil by challenging the authority of the teacher.

(5)   *Avoiding work.* Pupils can avoid the hardship of doing work by passive resistance, but they can also engage in disruptive behaviour that creates 'incidents' and subsequently offsets the need to do the classwork. The disruptive behaviour, again, serves a purpose.

These causes of pupil 'misbehaviour', it should be noted, do not make reference to subconscious motives or to psychological disturbance. Instead they treat the 'misbehaviour' as consciously motivated activity geared to a particular goal. And the same point applies to the activities of teachers. In so far as they are 'strategic actions' they are rationally conceived with explicit goals in mind.

Such goals suggest a second area of similarity between the specific nature of control activity in classrooms and the more general properties of action that is deemed 'strategic': both are essentially *problem-oriented* activity. Strategies arise in order to obviate, alleviate or overcome situations which actors regard as threatening or unpalatable and we have already established that, in the context of classrooms, both teachers and pupils regard control as something of a problem (even if for different reasons). Three points arise from this 'problem orientation'. First, to the extent that it is strategic, action which is directed at such problems carries with it no guarantee of success and it involves an inherent element of *uncertainty about the outcome*. If actors could be absolutely sure that a given kind of action would evoke a particular response there would be no element of risk and no sense of the 'creative, informed guesswork' that underpins the idea of strategy. In classrooms, the intensely social and interpersonal nature of the setting serves to assure that neither teachers nor pupils can operate with total confidence that their actions will achieve the anticipated result and, here again, the vision of control activity as strategic activity would seem to be well founded.

Second, both the nature of the problems and the nature of the strategies that are conceived to remedy the problems are shaped by the circumstances in which they occur. They are, in other words, *context specific*. Under certain circumstances certain problems arise and certain solutions offer themselves as possibilities. So far as the classroom environment is concerned, as we argued in Chapters 2 and 3, the social and organizational environment is responsible for creating some of the major problems associated with control – class size, low technology, architecture, and so on – and just as powerfully the social and organizational environment moulds the strategies that are acceptable and appropriate. The closed classroom environment engenders problems like those of 'man-management' and, at the same time, invites solutions that rely on strategies that retain the autonomy of the subject teacher.

It is worth emphasizing on this point, as do A. Hargreaves (1978, 1979), Denscombe (1980b, 1981) and Pollard (1982), that the structural constraints on classroom strategies stem from things like the historical location, material resources, organizational factors and pupil resistance, each of which has origins outside the immediate, proximate occasion of the use of the strategy and this accounts for the third of the points that follow on from the problem orientation of strategic action. Though the participants are unique individuals, the problems they face and the strategies they use are not. Teachers and pupils use strategies which, though generated by themselves as individuals and thus having some element of uniqueness, are also the product of shared pressures from the social and organizational environment. This explains the existence of *shared patterns* of strategic action covering a variety of teachers, pupils and lessons, and underpins the whole enterprise of trying to analyse kinds of strategic activity in classrooms.

This reference to shared patterns of strategic action perhaps needs some elaboration in order to avoid the impression that *all* participants in the classroom experience the same pressures and problems and adopt similar strategies to resolve them. Clearly, teachers and pupils – the parties to classroom interaction – are in very different positions and though they may share certain kinds of problems amongst themselves one of the distinctive features of classrooms is the way the parties operate with *'oppositional interests'*. Normally, teachers and pupils get depicted as protagonists in the school venture, each attempting by guile or force to impose their will at the expense of the other. If not at loggerheads or open conflict on each and every occasion they meet, they are, at least, portrayed in terms of an underlying hostility. The notion of 'strategy' is useful in this context because it captures the idea of teacher and pupil activity being geared towards the domination of the opponents and the direct suppression of behaviour deemed to be in the interests of the opposition. It clearly conjures up an image of classroom activity as an attempt to impose control in an 'us and them' situation where any sign of weakness will be mercilessly exploited and where survival depends on strength and bravery. As Willard Waller expressed the point in his classic portrayal of teaching:

> Teacher and pupil confront each other with attitudes from which the underlying hostility can never be altogether removed. Pupils are the material in which teachers are supposed to produce results. Pupils are human beings striving to realise their own results in their own way. Each of these hostile parties stands in the way of the other; in so far as the aims of either are realised, it is at the sacrifice of the aims of the other.

> (Waller, 1932, p. 196)

But the concept of classroom strategy, though drawing attention to the oppositional interests of teachers and pupils and being equally applicable to either, does not consequently suggest that *power* is equally distributed in the classroom.

> To argue for the importance of strategic interaction and negotiation processes does not mean denying the importance of differences in the weight of the power resources available to different actors and organisations. The area which is open to negotiation or gains by strategic action will vary according to the weight of power resources controlled by the different sides.

> (Hammersley, 1976, p. 114)

In effect, legal and institutional authority give teachers a superior power base yet it is obvious that teacher strategies for control do not operate on a passive body of pupils. As Waller said, 'Pupils are human beings striving to realise their own results in their own way'. They engage in counter-strategies geared towards their own interests in the classroom situation and use ploys to limit the nature and extent of (teacher) control which is feasible in class. They are an active force in classroom control between teacher and pupils. So, though the balance of power rests with the teachers, resistance by pupils cannot be ignored as a vital feature of control in classrooms.

This leads us to the final point about strategic action for control. The vivid and striking picture of confrontation in the classroom is one which needs to be tempered somewhat if it is to accord with the situation experienced by most pupils and teachers. As Waller went on to point out, conflicting interests in the situation need not lead to a persistent battle, and to state that teachers' and pupils' interests are in opposition is *not* to imply that classrooms are arenas of perpetual and overt struggle for supremacy. What it does imply is that the order which exists in the classroom is not very stable. In Waller's terms it is a despotism in a precarious state of balance. As with guerrilla warfare, opposition to the ruling regime is localized and sporadic, rarely erupting into a wholesale challenge to the rule of the dominant party. For much of the time there is a fragile truce.

This 'fragile truce' is precisely the kind of situation noted by ethnographers of the classroom. As ethnographers have shown, the truce rests on informal assumptions about conduct that get established over time through interaction between the parties to become the negotiated order of classroom life (Ball, 1980; D. H. Hargreaves *et al.*, 1975). This order is delicately preserved and sometimes ruptured by the actions of teachers and pupils but perhaps the crucial point to notice at this stage is the way the order of classroom life depends on informal negotiations rather than the simple imposition of superior institutional power by teachers on pupils. Because pupils can, and do, engage in informal modes of resistance which are quite effective, teachers are not really in a position to ride roughshod over pupils' wishes without risking severe consequences and can hardly afford to ignore the attitudes and expectations of those with whom they are interacting. In practice, teachers have to bear in mind the reaction of pupils, in particular the extent to which the pupils view the teacher's activity as 'legitimate' because such 'legitimacy' directly affects the success of the teacher strategy employed. They have to bear in mind an unwritten code of conduct covering the strategies used by teachers – a code that is fairly clear and consistent amongst pupils from a variety of settings.[1] Pupils expect teachers to be:

(1) *Firm:* first and foremost the 'good' teacher is willing and able to exercise control over individuals and classes. But the methods used to achieve this control also serve to separate the good from the bad.

(2) *Fair:* the good teacher does not give punishments that are seen as too harsh and is careful to give punishments only to 'guilty parties'. He/she also avoids the use of adverse comparisons between individuals or groups of pupils as a means for achieving control.

(3)   *Respectful* to pupils: the good teacher allows pupils to retain a sense of dignity which is especially valued by adolescent pupils.

(4)   *Friendly:* the good teacher is not aloof or distant. He/she must be able to 'have a laugh' and be able to 'take a joke'.

(5)   *Explains things well* and *gets work done:* the good teacher establishes productive lessons and avoids boring lessons so that pupils feel they have achieved something and are interested in the subject.

The acceptability to pupils of particular teacher control strategies makes certain strategies more attractive than others depending on the time, the place and the people involved and, as we see when exploring 'domination' strategies, 'classwork management' strategies and 'co-optation' strategies, these features of pupil thinking are rarely far from the minds of those who would use the strategies. They recur time and again as considerations guiding the use of strategies by teachers.

Domination strategies

In the nineteenth century teachers in elementary schools were put in a position of either exercising control over their pupils or effectively failing at their job. As Grace (1978) puts it:

> The classrooms of urban elementary schools were ... arenas in which were enacted basic struggles for dominance. The physical context and the expectations of colleagues, parents and pupils that the first business of a teacher was to govern, made this a paramount reality of the teacher's world.
>
> (Grace, 1978, p. 36)

Faced with such pressures, the teacher had little alternative but to adopt an awesome image that would leave no doubt about who was in charge of the situation. Times change, however, and the draconian teacher – fierce, intimidating and vigilant – might seem ill-suited to the present-day school. But the legacy of a time when the teacher's word was law still haunts the contemporary classroom and domination strategies are far from extinct (Woods, 1977, 1979). There are strategies regularly employed by teachers which help to establish a situation where resistance is bludgeoned out of existence and a begrudging passivity is elicited from the pupils.

The *'drill-sergeant' strategy* referred to by Webb (1962) provides a good example. Using the strategy, teachers unilaterally impose an order to events, insist on a high level of regimentation and demand an automatic obedience to their commands and instructions. The advantage, argues Webb, is that the rigid order imposed in this authoritarian manner minimizes that prospect of uncertainty, confusion and chaos erupting in the classroom and thus allows the teacher to assert control in an essentially hostile environment. And Webb makes no bones about it – the drill-sergeant strategy responds to a climate of hostility between the parties where teachers should expect to be respected rather than liked by the pupils. Similarly the *'policing' strategy* identified by A. Hargreaves (1979) is one which operates in a 'low trust' climate where the only alternative to absolute control by the teacher is chaos. Answering the need for total control, the 'policing' strategy involves 'rigorous and systematic control over pupil talk and bodily movement', 'an explicit articulation of the rule system and a public display of the hierarchical relationship which obtains between teacher and pupil', and a transformation of decisions about the curriculum and pedagogy into immediate decisions in classrooms in a way which reinforces social control and averts threats to order.

Domination strategies like these share the view that despotism in the classroom is vital for order to exist (cf. Waller, 1932) and, rather like Hobbes's *Leviathan*, any weakness on the part of the teacher is seen as ensuring a tenure that is 'nasty, brutish and short'. The methods used to achieve this domination involve a rigorous and unrelenting insistence on 'rules, rituals and regimentation' in class. By pursuing these 'three Rs', the teacher allows no fragment of the underlying hostility to become manifest in the pupils' behaviour so that lessons proceed with the institutional authority of the teacher surviving apparently intact and unchallenged. At the same time, the teacher also creates a certain routine to classroom life which, as Woods (1979, p. 162) points out, can prove useful in its own right because 'Routine imposes a structure on school life which pupils and teachers almost automatically come to accept'. The routine becomes embedded in the consciousness of those involved and takes on the guise of a natural unquestionable feature of classroom life. Added to this, when deliberately exploited by teachers, the *habits and routines* which emerge as the by-product of concentrating on the three Rs of rules, rituals and regimentation also enhance the teacher's ability to cover syllabus material during lessons: the rigid structuring of events which serves to obviate pupil challenges to teacher control also helps to get work done. In essence, however, strategies of this kind are geared towards eliminating any opportunity for pupils to question, challenge or threaten the authority vested in the teacher by the institution. They allow no truck with questions about the legitimacy of teacher rule in the classroom and consist of commands by the teacher; edicts not to be qualified, justified or explained. They are intended to establish a state of affairs in the classroom where, despite the underlying and some would say inevitable hostility, pupils 'do as they are told'.

There is evidence to suggest that this 'laying down the law' to pupils can be quite a successful strategy for teachers and that those who tend to rely on domination strategies can avert some of the problems that other approaches invite. Torode (1976), for instance, has argued that where teachers try to justify their decisions to the pupils on the basis of personal choice and commitment they are likely to face greater discipline problems than where they issue commands as impersonal edicts which emanate from abstract principles and which demand obedience irrespective of the personal wishes of the teacher. Those who make their actions accountable to the pupils, in other words, would seem to jeopardize control while those who issue threats in terms of 'inevitable consequences' to a particular pupil behaviour in the classroom setting tend to achieve good discipline.

In part, this would seem to result from the *structure* which domination strategies impose on proceedings. They provide a firm, predictable environment in which pupils know what is expected of them in terms of their relationship with the teacher and where pupils are left in little doubt about the standards of classroom conduct that are required. But it also results from the way in which domination strategies fulfil the image of the *strong teacher*. Time and again, and in widely varying circumstances, pupils express a liking for the strong teacher who sets rigid standards and imposes firm control (Delamont, 1983; Docking, 1980; Marsh *et al.*, 1978). As a corollary, being seen as weak or soft is an arch failing for teachers. Marsh *et al.*, for instance, report that in their research

> Being a soft teacher was seen to be one of the worst categories of offence. The pupils are insulted by weakness on the part of those in authority who they expect to be strong.
>
> (Marsh *et al.*, 1978, p. 38)

Faced with such expectations, teachers are obviously under some pressure to present a tough image. Despite their personal views about how teaching ought properly to be conducted they find themselves in circumstances where a degree of toughness is essential for survival and here, of course, domination stategies would appear to be in their element. Such strategies automatically emphasize authority relations within the classroom and involve the kind of explicit demonstrations of power which are likely to prevent the teacher being labelled 'weak' or 'soft'. The real advantage of such domination strategies so far as the teachers are concerned, though, is that they combine an image of the 'strong' teacher with a firm and explicit structure to proceedings in class and, together, these prove to be mutually supporting factors in the quest for classroom control.

Domination by resocialization
Despite the advantages of 'structure' and 'strength' for classroom control, obedience achieved through the use of these strategies is likely to come from a begrudging passivity on the part of the pupils who go along with the system through fear and intimidation rather than any wholehearted commitment to the regime. Their response is a temporary and fragile acquiescence – a 'situational adjustment' as Goffman has called it – which facilitates classroom proceedings in circumstances where one party can muster sufficient social power to impose his version of events. Resistance, however, need not be 'bludgeoned' out of existence. There are more subtle methods of domination which can be used to overcome opposing expectations and aspirations in the classroom – methods that rely on reorienting pupils so that their thinking matches the teachers' requirements for the exercise of control. Broadly these can be seen as strategies for domination by resocialization.

One example of how pupils' thinking can be moulded to fit the (teachers') needs for control can be found in the work of educational psychologists who, faced with 'problem' pupils, argue that bringing pupils into line can be achieved in a Skinnerian fashion through a process of stimulus–response learning (for example, O'Leary and O'Leary, 1977). Such *behaviour modification* in class can use fear, guilt, embarrassment or inconvenience as methods for negatively reinforcing types of mis-behaviour by pupils and effectively working as aversion therapy to prevent the recurrence of behaviour the teachers regard as undesirable. As a strategy for control this continues to be rather heavy-handed because it still relies on teachers handing out 'deterrents' that pupils, against their wishes, feel compelled to suffer. The co-operation that gets elicited, as a result, might expect to be less than wholehearted.

A more effective method is to dominate by generating in pupils a definite enthusiasm for the regime the teachers are trying to impose. This, in fact, is something that most schools recognize. At the one extreme there are boarding schools (particularly the public schools) whose influence tends to be 'all-encompassing' and where conscious efforts are made to mould the pupils' commitment to the school. As Lambart (1966) points out, such boarding schools do not coerce conformity, but attain a school-goal orientation but using 'subtle normative means [and] instilling expectations and standards, so that its values become accepted and enforced by the pupils as the ordinary or "done thing"' (Lambart, 1966, p. xxi). As Lambart and his colleagues have demonstrated, boarding schools tend to take on features of what Goffman (1968) has called 'total institutions' (Lambart, 1966, Lambart and Millham, 1968; Lambart *et al.*, 1970, 1975). These institutions typically seek to achieve acquiescence on the part of their inmates by breaking each inmate's image of 'self' and resocializing it to fit the regime. Entrants are systematically stripped of those things which reflect and enhance normal images of a unique identity – clothes, hairstyle, jewellery, names – and have these replaced with a corporate identity – uniforms, numbers, regimentation. Through a 'mortification of the self' the institution desocializes then resocializes the newcomer so that the expectations they hold complement those of the staff regime.

Boarding schools, to the extent that they entail both isolation from other social circles and regimentation and strict control over personal identity and freedom, correspond with this idea of a total institution. But in fact most schools reflect the total institution to some extent because things like compulsory attendance, isolation from the community, regimentation, uniforms, lack of personal freedoms, all are common features of schooling. So, the possibility of resocializing pupils, rather than achieving compliance by intimidation or brute force, is something available to nearly all teachers and is not restricted to use in boarding schools. Although the potency of this strategy for control will vary according to the circumstances of particular schools and the extent to which they allow the teachers to isolate and 'remould' their pupils, clearly most schools can, and do, attempt to get compliance by instilling in their pupils a general commitment to the school, its rules, its values and its regime.

Domination and interaction in classrooms
Apart from resocializing pupils, teachers can also dominate pupils without being too heavy handed by paying careful attention to the way they communicate with the pupils and the kind of interaction they allow during lessons. For example, by their demeanour in class teachers can go a long way towards communicating to the pupils that authority rests clearly and unequivocally with the teacher. As Robertson (1981) argues, this 'communication of authority' requires them to demonstrate and reinforce their status as 'teacher' and 'adult' and this can best be done, he says, through shrewd use of body language and control of talk. Using appropriate postural cues, gestures, eye contact and positioning in class, they can immediately communicate (or fail to communicate) that it is they who hold the whip-hand. Standing in a prominent position, appearing relaxed not tense, moving freely away from the 'safe zone' at the front of the class, using eye contact to sanction pupil talk – these are just some of

the repertoire of interpersonal skills that teachers can acquire and use to get classroom control.

Domination, however, depends not only on *what* is communicated but also on *who* does the communicating and who controls when it occurs. That is why when teachers use domination strategies they put themselves in a focal position in the classroom. For the duration of the lesson they insist that all communication should be channelled through them and that they have the sole right to initiate interaction. This point is particularly evident in the '*chalk and talk*' and '*recitation*' strategies where the teachers' attempts to control the class quite clearly revolve around their efforts to govern classroom interaction. With the 'chalk and talk' strategy we find teachers at the focal point of proceedings, initiating and monitoring interaction in a way that allows them to both express and exercise dominance over the pupils. And the same is true of the recitation strategy. 'Recitation', as Hoetker and Ahlbrand (1969) indicate, does not simply mean a process of reciting. Particularly in the US context, it has come to refer to the classroom practice of question–answer routines where teachers deliver information and then question individual pupils to find out what he/she has learnt. As they point out, it is an approach which has retained favour and is nearly as familiar today as it was fifty years ago, despite the fact that it has long been regarded by educationalists as a poor method.

> Each successive generation of educational thinkers, no matter how else they differ, has condemned the rapid-fire, question–answer pattern of instruction. This opens a number of interesting avenues of inquiry. What is there about the recitation, for instance, that makes it so singularly successful in the evolutionary struggle with other, more highly recommended methods? That is, what survival needs of teachers are met uniquely by the recitation?
>
> (Hoetker and Ahlbrand, 1969, p. 163)

The answer, not in fact provided by Hoetker and Ahlbrand, is that recitation continues to be used because, at one and the same time, it helps teachers to control the class and also to present and cover a body of material (Westbury, 1973). Particularly in the conventional classroom setting, with the specific pressures this entails, there are solid practical reasons for teachers sticking to the strategy. As Dreeben points out:

> Given the spatial constraints of self-contained classrooms and the need for teachers to gain and keep the attention of their pupils (both for administrative and instructional reasons), it is not surprising that the

recitation (strategy) has emerged as an adaptive solution because it can serve both as a means of disseminating knowledge and as a means of control at the same time in a setting whose major parameters are

(1)   spatial containment and crowding,
(2)   the inclusion of variously motivated children of different abilities and interests, and
(3)   the occupational and administrative injunction on teachers to teach-direct an instructional programme.

(Dreeben, 1973, pp. 467–8)

Using the 'recitation' strategy, then, teachers can satisfy the demands placed upon them to exercise the positional authority entrusted in them and also fulfil their duty of transmitting curricular knowledge. Whether or not pupils actually imbibe the knowledge is another matter but, so far as their accountability to external agencies is concerned, the syllabus is covered and the teacher appears to be in command of the situation.

Using strategies such as these, teachers tend to monopolize the classroom talk (Sinclair and Coulthard, 1974) and strive to minimize the amount of pupil-initiated talk. This does not mean, though, that pupils are prevented from talking in class. Indeed, as Hammersley (1974) argues, it is important for teachers to elicit answers to their questions and to ensure a sufficient level of responsiveness to teacher talk. But as he goes on to note, the nature and extent of pupil talk needs to be carefully monitored if classroom control is not to be threatened. Too many pupils participating at once, or unsolicited pupil participation, can effectively ruin the lesson and undermine the teacher's control of the situation. Over-participation, in fact, provides a pupil strategy for countering and challenging the teacher's control and, from the teacher's point of view, needs to be avoided at all cost. If pupils begin to talk amongst themselves spontaneously it poses a problem because it moves the *focus* of interaction away from the teacher and it takes the *initiative* for interaction away from the teacher – both of which are regarded as vital for control through domination.

Methods to limit the amount of talk between pupils, of course, must be available to teachers who wish to achieve dominance by governing classroom interaction. Obviously, they can use the simple and straightforward method of stating categorically that such talk is not permitted in the classroom and reiterate the rule when necessary. Backed-up with sanctions this may go some way to ensuring that they remain the focal point and sole instigator of classroom talk. Alternatively, or even as a complement to such measures, they can utilize the effects of classroom ecology and manipulate *seating arrangements* to control pupil interaction in the classroom (Adams and Biddle, 1970; Breed and Colaiuta, 1974; Sommer, 1967). The strength of this strategy comes from the point, as Waller once observed, that

> There appears to be a characteristic ecology of the classroom. ... In large classes where students are left free to choose their own positions the author has found a certain distribution to recur. In the front row is a plentiful sprinkling of over-dependent types, mixed perhaps with a number of extremely zealous students. In the back row are persons in rebellion.
>
> (Waller, 1932, pp. 161-2)

More recently, Walberg (1969) has subjected this observation to rigorous research and confirmed that:

> Students in the front were not only more enthusiastic about school work than the other students but more [enthusiastic] in learning, reading and creativity generally. Those who said they do not care where they sit gave responses similar to students in the front but not quite as extreme. Students who select places in the back or near a window expressed in their responses a general negation of school learning and their own interest and capacity for success.
>
> (Walberg, 1969, p. 69)

This point does not escape the attention of practising teachers whose experience has taught them that the manipulation of seating arrangements can have a considerable impact on the behaviour of pupils and consequently on the teacher's ability to gain control. Teachers often insist, for instance, that 'troublemakers' do not sit at the back but come to the front of the class where the teacher can keep an eye on them, and the potential of seating arrangements to aid teacher control was clearly in the mind of an English teacher at Beechgrove as she recalled how it had helped her with a particular group of pupils:

> I had a class and they were hell ... couldn't do anything with them. They were real sods ... girls, all girls ... and they really hated my guts. And there was no way I could get them to stop talking. And somebody worked out ... worked out this brilliant idea.
>
> And it was a needlework room I took them in, and I set all the chairs ... only about 20 of them ... all the chairs in a line. It was a rotten thing to do. And each chair slightly separate from the next, but in a line. And, do you know, it worked! 'Cos they were cut off from each other, you know.

The use of seating arrangements to aid control depends, of course, on certain conditions. Principally it requires a situation in which the teacher is not afraid to dictate where pupils sit and in which the teacher has no qualms about appearing authoritarian. In other circumstances, its potential is markedly reduced. For example, in the humanities lessons at Cedars where about sixty pupils come together in 'lead' lessons, teachers found it difficult to use the conventional seating strategies. Especially when the class was watching a video and pupils were huddled around the screen, there were certain pupils who seemed adept at hiding themselves in the crowd and keeping 'out of reach' of the teachers. During the lead lessons, there were blind-spots in terms of teacher control – areas effectively outside the action zone of the teachers, such as an inaccessible corner, behind a cupboard or any other such place created by the particular furnishing of the room. As the teachers acknowledged when the issue was discussed informally at a staff meeting, disruptive pupils managed to place themselves so that they could prevent the possibility of eye to eye contact with the teachers and thus avoid the use of a hard stare or any other facial signals by the teachers to make them stop whatever they were doing – normally passing comments and looking about. Nor could teachers tap them on the shoulder to get them to stop because their position left the disruptive pupils surrounded by other pupils. The teachers were left with the prospect of shouting to the pupil(s) but this, of course, meant adding a further interruption to the lesson. Inaccessibility, however, was not simply a product of physical positioning in the classrooms. Its strength as a defence against teacher control also depended on the fact that members of the team were constrained in their ability to stop pupils misbehaving because they did not want to expose an authoritarian position. It was important to the teachers to operate in a collaborative fashion and, as the pupils realized, this limited the teachers' willingness to raise their voices. It was this that made shrewd positioning during lead lessons a particularly effective counter-strategy to control in the context of Cedars.

Pupil reactions to domination strategies

It would be false to regard domination strategies as potent and predictable tools for eliciting passivity on the part of pupils at the expense of considering the potential counter-strategies that arise. Pupils, after all, can be skilled manipulators of the classroom situation and any acquiescence to the strategy of dominance on their part deserves to be treated as a precarious and possibly superficial accomplishment by the teacher. Just as teachers can use eye contact, postural cues, gestures and control over talk as a means for getting control, so too can pupils. They can refuse to answer questions or answer in monosyllabic terms. They can turn away from the teacher or studiously avoid eye contact when being spoken to. They can adopt poses and use gestures that effectively ridicule or insult the teacher (sometimes without the teachers being aware of it). All of which can put the teacher in a very awkward position because such tactics can prevent the teacher 'getting through' to the pupil or make the teacher feel belittled in front of the pupils. In subtle ways teachers can find themselves being ignored or put down by pupils and having their authority challenged in a way that proves difficult to pin down yet which is none the less evident to those concerned.

The strength of this form of resistance rests on two points. First, the fact that the pupil behaviour might be sufficiently *ambiguous* to prevent direct accusations of insulting behaviour. Second, that it might alternatively be '*sub-reactional*' (D. H. Hargreaves *et al.*, 1975) so far as the teacher is concerned. Either because the teacher wants to avoid provoking the pupil and escalating a seemingly trivial matter into a big event, or because the behaviour in its own right is not really serious enough to warrant action, pupil(s) can use *sullen resistance* as a counter-strategy which draws on the kind of body language and control of talk that teachers themselves would hope to use in their own pursuance of control.

Counter-strategies of this kind do not normally involve a full-scale confrontation between teacher and pupil(s). Resistance to teacher domination more commonly involves pupil manoeuvres that are like guerrilla warfare rather than open rebellion. In many respects the opposition is limiting rather than revolutionary, and rarely is the teacher's institutional authority totally ignored or rejected. In fact, domination strategies, as a genre, are generally founded upon the assumption that, in the last instance, the teacher will be able to quell hostility and count on pupils giving in to his/her commands because, no matter how begrudgingly, pupils will be 'willing to be forced' into the appropriate pattern of behaviour.

Yet ironically there is a potential in the strategy to foster rebellion as much as quell it. Clearly domination strategies can be used as a *response* to pupil initiatives where pupil expectations set the pattern and teacher strategies simple try to cope with the situation. Webb (1962) emphasized this point in his account of the drill-sergeant strategy, arguing that the rules, rituals and regimentation it entails, allows for, indeed fosters, a solidarity-in-opposition on the part of pupils and thereby matches the expectations they derive from their culture outside the bounds of school. In essence it conforms to the 'us and them' syndrome. At the same time, however, domination strategies can have the effect of enshrining the element of pupil opposition and giving it credibility if not respectibility.

And this puts teachers in something of a dilemma. While they might be prepared to recognize and respond to the fact that pupils expect strength and toughness on the part of the teacher, and use methods which correspond with these expectations, it is obvious that the very pupils who promote the idea that the strong teacher is the good one are those who will tend to go furthest in challenging and flaunting the institutional authority of the teacher. Their appreciation of the strong teacher, in other words, really only reflects the fact that the strategy involves *methods* which they appreciate. Yet in such appreciation there is little guarantee that they will be distracted from perpetual battles of strength in the classroom. Domination strategies, in attempting to suppress opposition, reinforce the image of antagonism between teacher and pupils and can, therefore, serve to exacerbate or even create conflict rather than avoid it.

This paradox is not the only difficulty facing the use of domination strategies. For male teachers whose stature is small, thin or frail, for elderly teachers and for many women teachers, it may be far from easy to present an awesome image with which to intimidate pupils especially when they reach the secondary school. In fact, the ability to rely on domination strategies, at least in their cruder forms, is really restricted to a minority of teachers. The rasping voice and menacing posture need to be convincing and not that many teachers are endowed with what it takes to act the part. The point was brought home quite sharply by the case of a male PE teacher at Beechgrove. He had a reputation as a 'hard man' and had little difficulty in controlling even the most aggressive pupils, according to colleagues in the staffroom. The reputation seemed to follow a legendary incident on the bus taking pupils to the playing fields. As the story goes, some fifth-form boys were being generally rude and rowdy. When confronted by the PE teacher they threatened to beat him up. He then challenged their toughness by inviting any of them to hit him in the stomach as hard as he could. One boy took up the challenge – and broke his wrist. The PE teacher was unhurt. Machismo here had been exceptionally fruitful in preventing this teacher facing future control problems, but the strategy is not, perhaps, to be recommended in most cases.

Quite apart from the physical problems of using 'strong-arm' tactics there are other constraints which limit the use of domination strategies. From the available studies of what pupils expect of a teacher it appears that, across the whole spectrum of school situations, pupils not only revere a certain strength in the teacher's approach but equally they insist that the teacher ought to be *fair* in dealings with pupils and be prepared to temper any sternness with a sense of *humour* in the class (Docking, 1980). Brute domination is clearly not acceptable to most pupils. While respecting and requiring a degree of strength in the teacher's approach they are adamant that it must be exercised consistently and fairly, avoiding all signs of arbitrary or vindictive use of power. As a result, any teacher who places too great an emphasis on strength at the expense of fairness and humour is likely to end up being rejected by pupils as someone who is haughty, high-handed or arbitrary (cf. Marsh *et al.*, 1978).

These additional constraints can pose particular problems for the use of domination strategies. It is not simply that teachers need to be conscious of exercising domination in a fair way and without excluding any semblance of humour from the classroom. These are problems enough, but, because domination strategies tend to rely on a class-orientation with all the pupils being involved in the same event, the teacher faces the further problem that whatever action is taken is exposed to *all* the pupils in the class. Strategies which rely on the teacher being the focal point of attention make the decisions of the teacher completely public. As Bossert (1979) argues, this puts considerable pressure on teachers to be meticulously impartial in their dealings with the pupils – more than in the case of group-work or project work where teachers abscond from the limelight and work at a far more private level. Here, teachers are more free to adjust their reactions to the particular circumstances of the group or the individual and can concentrate on criteria of relevance to the needs of the individuals rather than on criteria of fairness to the whole class. However, because domination strategies generally depend on a class-orientation, issues of consistency and fairness take on added significance and are vital to the success of the strategy and, although domination strategies appease the pupil demands for a structured lesson in a classroom controlled by a strong teacher, the exercise of that domination needs to be scrupulously fair and compassionate if it is to be considered legitimate by pupils.

Teachers, therefore, find themselves constrained in a number of ways in their use of domination strategies. It is not just that their exercise of dominance needs to be coupled with fairness and a sense of humour but, as we have seen, domination strategies also carry with them the hazardous potential to institutionalize and exacerbate confrontational tactics in class. Pupils can turn this to their advantage and, adopting much the same rationale as that used by the teachers, they can undermine the teachers' prospects of getting control by refusing to acknowledge the teachers' authority, by taking on the teachers at the machismo game. Coupled with this, of course, there are the social, legal and professional limits on the extent to which teachers can resort to force and, clearly, teachers are not often in a position to depend exclusively on the more crude forms of domination. Although they can generally strive to dominate by resocializing their pupils or by controlling interaction and communications in class, they have been obliged, for practical purposes, to look for alternative strategies which facilitate classroom control yet which do not necessarily depend for their success on a combination of fear and pupil reverence for the institutional authority of the teacher.

Co-optation strategies

Attempts to entice pupils into becoming personally committed to the order and structure of classroom proceedings can be attributed in large part to teachers' disenchantment with strategies of dominance. Particularly at the secondary school level there has been an erosion of pupils' willingness and teachers' ability to rely on pure domination and, as Swift has observed about the effect of this trend in the United States,

> faced with problems of retention and control and unable to use traditional methods of maintaining order, new procedures were necessary. Instead of using force and coercion the public schools now sought the pupils' willing participation.
>
> (Swift, 1971, p. 49)

The point that Swift makes is that the selective adoption of tenets associated with 'progressive' teaching within current conventional practice owes as much to the substantial realities of school life as to any autonomous change in pedagogic beliefs, and the selective adoption suits the purposes of teachers particularly with respect to classroom control. The fact is that schools have been unable to resist the pervasive influence of social change, unable to insulate themselves against the changing attitudes and expectations of the world in which they exist. And faced with a growing discrepancy between traditional school values and the new expectations of pupils, teachers have found it prudent to adapt their aspirations to meet the new circumstances. Rather than fight the changes and attempt to suppress the emerging trends – a losing battle – teachers have increasingly sought to incorporate the new culture, to adapt and use it to their own ends.

Incorporating oppositional forces within the dominant framework is a widely used strategy for maintaining control, whether it be in classrooms or large organizations (Selznick, 1966), but in the classroom situation it specifically refers to the attempt to neutralize the damaging effect of pupil expectations which challenge the domination of teachers. In this light, co-optation is clearly a strategy for control. Without directly confronting the opposition or attempting to combat it, co-optation limits conflict by bringing the oppositional forces under the auspices of the established framework – using it rather than fighting it.

Coleman's (1961) recommendation on the basis of his research in the United States provides a good illustration of how this might work in practice. He argued that pupil expectations constitute an oppositional force in schools because pupils no longer look to adults – teachers or parents – for approval and self-esteem. Instead, they strive for status in the eyes of other pupils. This status, Coleman points out, results primarily from success in sporting competition (boys) or the ability to date a sporting 'super-star' (girls) rather than academic abilities. Indeed, the quest for status through sporting prowess and the orientation to peers not adults are identified by Coleman as distictive features of an 'adolescent culture' – a culture of pupils which transcends social class, neighbourhood and school. This culture, of course, poses considerable problems for teachers who find that pupils no longer regard academic success or respect in the eyes of teachers as vital motivating factors. It undermines deference to their authority and the desire of pupils to excel in school work. His answer, however, is not to suppress the pupil culture but to harness essential features of the culture to the development of academic work. Through 'inter-scholastic competition' between groups of pupils, Coleman recommends that the elements of competitiveness and status-amongst-peers can be incorporated into the organization of academic work and thus used to reconcile the disparity between pupil culture and the need to develop academic abilities.

Pupil participation
An alternative method of incorporating, and thus neutralizing, opposition is to promote a high level of participation by pupils in the policies of the school. By getting pupils to participate in an active way there is possibly more chance of them becoming involved in, and committed to, the other of things which they had a hand in creating. This is one facet, indeed, of *school councils* with elected pupil representatives which meet to discuss and make recommendations on the running of the school. On the surface these councils would appear to move some way towards democratizing the organization and to offer a safety valve, human relations exercise and source of experience about political decision-making all in one go. But they also appear to invite pupils to involve themselves in the regime rather than stand outside in opposition to the established order. Like other co-optation strategies the democratization tends to be illusory and is geared primarily to securing a certain commitment on the part of pupils to the existing social order. It is essentially a facade simply because the participation constitutes a strategy for teachers to legitimize and

institutionalize their control and effectively neutralize expressions of grievance by pupils. As Hunter puts the point,

> the rhetoric of participation is frequently used in schools to encourage pupils to be involved in the process of their 'social development' and for teachers to enlarge their traditional pedagogical sphere of influence. At the implementational level, however ... the concept is being used as a legitimating strategy for forms of social control.
>
> (Hunter, 1980, p. 213)

Reasoning

As it happens, this political form of participation is actually rather peripheral to teachers' use of participation as a strategy for control. For teachers it is the co-opting potential of participation *at the classroom level* which is the significant issue and the thing around which the strategy mainly revolves because it is at this level that any lack of involvement or commitment on the part of the pupils can have a devastating effect. One way of encouraging participation at this level is for teachers to discuss the issues and attempt to 'reason' with the pupils. As Robertson has described the strategy, 'Reasoning includes describing the consequences that the pupil's behaviour may have for others and explanations why specific demands are made of him' (Robertson, 1981, p. 105). In the spirit of co-optation strategies, such reasoning appeals to the pupils' logic and suggests, at least superficially, that what the pupil has to say might also have some credibility and persuasive potential on the teacher. It gives some recognition to the ideas and ambitions of the pupils, even if the teacher's aim is ultimately to transform or neutralize them.

As a control strategy, though, there are two points that need to be made about 'reasoning' with the pupils. First, although it appeals to the rationality of the pupils, any defence they might offer of their position is unlikely to win over the teacher to their way of thinking. More realistically the teacher invites the pupil(s) to explain and justify their position and tries to demonstrate that there are reasons behind the teacher's wishes which are better. So, like participation in the school policy-making machinery, it tends to be something of a sham as far as any genuine dialogue is concerned and is likely to be regarded with suspicion by pupils who recognize the 'tokenism' involved.

The second point is that, as a strategy, reasoning is a rather hazardous venture. As we have already mentioned in connection with domination strategies, teachers who try to justify their demands to pupils appear to face more discipline problems than those who do not. One explanation for this, as Robertson warns, is that pupils can choose to adopt and use reasoning as a counter-strategy to control. 'Some teachers', he writes, 'are too easily trapped into the "reasons game" by pupils whose objective is to argue their way out of trouble if given the opportunity. This exercise can waste a good deal of time and slow down the pace of a lesson' (ibid, p. 105). That, of course, might be exactly what the pupil(s) intended. Though the teacher probably aims to initiate a reasonable discussion with the intention of persuading the pupil(s) that the teacher's commands are in the pupil's own interests and quite justifiable, the pupil(s) can latch on to this new found opportunity and use it to waste time. They can turn the teacher strategy for control back on to the teacher and use it, ironically, as a means for controlling the teacher.

Motivating the unmotivated
In practice, teachers rarely, if ever, rely exclusively on the existence of a formal participation machinery or on straightforward reasoning with pupils as ways of co-opting pupils into participating in classroom matters. More important from their point of view is a co-optation strategy that tries instead to foster pupil participation by arranging lessons in such a way that the lessons literally 'capture' the pupils' interests. In so doing, the teacher can hope to involve those pupils who might otherwise find themselves disenchanted, bored and distanced from the work and thus motivate them to feel some enthusiasm for proceedings in class.

As a co-optation strategy, this depends in essence on 'motivating the unmotivated'. It is not concerned so much with those pupils who are 'achievement oriented' and who would be prepared to apply themselves to lesson work irrespective of whether the content happened to be immediately appealing, but to those pupils who are 'unmotivated' to suffer present boredom as the price for some future qualification. It is these latter kind of pupils who pose the problem for teachers because it is those who, for whatever reason, are unmotivated to do the work who are most likely to cause problems for the teacher and most likely to misbehave in class. It is they who tend to be rebellious and challenge the authority of the teacher and it is they who consequently tend to become control problems in the classroom. This is why methods for getting these pupils motivated are considered by teachers to be so important.

The task of motivating the unmotivated, of course, assumes added significance for teaching where large proportions of the pupil population are regarded as unmotivated. Particularly in schools like Ashton and Beechgrove with a 'low achievement orientation' – where pupil aspirations and teacher expectations complement each other to generate a mutually held, limited academic orientation – the task tends to become a rather prevalent feature of the routine work of teachers. Under such circumstances, the teachers feel there is extra pressure on them to make the work *relevant and interesting* because, if the pupils see the work as relevant to their lives and if they consequently regard it as interesting, there is more chance of being able to integrate the pupils' own aims and ambitions within the structure of the lesson. As a social studies teacher at Ashton indicated, this could prove to be the cornerstone of successful teaching:

> These kids need real things, you know, not the needs we are telling them to ... or that the system generally is telling them to want. So I find – I sound a bit arrogant about this – but I think my teaching is very successful in this way ... because I use what's relevant for these kids and get them interested that way.

Such relevance is not easily attainable in every subject. Motivating such 11 year olds to learn French, for instance, can pose particular problems because

> They remain, for the most part, impervious to arguments concerning a European cultural heritage, flippant towards suggestions about continental cousins and the 'entente cordiale' and positively blank in the face of the Common Market. The point ... is that the impetus to learn the language springs largely from the teacher, and he cannot rely on a latent fund of self-interest to come to his aid.
>
> (Warnes, 1975, p. 100)

The nature of the subject, that is, exacerbates the practical teaching problem of motivating the unmotivated. This was felt to be a sizeable problem by the head of French at Ashton who emphasized that

> What you have got to realize is that in this particular area which is a fairly working-class area, with a large immigrant population ... obviously we are going to have problems with a subject like French, problems which perhaps don't arise maybe with other subjects ... and certainly London comprehensive schools being what they are ... certainly we are having difficulty in motivating interest in the subject, the relevance of which is not immediately obvious.

These were sentiments echoed and expanded by a language teacher at Beechgrove:

> I think the fact is that [working-class pupils] have very little potential

use of French. You know, with Spanish ... the reason I teach it really is that ... er ... lots of working-class kids now go on package holidays and they at least, you know ... they do go to Spain. They at least get the chance of communicating even if it's with the people in shops and waiters – and they don't get conned so easily if they can speak a bit of Spanish and they get quite a kick out of speaking a few words of the language. But with French ... um ... going to France on holidays is a very bourgeois pastime really.

The nature of the problem facing teachers, however, is not simply that pupils who are unmotivated are less inclined to learn the subject. Although this is certainly a part of the teachers' concern, their anxiety is sparked off equally by their fear that *where pupils remain unmotivated they pose a threat to classroom control*. A social studies teacher at Ashton was quite explicit about the association which existed between interest and control when saying

I think interest does play quite a role in enabling you to keep control, in the same sense that ... in the sense that the kids who are interested in the subject will not play up as much as those who aren't interested. ... It's the kids who are just blatantly not interested – I mean, you can see that they're not interested – who are creating the problem.

Evidently, then, where teachers managed to motivate the unmotivated by making the work relevant and interesting, they could hope to obviate disruptive behaviour by keeping potentially disruptive pupils (specifically those with a low achievement motivation) interested and involved with the classwork. These pupils will be less likely to challenge the teacher's authority or disturb the flow of the lesson because there is less chance of their being bored by the lesson and, vital to the success of the strategy, there is an increased *tolerance* on the part of these pupils which stems from their interest in the subject. It is this tolerance which makes the teacher's task of controlling the class slightly less arduous.

This is a point taken up by Spender (1982) who, along with writers such as Clarricoates (1978) and Stanworth (1983) argues that:

In today's classrooms, the point of view of students is often taken into account – in some areas – far more than is generally acknowledged and it makes common sense to many teachers to enlist the co-operation of their students.

But many males will only co-operate when it is their interests that are taken into account. This means that teachers are not always free to introduce either the forms of discussion or materials they would like.

Rather than catering for the class as a whole, in mixed-sex classrooms they may find that they are being manipulated by a group of boys who will engage in uncooperative and disruptive behaviour if they do not get the material they find interesting.

(Spender, 1982, p. 57)

The result is that the strategy of co-operation has an inbuilt tendency to focus on boys' interests rather than girls' – implicitly denigrating the value of the girls' interests and their potential contribution to the lesson. This may not be an intentional sexism on the part of the teacher who, as we have already argued, is responding to the practical imperative of establishing control but the end product, none the less, serves only to reinforce patterns of sex inequality in the wider society.

Co-optation strategies can also involve an element of 'unintentional racism' (cf. DES, 1981). Carrington (1983), for example, found in his research in an urban, multiracial comprehensive school that teachers not only regarded West Indian pupils as more troublesome compared with Asian or white pupils, but also were 'more likely to stereotype this group as having superior physical and practical capabilities and have higher expectations of their potential in areas such as sport, drama, dance and art' (Carrington, 1983, p. 44). The opportunity to tap these perceived strengths and interests by channelling West Indian pupils into sports and expressive subjects carries with it the prospect of integrating the West Indian pupils into the school culture – benefiting the school's sporting reputation and, all too significantly, reducing the amount of disruptiveness in class. If the pupils enjoy sports and are good at sports then the teachers can use the pupils' involvement in sporting activity as a strategic device to encourage, cajole or threaten the pupil in other spheres of school life. Whether such sporting involvement is ultimately of educational or career value to the pupils is, of course, open to doubt but the potential of such involvement to entice less disruptiveness is perhaps a key attraction from the teachers' point of view.

Friendliness

Harnessing pupil interests to facilitate classroom control can also be accomplished through the strategy of friendliness. Forsaking the draconian image and discarding the strategy of domination, teachers can use a friendly approach to pupils as an alternative means for eliciting co-operation from pupils. As Woods has indicated on this matter,

a prominent survival strategy [for teachers] is to work for good relations with the pupils, thus mellowing the inherent conflict, increasing the pupils' sense of obligation, and reducing their desire to cause trouble.

(Woods, 1977, p. 281)

Friendliness, in this sense, is not simply the unplanned and fortuitous product of personal relationships between teacher and pupils but is to some extent engineered by staff as a deliberate method of coping with events in the classroom.

There are two facets to this friendliness strategy. First, there is what Woods (1977, 1979) has termed 'cultural identification'. This relies on the possibility of establishing a sympathetic rapport between staff and pupils through emphasizing the shared aspects of their respective lifestyles. This, of course, will be a strategy particularly useful to young teachers who can hope to draw on areas of common interest with pupils but it is available also where the content of the lessons *per se* lends itself to the discussion of areas of mutual interest. Humanities, social studies, liberal studies and general studies teachers are at an obvious advantage in this respect, but this does not preclude the possibility of teachers in other subjects dealing with topics in a way which utilizes interests shared by both parties. Teachers can use the opportunity afforded by these shared interests to present themselves as 'real people' with personal identities, and as members of the same community and neighbourhood, supporting the same football team, having similar tastes in music, films, clothes, and so on. Cultural identification, in effect, allows a point of contact and communication between teacher and pupils which can be fabricated as a resource upon which teachers can draw in their efforts to control the class.

This resource is used and refurbished in association with the second significant facet of the friendliness strategy – that of humour (Woods, 1983). As a social control mechanism, the use of humour is well known to teachers, with sarcasm and irony being well-established features of teacher talk in the conventional classroom. Pupils can be 'punished' and brought into line by the cruel wit of the teacher and can be embarrassed into acquiescence with the teacher's version of the classroom situation (Woods, 1975). Sarcasm or the use of embarrassment provide teachers with a strategy which aids classroom control but, because the humour tends to be at the expense of one or more of the pupils, it is ill-suited to the strategy of friendliness. It is something of a one-sided humour which demonstrates and recreates the institutional divide between teacher and pupil in the classroom. It is a humour whose poignancy for authority relations in the classroom is unlikely to escape the attention of those who are the 'butt' of the joke. Humour, however, can also be used to generate what Walker *et al.* (1973) refer to as an atmosphere of 'fun and conviviality' in the classroom. It can help to create a friendly atmosphere in the classroom and allow teachers to be privy to the kind of personal information about pupils which they might not glean under more formal circumstances (Stebbins, 1980; Walker and Adelman, 1976; Walker and Goodson, 1977; Walker *et al.*, 1973). Teachers in the humanities lessons at Cedars provided a good illustration of the use of this strategy because they were quite consciously dedicated to fostering an atmosphere of friendliness and conviviality in the classroom. It was evident that the pupils recognized and responded to this atmosphere, regarding the humanities lessons as more relaxed and friendly, and feeling that their relationships with the staff were more cordial than in other lessons. On the basis of a questionnaire administered to all the fourth-year pupils in three teams (over 200 pupils) the feeling of preference and advantage over the normal lessons experienced at their previous schools is shown in Table 4.1. The questionnaire responses also included comments such as:

The teachers are better than at my last school because they try to be friendly and don't shout so much.

In humanities they are easier than in other lessons. They treat you more like adults and you can reason with them.

You can chat with the teachers and they are easier to get along with than in other lessons.

Table 4.1 *Pupil attitudes to the open classroom: Cedars*

	%	%	
More relaxed	53·8	27·7	Less relaxed
More friendly	65·6	8·7	Less friendly
More easy to concentrate	11·3	65·5	Less easy to concentrate
Advantage	61·3	8·8	Disadvantage
Better relations with teachers	37·1	17·7	Worse relations with teachers
Prefer teams	36·9	50·3	Prefer individuals
Prefer open-plan	38·5	42·1	Prefer closed classrooms

Such an atmosphere of friendliness could have resulted from the personal preference of the staff and be nothing more than the product of a good relationship between pupils and teachers. It seemed, however, that this atmosphere was not entirely an unplanned and fortuitous product of personal and personality factors but was, to some extent, consciously engineered by staff. Friendly relationships were encouraged, sought after and, as a humanities teacher at Cedars indicated, even pursued relentlessly in lessons.

> Friendly? Oh yes, I'm *remorselessly* friendly,
> I'm friendly till it hurts.

Such calculated friendliness, as A. Hargreaves (1976) argues, need not signify the abdication of control – it merely shrouds its more obvious manifestations. Although appearing to emphasize personal relationships and negotiation about the conduct of lessons and fostering the impression of collaboration rather than dominance, the strategy of friendliness rests squarely on institutional disparities of power between staff and pupils. Its presence in the classroom is basically at the discretion of teachers and it is their option to facilitate friendliness – not the pupils'. Humanities lessons, of course, were particularly well-suited to this because, in accord with the tenor of the open classroom, the strategy provided teachers with a means of control which had no recourse to heavy-handed or authoritarian relationships between teacher and pupils. The nature of the humanities lessons, in fact, encouraged teachers to use strategies like friendliness, cultural identification, humour, flirting and indulgence because all of these provided teachers with a means for gaining the co-operation of pupils while at the same time appearing to go along with the idea of pupil self-determination. The context, after all, effectively precluded the use of domination strategies by teachers because these always rely on an overt expression of status differences between teachers and pupils and depend for their success on a recognition of power differentials in school. But, like most teacher strategies, the effectiveness of friendliness was limited by its potential to be employed by pupils as a method of asserting *their* influence on the situation. Pupils, ever adept at recognizing and coping with the hidden curriculum of the classroom, could exploit the teacher strategies and use them to gain some influence over the conduct and progress of classroom events. It was particularly interesting to observe how pupils in humanities lessons at Cedars used countering techniques to avert threatening situations and divert the teacher's focus of attention.

Teacher: Robin, you owe me some work. You still haven't handed in the last unit.
Pupil: Well, I had to go out last night ...
Teacher: That's no excuse ...
Pupil: No, well ... it was football ... City, you know.
Teacher: That's hardly the point ...

Pupil:	Have you seen them recently? They're coming on quite good now. You know ... they've got a lot of young lads in the side ... good they are.
Teacher:	Yes, I hear the average age of the team is twenty or so.
Pupil:	Makes you too old, doesn't it ...
Teacher:	Cheek. I've got a few years left in me yet.
Pupil:	Why, where do you play? Must be goalkeeper at your age.
Teacher:	Well, actually, if you must know ...

Such counter-strategies were useful for pupils not only in avoiding awkward moments. They could also be used to provide a 'legitimate' respite from the rigours of work. Where pupils could conjure up a humorous interlude, either in small groups or in the larger units, pupils could generate for themselves a situation in class where there was no onus on them to be working. Creating a joke, therefore, provided pupils with a means for negotiating their involvement in work. This again was well illustrated in the humanities lessons at Cedars when staff talked to individual pupils about their work. The interaction rarely attracted the attention of others in the classroom but, if the interaction produced some humour or laughter, those pupils nearby tended to get themselves involved. The numbers of those involved seemed to grow quite rapidly and, what often started as a private joke, had a tendency to increase in scope very quickly if laughter was heard. It might be argued that this snowballing effect was a response to the interruption suffered by the other pupils, but in the humanities lessons there appeared to be a desire to become actively associated with the humour. Additional quips would be offered from those outside the original group and the 'ripple effect' sometimes caused the teacher to intervene to restore some sense of decorum.

Quite apart from the issue of pupils' having their concentration broken, and quite apart from the pupils' genuine like of humour, the rapid spread of a humorous interlude in the classroom seemed to owe something to a pupil strategy for negotiating a legitimate pause from work and acceptable reason for breaking up the smooth flow of the lesson. The humour, in other words, was being used by pupils as a means for influencing the progress and conduct of the lesson.

This use of humour, it is worth noting, needs to be judicious. Pupils need to avoid using humour as a direct challenge to the authority of teachers. Humour in the classroom which is at the expense of the teacher challenges the institutional authority relations and poses a threat to the teacher's control of the setting. Where pupils exclude teachers from participation in the humour and/or treat teachers as the object of humour, it is likely to be interpreted as a direct challenge to the teacher's authority and an overt expression of the social gulf between teachers and pupils in classrooms more suited to the confrontation of domination strategies. Humour in the open classroom cannot afford to be of such a variety. It cannot be at the expense of either party because it would necessarily expose the divide and militate against the collaborative veneer of the co-optation strategy. Rather, the kind of humour needs to be that which reinforces friendliness and thus needs to be of a kind which is mutually conceived and in which neither party consistently 'suffers' the humour.

Classwork management strategies

Classwork management strategies provide a third, broad kind of control strategy available to teachers. This kind of strategy works on the principle that features of classwork such as the size of the workgroup, the variety of the tasks being tackled by the class and the degree of pupil choice over the content and schedule of work, are of particular importance because they affect teacher–pupil relationships in class. As Bossert (1979) has argued on the basis of his research, 'the structure of task activities – a classroom's organization of instruction – creates the context in which teacher and pupils interact and social relationships form' (p.12), and it is this property of classwork – its power to influence the social climate in class – which teachers can use as a means for achieving classroom control.

In a way, strategies of this kind have quite a lot in common with domination strategies. Both go along with Marland's (1975) belief that 'the central point is obvious: everything depends on good order. Without it every lesson will be a battle'. Also they share a dependence on using a tight-knit structure and order to events in class as the means for preventing threats against the teacher's control. Where they differ, however, is the way they impose that structure and order to events. As Marland goes on to point out, there are methods for getting good order in the classroom which do not rely on the thinly veiled force used by domination strategies but which rely instead on the organization of work during lessons. Rather than bludgeon the pupils into the required pattern, the teacher can just as well use shrewd management of the classwork to achieve the same ends. And this – the shrewd management of classwork – is precisely the thing which makes classwork management strategies a distinctive approach to establishing and maintaining control in the classroom. *Teachers have at their disposal some degree of control over the content and schedule of work done during lessons and this can be translated to a greater or lesser extent into a broader control over the conduct and discipline of pupils.*

Group management techniques

Faced with thirty or so pupils, each with a unique personality and his/her own ambitions, one of the major problems for a teacher is how to keep some sense of unity and direction to lessons. One answer, in tune with domination strategies, is to invoke teacher authority to douse the individual exploits of pupils but this cohesion in class, according to people like Kounin (1970), can be equally well achieved by careful attention to the way classwork is organized and presented by the teacher.

Initially Kounin had set out to study the impact of different commands used by teachers to stop pupils engaging in disruptive behaviour. On the assumption that some 'desists' would prove to be universally more effective than others, he observed a variety of teaching situations and the teachers' methods for controlling the behaviour of their pupils. The only kind of desist which he found to have any consistent effect, however, was 'anger and punitiveness'. Other reprimands failed to have any uniform or guaranteed impact – far too much depending on variations in the context and on the particular individuals involved. But what Kounin's research *did* reveal was that teachers who achieved good control and discipline in class tended to use specific group management techniques and he was led to the conclusion that 'there are different dimensions of group management that far outweigh disciplinary techniques in their power to influence the behaviour of children in classrooms'. Indeed, what emerges so clearly from his work is the fact that, across a variety of teachers and in a variety of contexts, the ability to achieve classroom control depends on group management rather than the quality or quantity of 'desists' issued by the teacher and that teachers who concentrate on group management techniques will be at an advantage in their efforts to control the classroom.

Efforts to control through group management, as Kounin goes on to point out, are closely tied in with the way teachers organize the work in their lessons. He suggests that lessons which support teacher control are those where the teacher takes into account the need for:

(1)   *Variety* A variety of content, seating arrangements, props, and so on aids classroom discipline, particularly if pupils are doing 'seatwork'.

(2)   *Progress* Over-dwelling on a topic, or the teacher talking too much, slows down the lesson and is a source of frustration for pupils. Where teachers keep things rolling and make it clear that work is moving on, on the other hand, pupils have a 'sense of progress' and are less inclined to become engaged in deviant behaviour. They are less likely to be bored.

(3)   *Group focus* Particularly when engaged in a chalk-and-talk

approach, teachers who maintain a group focus and keep the whole class involved are better able to keep control. Where teachers concentrate on one or a few pupils, the others become restive. Teachers need to avoid group-fragmentation.

(4) *Smoothness and momentum* A key to good discipline is the extent to which teachers avoid a jerky presentation and structure to the lesson. Teachers need to provide a smooth and orderly movement through the different phases of the lesson so that pupils know clearly what stage they are at. '*Dangles*', where teachers leave things unfinished and in mid-air, and '*flip-flops*', where teachers return to a previous phase of the lesson, give a jerkiness to the lesson which inhibits good control.

(5) *Withitness and overlapping* 'Withitness' refers to an apparent ability to see everywhere in the classroom and involves teachers demonstrating that they have 'eyes in the back of their heads'. 'Overlapping' is the ability to deal with two or more issues simultaneously. Together, withitness and overlapping are features of teachers' classroom activity which *demonstrate to the pupils* that the teacher is in command of the situation. For instance, knowing who is committing a deviant act, even with back turned to the class, demonstrates withitness and, if instructions are given to the pupils at the same time as the teacher is doing something else, like writing on the board, there is a degree of overlapping. As Kounin emphasizes, it is essential that the teacher is seen to be in complete command of the instant.

These points are also noted by Smith and Geoffrey (1968). Their research draws attention to the particularly complex social situation facing the teacher in the classroom, one which frequently demands instantaneous decisions on unpredictable events, and suggests that coping with the urgency and complexity of the classroom situation is a vital part of teachers' work. While this urgency and complexity cannot be entirely eliminated, they argue, life can be made easier for the teacher by careful structuring of the classwork (providing 'continuity' to events, 'sequential smoothness' and appropriate 'pacing' of the work), and demonstrating a certain withitness through the capable 'handling of multiple simultaneous facets of the classroom system' and by letting pupils know that they know what is going on.

In sum, what the detailed empirical observations of Kounin and Smith and Geoffrey highlight is that, in their quest for control, teachers are well advised to pay attention right from the start to giving a *structure* to the classwork. As a humanities teacher at Cedars put the point,

You've got to structure the work. If you know where you're going, they'll know where they are going ... it's really as simple as that. You have to have a plan of what you want to do ... I mean, in your head ... and be clear about how far you've got and what's to be done.

It would also appear that any such structure must be visible to the pupils and that teachers should equally be aware of the need to foster the *appearance of complete command*. Withitness and dealing with simultaneous classroom events demonstrates to the pupils that the teacher is in control while, on the other hand, dangles and flip-flops and a lack of smooth progress serve to demonstrate that the teacher does not have a clear grasp of what is going on or where the lesson is moving towards. Here, the words of a history teacher at Ashton illustrate the point:

I reckon the key to controlling a class is to let the kids see that you're in command ... I don't mean authority-wise, but in ... in the sense that *you* know what's happening and you're in charge of what's going on. Your're *wise* to what's going on.

Finally, group management techniques need to retain *a group focus*. The teacher needs to devote considerable attention to keeping the class as a unified 'cohort' and, as Payne and Hustler (1980) show, a good deal of teacher talk is, in fact, given over to this purpose. Much of their

directing,urging and reprimanding miscreant individuals may be seen as analogous to a shepherd moving a flock or herd along from one place to another. The concern is to have them *all* moved along. Those following behind or getting out of line are attended to in terms of how their activities relate to the scheduled activity for the collectivity.
(Payne and Hustler,1980, p.64)

Those whose attention wanders or who get out of step with the work pose a problem of course, because they are, wittingly or otherwise, evading the means for control being used by the teacher. The use of this strategy really depends, therefore, on the ability of the teacher to keep the structure of the lesson as the main guiding influence on the behaviour of *all* the pupils, *all* of the time. Or, to put it another way, classwork management strategies largely depend on 'keeping 'em busy'.

Keeping 'em busy
One of the interesting features of classwork management strategies, as we have already noted, is that the rigours imposed in the name of classwork

are not valued solely for their own sake but are valued as well for their impact on the social relations in class. So, although one of the main aims of imposing a tight-knit structure and order to the lesson is to ensure that pupils are kept busily occupied with classwork this is not the end of the story. A concern with 'keeping 'em busy' does not simply reflect the Protestant ethic that 'laziness is the enemy of the soul'. There are far more immediate and practical reasons for wishing to keep pupils busy – reasons which revolve around the classroom survival of the teacher rather than the spiritual salvation of the pupils. Busyness is not valued in itself so much as valued for what it *does* to help the teacher cope with life in classrooms and, as far as teachers are concerned, the most pressing and urgent reason for needing to keep pupils busy is the fact that it is those pupils who are not busily engaged in classwork who are seen as potential hazards for classroom control. By 'keeping 'em busy' teachers can help keep the pupils' minds off mischief.

But what steps must be taken to make sure that all pupils are kept fully occupied? First, the teacher must *pitch* the work at the right level for the pupils and, second, the work must progress at an appropriate *pace*. These, in effect, are the essentials for keeping all pupils busy because if lessons are pitched at the wrong level for the class, or if the pace of the work expected in class is too fast or too slow, the likelihood is that some pupils will lose interest and dissociate themselves from the classwork. They will end up being unoccupied because the pitch and pace of work is not sufficiently challenging or perhaps because the expectations are too demanding.

Teachers are generally aware of the point. In most of their deliberations on the best approach to their classwork it is easy to see their conscious efforts to fit the demands of classwork to the ability of the pupils and to ensure that all pupils are kept involved in the classwork for the duration of the lesson. But circumstances sometimes arise which make it difficult for teachers to do this. Things quite outside their immediate control can create situations where they feel unable to pitch and pace the work properly and such situations, not surprisingly in view of what we have said, cause a great deal of consternation.

Mixed-ability grouping and control
The degree of sensitivity shown by teachers to such 'external' threats against their efforts to keep pupils busy can be seen very clearly in their reactions to mixed-ability grouping. Mixed-ability grouping, as a feature of classrooms, is almost inevitably a product of policy and organizational decisions made at a school level. It is to this extent imposed on the classroom teacher whether or not he/she happens to support the idea and it is, therefore, a circumstance of the classroom over which the individual

has little control. There are, of course, as we noted in Chapter 3, a number of features of the classroom over which the teacher has little control but the point about mixed-ability grouping is that, not only is it externally imposed, but also it has particular significance for the way in which teachers approach their classwork. Because mixed-ability grouping brings together in one class pupils for whom the pitch and pace of work needs to differ widely, it militates against the use of a 'class orientation' in which the pitch and pace of the work is governed by some expectations about the average performance of the pupils. It operates, instead, in favour of using either a 'group or individualized orientation' where the pitch and pace of the work is geared to the ability of specific pupils within the class and where busyness is linked to the ambitions and targets of distinct pupils rather than lesson-scheduled norms for the class (Cohen and Manion, 1981; Kelly, 1974). The group or individualized orientation allows the pitch and pace of the work, at least in theory, to be automatically adjusted to suit the individual pupil and consequently to overcome the likelihood of boredom, or frustration arising from the nature of the work.

A class orientation, on the other hand, would appear less well suited to mixed-ability grouping. By aiming the work at the class as a whole it would seem to exacerbate the chances of some pupils finding the work too easy and others finding it too difficult and it is the potential threat to classroom control that accompanies this situation which, in fact, lies at the heart of many teachers' anxieties about mixed-ability grouping. For teachers who feel that they cannot, or do not wish to, adopt a group/individualized orientation to classwork but nonetheless, have to deal with such classes, mixed-ability grouping poses a major problem ... a problem not only in terms of pupils covering the syllabus material but also, and more pertinently in the context of the present discussion, because it constitutes a threat to classroom control.

At first glance, the idea that mixed-ability grouping might pose a threat to classroom control would seem rather ironic since it has been suggested on many occasions that one of the particular advantages of mixed-ability grouping is that it actually aids classroom control. Because it prevents a situation where those pupils least receptive to teacher authority get lumped together, mixed-ability grouping, it is argued, stops pockets of resistance from forming by splitting-up the troublemakers, more or less isolating them amongst the other pupils and reducing the likelihood of any 'appreciative audience' for their deviant acts (Kelly, 1974: Robertson, 1981). Recent evidence, indeed, suggests that this is one of the major incentives for teachers to adopt mixed-ability grouping (Ball, 1981; Reid et al., 1981). This is not the whole picture, however, and despite the way mixed-ability grouping diffuses control problems, not all teachers are persuaded of its benefits. At Ashton and Beechgrove, for instance, the teachers of maths and French generally argued against the adoption of mixed-ability grouping and, just as Ball (1981) found in his research at Beachside, teachers in these departments actively opposed the introduction of mixed-ability grouping, actually managing to retain 'setting' even though general school policy had shifted against such practices. For these teachers, mixed-ability grouping appeared to pose special problems. Cynically, it might be argued that their special problem was nothing other than the fact that mixed-ability grouping meant they had to deal with pupils who would not otherwise have been in their lessons. After all, the concentration of difficult pupils may well pose a problem for the teacher who takes the class but, by the same token, it is a positive boon for those who have the difficult pupils taken out of their classes. This, however, would not explain the situation of maths, where, certainly at Ashton and Beechgrove, and probably the vast majority of secondary schools, all pupils took the subject. What was special about these subjects was not just that they had hitherto avoided the problems of social dynamics associated with 'bottom sets' but that, according to the staff involved, mixed-ability grouping had a distinct disadvantage for them because of the particular way they needed to organize their classwork. Mixed-ability grouping, they acknowledged, depended heavily on individualized modes of classwork in which the pupils were allowed to work at their own pace and to the extents of their own ability but this, they argued, was not always compatible with the nature of the subject that was to be taught. In the case of French and maths the subject demanded an 'incrementalist' approach that could not be reconciled with mixed-ability grouping. As a French teacher at Beechgrove made the point:

> With lots of subjects you can have kids working at different speeds, at their own pace, and within their own particular field of interest within the subject. In a language course, it's so carefully structured, even if it's non-grammatical ... quotes 'non-grammatical' ... it is. You know, the grammar's introduced gradually without calling it grammar, and they have to build on what's gone on before and so on ... a continuous process. And they all have to work on the same thing all the time. There's just no way you can ... no way that I can see in the present courses where kids can sort of do otherwise.

The subject, in other words, demanded a class-orientation and class-progression and, so far as these teachers were concerned, this precluded the possibility of allowing pupils to develop at a variety of different paces. This was the crux of the problem facing these teachers because, as a maths teacher at Ashton explained.

With non-streamed classes it's more difficult I think to set a sort of pace, a pace at which you get through the work you know, set some sort of pace that's agreeable to everyone. It's too slow for the brighter ones and it's too fast for the ones who are less intelligent and causes, perhaps, boredom in the bright kids. And the slower ones get frustrated because they can only half understand something before you move on to a new unit of work.

Bored pupils and frustrated pupils, of course, hardly provide a recipe for classroom control. Far from it, according to the teachers at Ashton, Beechgrove and Cedars and, indeed, according to the everyday wisdoms of teachers, these are the very ingredients that need to be avoided like the plague because they lead to idleness – and idleness is premium fuel for classroom disruption.

In view of this, it is not surprising that some teachers were worried about the impact of mixed-ability grouping. Sets, streams and banding on the other hand, went some way towards limiting the range of abilities in class and were attractive, therefore, because they eased the problem of pitching and pacing the classwork in a way that kept all pupils occupied during lessons. So significant was this advantage, in fact, that teachers such as the head of French at Ashton could regard setting as absolutely vital to the successful teaching of the subject. Quite explicitly he argued that mixed-ability grouping had worked to the detriment of his subject because of the pitching and pacing problem and that, against general school policy, he had managed to reintroduce setting for his subject. In unapologetic terms he said

> We do our utmost to set them so that the better ones, the most able ones, come together in one set and then the less able in another set and the least able in another group. And then the teacher knows what level to teach at, you see, and he knows what level to prepare his material for.

He went on to express sentiments shared by many, in fact most, of those involved with teaching maths and French at Ashton and Beechgrove when he said that, in view of the particular nature of their subject, sets, streams or bands were beneficial because they aided appropriate pitching and pacing of the work for the class, and, helped the teacher to keep all the pupils in class occupied all of the time. We ought to remember, however, that the way these teachers justified their use of sets based on ability was not necessarily to argue that there was something inherently better in that kind of arrangement for grouping pupils but to point to certain factors over which they personally had no control and which subsequently led them to favour setting[2]. It was, as they pointed out, in the particular circumstances of their lessons that mixed-ability grouping did not work – specifically the incrementalist nature of the subject.

The logic of the subject was not the only factor presented by teachers as beyond their control and as creating conditions that led them to be anxious about the adoption of mixed-ability grouping. External examinations were also cited in this respect. When teachers were faced with the task of putting over a preordanied body of knowledge, the kind of syllabus requirement typical of most GCE and CSE mode 1 examinations, they felt that the onus was on them to lead the classwork, to direct it and schedule its progress, so that the pupils were adequately prepared by the time of the examination. Under these circumstances they felt there was little leeway to allow pupils to explore areas of particular interest to themselves or to permit pupils to develop to a pitch, and at a pace, suited to themselves as individuals. The teachers' duty was to prepare the class for the examination and this, inevitably, involved a fair degree of class organization. So, as the head of history at Beechgrove argued, while mixed-ability grouping might work at stages before external examinations came on the horizon, when the teacher needed to instil specific, syllabus-linked knowledge, it no longer served the purpose. As she said,

If you're not faced with the specific aim of getting over the information then you can try to construct a lesson which will be interesting for all of them and which the bright ones can go into at a greater level. It depends on what your aim is in your lesson; whether information and facts are the things you want to get across or if you're just trying to instil some sort of attitude towards the subject. But, if you've got exams to work for, then mixed-ability really does cause a problem. You've somehow got to get all the facts across to all of them.

As a result of all this, it is obviously wrong to suggest that mixed-ability grouping acts as an aid to classroom control without taking into account the particular nature of the lessons involved. Although mixed-ability grouping spreads the burden of difficult pupils, at the same time it creates new problems for these teachers who feel unwilling or unable to adopt individualized learning approaches.

The negotiation and control of classwork
The idea that classwork can be organized with a view to bolstering classroom control is based on the assumption that the teacher is in a position to influence and direct the work of the class. Particularly in the

traditional classroom this would seem to be a reasonable assumption because here it is generally taken as axiomatic that the content and schedule of work is to be dictated by the teacher. However, where the teacher adopts a different role, such as that of the 'facilitator' or 'catalyst' usually associated with more progressive approaches, the position is far less clear cut. Where the teacher becomes a facilitator to learning, the responsibility for choosing the pace of work, and even the content of the work to be covered, is delegated from the teacher to the pupil. Such pupil discretion in connection with classwork is characteristic of the whole gamut of approaches under the aegis of progressive education and, at least on the surface, it would seem to suggest the classwork management strategies might be ruled out of order in the progressive classroom. Under these circumstances the teacher would seem to forfeit control over classwork by allowing pupils to operate at their own level, at their own pace and on a topic which is of interest to them.

Appearances, however, are often deceptive. There are not many situations in which teachers are actually prepared to relinquish their control of classwork and, in practice, even where some concessions are made to pupil choice over the scheduling, there is usually some concern on the part of the teacher to retain broad control of the content of work done during lessons. Though pupils might be given some leeway over the level at which they work and the pace at which they cover the work, it is still the teacher who structures the available choice over the content. More than this, in light of recent research by Ball (1980), there is even reason to doubt whether teachers are prepared to sacrifice control over the schedule of work. In his study of the way teachers used *worksheets* with mixed-ability groups he showed that while worksheets suit the scheme of mixed-ability grouping by appearing to allow pupils to work at their own pace and at their own level, the element of pupil choice was, in fact, something of an illusion. In practice, rather than matching the work to the individual the teachers still made the individual adapt to a clearly defined schedule (as well as content) of learning established through the worksheet. From this point, Ball goes on to make the case that the popularity of worksheets in mixed-ability classes is largely because they allow teachers to retain a conventional control over schedule and content while having *appeared* to embrace wholeheartedly the principle of individualized work organization. Worksheets, in other words, are used as a strategy by teachers for retaining control over the pitching and pacing of work despite the adoption of mixed-ability groups.

The use of worksheets for this purpose, from what we have seen, has a clear explanation. Because management of the classwork is regarded as an important strategy for retaining classroom control, teachers are reticent to allow their orchestration of events to be undermined by a process which allows pupils to dictate the scheduling and content of their work. In this respect they are helped by the fact that their positional authority as 'teacher' gives them the initiative in granting or withholding the right of pupils to choose the schedule and content of classwork for themselves. But, as it was argued in Chapters 1 and 2 this official authority cannot guarantee that the teacher will be able to impose his/her will on proceedings in class. The harsh reality is that official authority actually turns out to be a fairly poor basis for asserting control and this, of course, is where classwork management strategies come in. As a source of classroom control, whether used in a traditional or a progressive context, classwork management strategies have a distinctive character. As a genre, they clearly involve an attempt to shift the rationale for classroom control away from matters of positional authority vested in the role of the teacher to issues connected with the demands of the work and the kind of arrangements which are needed in order to accomplish the work. In a Weberian sense, the legitimation of teacher authority depends on an impersonal kind of technical rationality rooted in the imperatives of work organization. Demands for obedience and the acceptance of teacher control, as a result, become justified in terms of the kind of classwork to be done and the nature of the syllabus to be covered – both of which are presented to pupils as things over which the teacher personally has little control. Such a rationale for classroom control, however, depends in the first place on whether or not the pupils are willing to be persuaded that they should be bothered with classwork at all. Obviously, if pupils decide that classwork is irrelevant and refuse to have anything to do with it, there is little chance of the teacher being able to use the classwork as a strategy. The only hope under these circumstances is to fall back on to domination strategies and trust that the pupils still hold some deference to the teacher's official authority, personality, age and, perhaps size. Luckily, as Woods (1978b) points out, most pupils can be persuaded that some manner of involvement in classwork is necessary even though their commitment can turn out to be rather shallow and sporadic.

In classes motivated to achieve in academic terms there is, to emphasize the obvious, a high level of commitment to classwork, which means that classwork management strategies are likely to play a prominent part in the way teachers strive to control the class. But as we move along the continuum towards pupils whose academic motivation is low, then we begin to encounter situations where a commitment to classwork rather than being taken for granted by the teacher, has to be consciously sought after and regularly bolstered if the teacher is not going to be forced to abandon the whole idea of such strategies. As many commentators have suggested, CSE exams have played an important role in this sense over recent years. The CSE exams have given teachers, especially those dealing with the lower ability or less well-motivated pupils, an addition to their armoury by providing an incentive for pupils to get involved with classwork where otherwise there might have been none. Pupils who might have seen little chance of exam success and thus opted out of any concern with classwork now have a 'carrot' dangled before them which, quite apart from what it means for their intellectual development, subtly integrates them into classroom affairs by placing upon them some obligation to conform to the demands of classwork. Such exams, therefore, increase the prospects of using classwork management strategies with the lower ability and (otherwise) lower-motivated pupils by increasing the chances of persuading pupils not to disregard classwork altogether.

'Opting-in' or 'opting-out' of such involvement presents rather a crude picture of what actually happens in class. More accurately, pupils spend some of their time involved in classwork and some of their time not. It is really a question in most instances of the proportion of their time pupils are prepared to give over to classwork rather than total involvement or total rejection of classwork. To complicate the issue further, there is also a question about the nature of classwork that pupils are prepared to undertake. These are both crucial to the way teachers can use the strategy and they remind us that, although classwork management strategies depend on some level of involvement in the first place, in practice they also depend on negotiations about the *proportion* of pupils' time in class which is to be devoted to classwork and negotiations about the *type* of work that is to be done under the rubric of 'classwork'.

The proportion of their time in class which pupils are willing to devote to work will depend on a large array of factors. It will depend, for instance, on the social background of the school and the particular pupil, the kind of lesson and the time of the day and week. Importantly it will also depend on the personal relationships established between teacher and pupils in class. Personal relationships, unlike the other factors over which teachers have little control, depend on the skill and endeavours of the teacher and are a source of influence on involvement in classwork that each teacher can try to exploit. By establishing suitable rapport with the pupils, the teacher can use the relationship as a basis for cajoling, persuading and encouraging the pupils to spend more time at their labours. But, like so many classroom strategies, it is double-edged. Personal relationships are not, in fact, simply a tool for teachers to control pupils because pupils themselves can use involvement in schoolwork as a manipulative device. As Woods (1978a) argues, the amount of work undertaken by pupils can be used as a lever on the relationships between pupils and teachers; work will be done for one teacher where it will not be done for another. On the basis of his research at 'Lowfield', he concluded that pupils' attitude to classwork

> put the emphasis not on the intrinsic qualities of work, the virtues of industry, nor primarily on the personal benefits to be gained. Motivation for these pupils was not to come from socialization into a work ethic, nor form an appeal to instrumentalism, but ... above all, the relationships with the teacher.
>
> (Woods, 1978a, p.174)

It is not, though, just a matter of quantity. When Woods writes about pupil attitudes to classwork it is obvious that the *nature* of the work is just as important as the actual number of minutes of each lesson devoted to it. Pupils, he argues, have a clear perception of the differences between hard work and an easy time. Recitation and chalk and talk, for instance, are hard work, while watching videos and the like are not.

The distinction between hard work and easy time is fairly easy to discern in more traditional teachings situations where there is the underlying assumption that hard work (recitation, chalk and talk and so on) forms the basis of real learning. In such situations the negotiations concern the pupils' involvement in the hard work element of lessons, by definition the less palatable and more arduous features of the learning process. Here, negotiations about the amount of work pupils do, as Woods (1977, 1979) has found, can take the form of an exchange in which the teacher can trade off a future 'easy' session against a current commitment to work or to behave well in class.

> Often the commodity the teacher offers in exchange for good order and a reprensentation of 'work' is escape from relaxation of institutional constraint – films, records, visits, outings, breaks, an 'easy-time'. In the pupils' reckoning, these are not 'work'. Nor are they always such in the teachers'.
>
> (Woods,1979, p.153)

Towards the more progressive end of the spectrum hard work tends to be less clearly defined because greater emphasis is placed on learning through methods pupils have conventionally regarded as 'easy time'. The result of this is a blurring of the distinction between the two kinds of work. This blurring does not, however, negate the possibility of pupils negotiating about the classwork. At Cedars, for instance the relative openness of the humanities syllabus provided a strategy for gaining control over the amount of work which was done by facilitating, if not promoting, discussion between pupils. The very interest and relevance of the topics, combined with a teacher tolerance of talk in open classrooms, allowed pupils to engage in 'legitimate' course-based discussion which in more conventional circumstances on less pupil-centred topics might be regarded as 'idle chatter'. Notwithstanding the potential pedagogic advantages accruing to relevant and interesting material, from the pupils' point of view it blurred the boundaries between 'proper work' and 'having a chat' in a way which could be exploited in the negotiation of work[3].

Teacher:	Jean, Allison, you've been doing a lot of talking. Get on with some work.
Pupil A:	We're talking about work.
Teacher:	I've heard you chatting about clothes
Pupil A:	Yes, well that's it isn't it ... We're talking about fashion. It's part of the unit.
Teacher:	Still sounds like chat to me. Anyway, how much have you written? It's got to be written down for the units ...
Pupil B:	But we've got to discuss things first.

Because conventional methods of distinguishing between 'hard work' and 'easy work' became less appropriate in the humanities lessons, pupils had at their disposal a means for negotiating with teachers about the amount of work they did – a means specific to the open classroom situation.

Involvement in classwork, then, does not simply reflect the demands of the syllabus or the wishes of the teacher. Despite the fact that teachers have a vested interest in high work-loads in order both to cover the syllabus adequately and to enhance the prospect of classroom control, the amount of work actually undertaken depends on a process of negotiation between staff and pupils in which pupils can, for example, trade off obedience and involvement in 'hard-work' against the promise of 'easy sessions'. But any such negotiation depends at heart on the personal relationships between teacher and pupils, and this serves to complicate matters for the teacher. While classwork management strategies tend to present the rigours of work organization in the guise of abstract imperatives, the process of negotiating any work-involvement in the first place might well reintroduce a personal element. This would suggest crucially for teachers' use of classwork management strategies that they cannot assume that the logic of the subject or the incentive of exams is sufficient guarantee of pupils' involvement in classwork and the chances are that some element of a personal relationship will be needed to get the involvement which then, and only then, can be used to foster classroom control.

Conclusion

The advantages of classwork management strategies, from the teachers' point of view, stem from the way they justify control on technical grounds rather than by the 'right to command' vested in the position of teacher as such. The idea is still to provide an explicit structure to lessons but, in this case, the rules, ritual and regimentation of classroom life are not so much a strategic attempt to numb resistance out of existence but a rationalization of classroom proceedings towards the end of the efficient production of work. Used in this manner, the issue of control loses the appearance of a personalized struggle and tends to present itself instead as an organizational matter. *The rationale for control, that is, shifts from personal edict to organizational imperative* – imperatives which exist beyond the wishes of teacher or pupil and to which both parties are obliged to accede. Teachers in this way can present their commands as part of a wider logic and argue that pupil resistance is futile because the commands do not reflect a question of choice on the part of the teacher. Used in this way, the strategy actually serves to circumvent the problem of charisma by locating the need for control beyond the realms of the individual.

However, although staff might use the technical rationale as a mask for their control, it seems that they cannot always rely on appeal to calculative and instrumental feelings on the part of pupils. It cannot be assumed that the organization of classwork provides sufficient grounds for pupils to discard their interests in favour of the imperatives for 'getting things done' and pupils are not always prepared to play along on this score. They are, as we have argued, adept at repersonalizing the whole issue of how much work is to be done and what kind of work this should include and frequently use this repersonalizing as a counter-strategy to teachers' use of classwork management strategies. In fact, the whole process of the negotiation of classwork, to the extent that it reintroduces the personal element, hinders teachers' attempts to present the rules of the classroom in the guise of technical imperatives – whether in the open or the closed classroom. Where such negotiation exists, it is almost inevitable that classwork management strategies will provide only a partial source of classroom control and will need to be used as part of a repertoire of strategies that include domination strategies and co-optation strategies as well.

Strategic dispositions

Strategies for classroom control, by their very nature, provide no certainty of success and, as we have emphasized in the discussion of control strategies, teachers can be frustrated in their efforts to secure classroom control by pupils who either refuse to revere the official authority of teachers or use their own counter-strategies to limit the extent of control achieved by teachers. As a result, the prospects of teachers' being able to mould situations to suit their own requirements are not always good and, as Dreeben makes the point so clearly, teachers often end up reacting to events they neither initiated nor could they foresee.

> The teacher's exercise of authority resembles not that of the director who gives the orders, the foreman who supervises, or the professional who attempts to apply his expertise to the problem; rather, it is an attempt to instruct ... , to identify and stop violations of rules and conduct, and to play fair – all under pressure. With the endemic uncertainty and unpredictabililty of classroom events, the teacher, in attempting to instruct and maintain order, becomes more the reactor to than designer of classroom activities.
>
> (Dreeben, 1973, p.463)

This means, as Woods (1977) has argued, teachers are often obliged to 'accommodate' their vision of what they could or should be doing within the harsh limitations imposed by the real, practical workaday circumstances. They have to do what is possible in view of the events that arise rather than simply supervise, monitor or direct proceedings towards a preconceived end. This inevitably creates some degree of tension and anxiety for those teachers who experience the situation and, not surprisingly, calls for some way in which teachers can reduce their sense of frustration and impotence. *'Strategic dispositions'* serve this purpose.

Cynicism

One such strategic disposition involves a degree of cynicism about the whole teaching enterprise. To alleviate the pressures and contradictions they experience, teachers can adopt a stance which distances them from the turmoil and which allows them to take a rather detached attitude towards the problems they face. Essential features of this cynicism are the denial of responsibility for the circumstances coupled with a resigned attitude towards the situation. To adopt a cynical outlook on school life allows a kind of rhetoric in which the frustrations and failures of everyday classroom life can be attributed to the faults of others, or the faults of the system. Pupils, parents, senior staff, politicians, each serve as a 'scapegoat' which explains and justifies the horrors of the situation.

When new teachers arrive in my department I always give them one piece of advice. I had to give it to Miss Adams the other day when she was anxious and upset about the way things were going with her third-year class. 'It's never your fault – it's always theirs.' You've got to adopt this attitude to manage with the situation. I told her, 'You're just doing a job. You've got to look out for yourself if you're to survive.'
(English teacher – Beechgrove)

This kind of disposition, in a sense, serves as a *morale booster* for teachers and, as Woods (1977,1979) argues, it unites teachers in the face of a common enemy and allows an *esprit de corps* to be reinforced when morale runs low. It allows teachers to laugh in the face of adversity and provides the basis for much of the staffroom banter and in-group jokes. '*Having a laugh*', of course, is not necessarily symptomatic of having a good time and, on the contrary, can be the direct outcome of working in unpalatable circumstances. In this case its function is to provide a means of alleviating the kinds of pressures and contradictions experienced in the school (Stebbins, 1980; Walker *et al.*, 1973; Willis, 1977; Woods, 1976a,1977, 1979).

Withdrawal
The tensions, frustrations and contradictions facing the classroom teacher can become awesome and, on occasion, beyond the anaesthetizing effect of dispositional strategies. At this juncture, perhaps the 'one certain way of ensuring survival is to absent oneself from the scene of potential conflict' (Woods, 1979, p.159). In its most literal and extreme form, this entails leaving the occupation to work in a less hazardous environment. Stewart (1972) provides an illustration of how prominent a strategy this can be. Reporting on her experience at Elliott Comprehensive School in Putney, London, she identified the turnover of staff as a major problem and attributes a significant part of it to 'withdrawal' by teachers.

[A] teacher told of a woman member of staff who had a desk thrown at her. She left the school with a broken arm and was never seen again ...
A music teacher arrived a Elliott. She took a couple of classes and left the same afternoon. 'She was so appalled', a member of the staff told me.
One night after school had finished I met a woman who had been formerly on the staff at Elliott. She had come to visit old friends, and had tea with us. She said: 'I am working in a supermarket now ... I left

because I could not go on taking fourth-year leavers any more. I had done eleven years with them and I asked for other classes. I felt my nerves were stretched to breaking. I also requested a sabbatical. Both things were refused so I left. I am getting terribly in debt. But at least I am not a teacher! ' The others said she had been an excellent teacher ...

The staff reply to the strain on their nerves by going sick – quite frequently. That is when they do not leave altogether.

Now although such reportage is open to the allegation that it is sensationalist and based on restricted and localized evidence, it draws attention to the use of absenteeism, or leaving the job altogether, as a device for overcoming the stresses and strains of teaching.

Complete withdrawal from the situation is, of course, a rather drastic and negative strategy and will be prevalent only in localized or extreme instances. But withdrawal also has a more subtle facet used by those who remain at work. Teachers often choose to ignore or actively avoid situations which they know would place them in an invidious position, especially those that require them to impose control in awkward or difficult circumstances.

I don't go looking for trouble. Some staff, you know, go to the toilets where they ... they know someone's likely to be smoking. They know they'll get someone sooner or later ... and afterwards they'll come back to the staffroom and have a cigarette themselves!

I don't try to find them out. If a kid walks around smoking, you know, blatantly ... well then he's forcing me to do something about it. But unless I'm pushed into this kind of situation, it makes life a lot easier if you turn a blind eye to some of the less serious 'offences'. It's no fun being at loggerheads all the time with kids – it's exhausting and it's frustrating.

(French teacher: Beechgrove)

Over-zealous teachers, indeed, are likely to find themselves under pressure from both staff and pupils not to seek out misdemeanours or go looking for confrontations. Part of the competence of the teacher is to know when and where to turn a blind eye and thus in a sense withdraw from a situation which would oblige them to instigate a control mechanism.

Two points arise from this. First it is evident that some members of staff tend to overuse the strategy, at least in the eyes of staffroom colleagues. At Ashton, Beechgrove and Cedars it was clear that certain staff had been labelled as those who had 'copped-out' on matters of control. They would not involve themselves in matters of control in the 'neutral' zones of corridors and playground where no specific responsibility for control was given by the official set-up. The second point is that the withdrawal strategy is not entirely a random or idiosyncratic phenomenon, but can be attributed to the social context within which the potential confrontation occurs. If a pupil or group of pupils breaks certain explicit or implicit rules in the closed classroom, the individual subject teacher is unequivocally responsible for dealing with the matter. Yet, because it is a closed classroom, the teacher also has the discretion *not* to intervene if he/she feels that intervention might prove more disruptive than letting the incident go by without intervention (cf. D.H.Hargreaves *et al.*, 1975; Stebbins, 1970). The closed classroom context, that is, is a context which on the one hand renders specific teachers responsible for events (and thereby eliminates one form of withdrawal) but on the other hand facilitates discretion in whether to react or not.

In the team teaching situation the opposite is true. Though no one individual teacher is responsible for control, the events and withdrawal strategies become public and possibly subject to less discretion. Corridors and playgrounds offer other contexts where individual responsibility is less obvious and thus a situation where withdrawal is facilitated through an ambiguity of responsibility. Yet again, although the situation offers more potential for withdrawal it is also a public arena in which the strategy becomes apparent to colleagues.

On duty during breaks and lunch, the discretion for withdrawal is also to be found. Where no explicit tour of duty is provided, the member of staff can choose *not* to visit areas which, in his/her opinion, might invite a control confrontation. Outside school as well, teachers may find themselves in a context which allows, if not necessitates, a strategic withdrawal. The following interview extract explains the point.

We were sat in a pub the other night when two fifth formers walked in and got some drinks. They saw us but they didn't kind of hide the fact that they were drinking. And we knew they were under age. Well they sort of looked our way to say 'Hello' – a bit cocky I felt they were. Anyway ... um ... we felt a bit awkward. We avoided them and left soon after. I mean it could prove embarrassing if someone locally found out we'd sort of condoned their drinking. But we couldn't take them on there and then about it, I mean the landlord probably didn't want to know. And it would just spoil our evening – and theirs. It would all have been too much fuss and bother – so we took the easy way out.

(Humanities teacher: Cedars)

This strategy, like most, however, can be exploited by pupils in their attempts to limit the control of teachers. If pupils are aware that teachers would rather withdraw from confrontation than engage in embarrassing or protracted efforts to assert control they are in a position to achieve a degree of autonomy and counter the control of staff.

Indulgence
The same is true of 'indulgence'. Indulgence is a teacher strategy in which pupils are allowed to go beyond normally accepted bounds of behaviour and where teachers decline to enforce general classroom rules.

In a general sense, it has been observed that teachers do not always intervene when interruption occurs. On occasion they foresee that the intervention would cause a greater disturbance than was warranted by the initial disruption, or they might see the intervention as exacerbating the situation (D.H. Hargreaves *et al.*, 1975; Stebbins, 1970). Teachers are occasionally prepared to indulge forms of behaviour, especially where the take into account the identity of the perpetrator of that behaviour. Teachers respond to behaviour by taking into account *who* was involved and what would be the *likely outcome* of remedial action applied to this particular pupil. Where they come to regard the behaviour as 'normal' for the particular pupil or class, there is a tendency to indulge the behaviour and cease attempts to remedy the normally unacceptable behaviour.

As used by Woods (1977,1979) such indulgence is applied by teachers to the behaviour of the whole class, but it is worth noting that indulgence can be just as applicable to the behaviour of individual pupils within a class who, for whatever reason, come to be regarded as a special case and worthy of special treatment. At Cedars, for instance, in a fifth-year Humanities class, one boy spent the majority of his time walking around talking to other pupils. In the open-plan units movement around the class was not prohibited as such, but there were tacit amounts of movement deemed appropriate. In every sense, the movement of this pupil contravened this tacit rule for his classroom presence was typified by movement around the room with occasional sorties to his desk rather than vice versa. On his travels the pupil stopped with groups of pupils, chatted with them, walked off with pens and rulers and created interruptions for the groups he visited.

The indulgence with which this behaviour was treated, however, was the product of both teacher and pupil strategies. Accounts of the situation by the teachers drew attention to the fact that movement *per se* was not prohibited in the classroom and that this particular boy had learning difficulties which would probably become behavioural problems if he were made to stay in one place. They also noted the general pleasantness of his character. Looked at from the pupil's point of view, his success in countering normal modes of control by teachers stemmed from the combination of a number of factors. Had the staff attempted to force the pupil to stay in one place it might have provoked the kind of confrontation which could expose the essence of power relations in the classroom and explode the facade of friendliness. The staff not only disliked confrontation of itself, but also were aware of the broader implications for the tenor of the whole classroom. Added to this problem was the fact that he was regarded as a likeable fellow – much in the style of the 'amiable idiot'. Yet this pupil's use of the indulgence strategy exhibited some considerable sophistication. When talking to a small group of pupils he provided for them a source of brief respite from work but his interruptions were essentially temporary; after a short time he would move to disturb someone else. From the point of view of the other pupils his wanderings were more of a relief from work than a hindrance to it. Even when he walked off with someone's pen or ruler, he exhibitied a delightful sense of timing in giving it back just before the protestations of the owner became serious enough to attract the attention of the teachers. This pupil, in fact, exemplified the manner in which indulgence could be used to avoid work and how it relied on an ambience of friendliness and good humour in the classroom.

From the teacher's point of view, indulgence and withdrawal are strategies for coping with problem situations. By avoiding situations or turning a blind eye to particular events, teachers can sidestep the need to confront and control the activity of pupils, particularly where such efforts would be difficult, time consuming and embarrassing. Depending on both the prediliction of the teacher and the context of the event, teachers can use, and may be pressured to use, such dispositions as a means for maintaining the veneer of consensus and normality in their relations with pupils.

Pupil dispositional strategies

Faced with situations that do not match up with their expectations and obliged to attend situations they find nasty and unfair, pupils can adopt dispositions – in fact, may well *have* to adopt dispositions – which help them to 'make out'. The pupil counterpart to cynicism, for instance, would be an anti-school disposition which allows the teachers, the school and all it stands for to be treated with disdain and contempt. To overcome the prospect and reality of failure in the academic hoops and hurdles of school life, pupils can retain a sense of self-respect by rejecting the establishment's criteria for success and instituting subcultural criteria for status and success which are at variance with the school's. Pop culture

(Sugarman 1967) and a variety of machismo dispositions (Coleman, 1961; D.H. Hargreaves, 1967; Webb, 1962; Willis 1977) exemplify the manner in which pupils can opt out of the system and consequently survive on their own terms of reference. (See also Fuller, 1980, 1982, 1983).

These examples of pupil dispositions, however, are not necessarily a response to intolerable circumstances at school. Certainly they provide an avenue of escape for those who would wish to exploit them but they may be just as well a product of cultural factors unrelated to school experience as such (Coleman, 1961; Lacey, 1970; Sugarman, 1967), as manifestly opposed to the dominant school standards yet caused by factors remote from the social organization of the school. There is no necessity, in other words, that such dispositions constitute a *strategic* response to the school situation.

There are, on the other hand, certain dispositions which are not only open to all pupils to explore but also necessary that all pupils adopt if they are to survive in classrooms. As Jackson (1968) argues, given the crowding, the constant evaluation, the power differences between teacher and pupils, and the organizational difficulties in the distribution of materials in lessons, *all* pupils need to adopt the '*strategy of detachment*':

> the crowds, the praise and the power that combine to give a distinctive flavor to classroom life, collectively form a hidden curriculum which each student (and teacher) must master if he is to make his way satisfactorily through the school.
>
> (Jackson, 1968, p. 34)

Such a disposition is less a matter of choice, more a matter of necessity. Like Goffman's (1968) 'situational withdrawal', the strategy of detachment allows pupils to survive the threatening reality of institutional life by creating a psychological distance between the 'inner self' and the role of pupil. The waiting, the impersonality, the surveillance, the evaluation that Jackson identifies as characteristic of classrooms are strongly reminiscent of the features of Goffman's 'total institutions' and pupils, like inmates, have at their disposal dispositions which are necessary in order to cope with the unsavoury demands of the situation. Detachment allows pupils, in the face of what Jackson found to be an 'embarrassing, cruel experience suffered from malicious and insensitive teachers' and the 'boredom of meaningless class routine and work situation', to present a facade of conformity hiding an uninvolved and resentful soul. It gives the appearance of going along with teacher edicts and thus allows pupils to do 'easy time' while, at the same time, distancing them from events and retaining a thorough going lack of commitment to the regime. Pupils can *appear* to be fully involved in the proceedings while really not paying attention at all. They realize that gazing out of the window or talking across the room to another pupil will be treated by the teacher as evidence of a lack of attention but can become quite adept at manipulating such symbols of involvement in order to give the impression of going along with the teacher's regime (cf. Hammersley, 1976).

Summary and conclusion

Schoolteachers live in a world where classroom control is deemed vital to their occupational survival. Yet, as we have seen, their ability to win this control is precarious. They cannot depend too heavily on their official position of authority to guarantee their success and what they have to do instead is develop certain classroom strategies which help them in their ambitions to establish and maintain the necessary control during lessons.

These strategies seem to fall into three broad categories: 'domination', 'co-optation' and 'classwork management'. *Domination*, we noted, uses the official authority of the teacher as a backdrop to impose control in a very blatant and exposed form. It relies on, and exaggerates, institutionalized disparities in power. *Co-optation*, as a control strategy, seeks the willing participation of pupils by incorporating the interests of pupils and using methods of getting them involved in the process of the lesson. The aim is to harness those forces emanating from pupils which threaten an armageddon in the classroom and use them instead, to bolster the existing order. *Classwork management*, on the other hand, involves the attempt to gain control through the intrinsic rationale of particular forms of work organization. Emphasis is placed on the way different types of classwork affect the behaviour of pupils and can be used to alleviate or obviate threats to teacher control.

On the surface, the three kinds of strategies would appear to offer stark contrast. It is easy to see that domination stratagies are more readily associated with traditional teaching styles and that co-optation strategies can be tied in with progressive pedagogy. Yet, beneath the obvious differences in teacher approach which they portray, it can be argued that there is a deep-rooted link which explains why they all persist and why the individual teacher can switch between the three depending on the particular situation. *The possibility of coexistence and the possibility of interchange between the strategies exist simply because the strategies all serve similar functions.*

First, they all help the teacher to satisfy the dual facet of the job. They aid both semblance of classroom control *and* the appearance of covering a particular body of work. Their success and persistent use, in other words, is because they all go some way towards satisfying the necessities of control and work output, and do not facilitate one at the expense of the other.

Second, the strategies all do something to minimize the uncertainty of classroom events. Teacher control must entail some measures to give a pattern and predictability to proceedings during lesson-time and help the teacher to cope with potential chaos in the classroom. There is a concern, as it were, for order because order is at one and the same time a symbol of control and a prerequisite of control.

Third, and possibly most important, all the strategies involve an attempt by teachers to present a rationale for control which exists independent of the teacher's personal wishes. The appeal for compliance is taken away from the wishes of Ms Jones or Mr Green and located elsewhere. Domination strategies put the rationale for compliance in the form of immutable rules and traditional authority, while co-optation appeals to pupils themselves as the ostensive source of control. Participation and the involvement of pupils serve to give the impression that compliance is less problematic and, in any case, is a two-way process with teachers readily acceding to pupil interests. Classwork management places the emphasis on the imperatives of technology or work organization and teachers, in this case, can appeal to the rational authority of their demands. So, rather than rely on charisma to achieve control of the classroom, all three kinds of strategies seem to depend on methods geared to reducing any reliance on personality or personal relationships as a means for eliciting control. The strategies can in fact be regarded as the routinization of charisma – as reasonable and practical ways of coming to grips with the fact that not all teachers can be 'naturals'. In the present-day mass education system the naturally gifted teachers who can rely on their own charisma to command obedience are few and far between. They do exist, but *for the majority of teachers, there is a need to devise strategies which aid control by legitimizing their authority in ways other than appeal to charisma.* This does not mean that all teachers are striving in all their dealings with pupils to depersonalize the relationship. Obviously, approaches to the task will depend to some extent on the particular personality and pedagogic beliefs of individual teachers. But what *is* being suggested is that most teachers working under normal conditions strive to bolster control by down-playing the charismatic demand for obedience and by building upon alternative rationales to legitimize their command position. In this sense, of course, 'impersonal' is clearly a reference to the *basis for control* and does not signify a haughty or detached approach by staff.

There are instances where teachers deliberately promote the personal basis for control. At Cedars, as we have already seen, the staff placed emphasis on personal relationships, first-name terms and a friendly atmosphere; a conscious effort to reduce the institutional authority relations between teachers and pupils. Swidler (1979) describes a more extreme example when she reports on an ethnographic study at two 'free schools' – 'Group High' and 'Ethnic High'. Both schools, although part of the Berkeley public school system, made a special and concerted effort to be non-hierarchical and anti-bureaucratic in terms of their official organization and their teacher–pupil relationships. As Swidler is quick to point out, though, free schools 'do not *escape* the problems of power and social control that drive other organisations, but their members operate with different rules of the game' (p. 7). Instead of control based on hierarchical authority positions, she found three alternative forms of social control being used at 'Group High' and 'Ethnic High' : *internalization* – where students were encouraged to embrace the ethos of self-directed learning and identify with the aims of the school and its staff; *group pressure* – where collective incentives were used to foster a group solidarity that kept pupils integrated with class goals (that is, where peer pressure was approved by the teachers as a way of keeping disaffected students 'in line'); and *personal influence and charisma* – where teachers created personal allegiance and loyalty as the basis for control.

Swidler argues that all three substitutes for positional authority caused problems for the teachers involved since, 'although they have agreed to do without authority, [they] still want to maintain the schools where they teach and to influence, stimulate, and involve students' (p. 4). But personal influence, in particular, involved a high cost for teachers. The spark of being 'unpredictable, exotic and complicated' was difficult to keep kindled in the face of the mundane aspects of routine teaching. There were diminishing returns to the use of personal intimacies and anecdotes – especially since teachers were stripped of their special status and, as a result, the staff at Group High and Ethnic High often found that their efforts to influence proceedings left them 'exhausted, drained and sometimes neglected'. Charisma, in other words, proved a difficult and tiring alternative to positional authority. If this is true of free schools in Berkeley, it is hardly surprising that the teachers at Ashton and Beechgrove seemed reticent to rely on charisma as the basis for their classroom control and preferred, in general, to depersonalize their efforts for control.

Reference to Swidler's research is valuable at this point not just for what it tells us about teachers' use of charisma for control. It also reminds us that strategies for control arise in a particular context and because any context involves certain demands and obligations, problems and opportunities, there is a need to match the strategies to the context.

Strategies, for this reason, are always *context-specific* and should never be regarded as universally applicable. This is true of the kinds of teacher strategies identified so far – 'domination', 'co-optation' and 'classwork management'. As worthwhile strategies for control they respond to a particular context of teaching. In general, the strategies we have identified constitute a specific response to a context characterized by:

(1)   the closed classroom with its pressures on the individual teacher to be held responsible for events,

(2)   the minimal amounts of resources and technology available to help the teacher, and the consequent pressure this puts on the teacher in terms of his/her man-management function – a pressure exacerbated by

(3)   the large size of classes and the high staff–pupil ratio,

(4)   the changing and novel situations which teachers confront during lessons (the element of uncertainty) and,

(5)   the fact that pupils are not always willing partners to classroom proceedings (the element of opposition).

In this 'normal' context, the elements of *uncertainty and opposition* emerge as key threats to teacher control. This makes the notion of 'strategy' particularly appropriate for dealing with the methods adopted by teachers. Because strategic action is essentially concerned with opposition and uncertainty it therefore provides an appropriate image of the methods used by teachers to gain control – and, of course, the methods used by pupils to challenge and limit that control. The counter-strategies adopted by pupils, remember, tend to depend on trying to retain or reintroduce the personal element or the uncertainty element.

Notes

1   See, for example, Davies (1978), Docking (1980), Furlong (1976), Gannaway (1976), D. H. Hargreaves (1982), Marsh *et al.* (1978), Nash (1976) and Woods (1976b, 1979).

2   Reid *et al.* (1981) found in their research covering twenty-nine schools that maths teachers were divided between those who shared with the teachers at Ashton and Beechgrove a view of the subject as 'sequential' and who therefore considered the subject ill-suited to mixed-ability grouping, and those who favoured an individual, resource-based topic approach for whom mixed-ability grouping provided a suitable organization. This suggests that, at a general level, it would be wrong to see teacher responses to mixed-ability grouping in subjects like maths as showing complete agreement. In fact Corbishley *et al.* (1981) and Evans (1982), on the basis of their research covering mixed-ability grouping in maths in London comprehensives, make the point that some teachers deliberately adopted individualized modes of instruction to accommodate the demands

and pressures coming from the use of mixed-ability grouping. Rather than change the mode of class organization they changed their style of teaching.

3 Such a manoeuvre would fit Woods' (1978b) typology as part of 'open negotiation' about schoolwork between teacher and pupils.

5

The Significance of Noise

Jackson, in his perceptive account of the social organization of classrooms, draws attention to the fact that 'Classrooms, by and large, are relatively quiet places and it is part of the teacher's job to keep them that way' (1968, p. 105). The observation is not startling and those who have experience of conventional schooling might be forgiven for wondering whether this is anything more than an unremarkable comment on the obvious. Taken for granted truths, however, often shroud vital issues and Jackson's point is, in fact, far from trite. It reminds us that despite containing something like thirty pupils, each with particular interests and energies, classrooms are not normally riotous settings. They are not normally like playgrounds with their cacophony of sounds but are (under the circunstances) remarkably subdued and frequently silent places.

The reason for this is not hard to find. The main, if not the only, reason that classrooms are relatively quiet is because teachers strive to make them that way. Teachers devote a considerable part of their energies to the prevention of loud disruptions and spend much of their time exhorting pupils to 'keep the noise down' or 'keep quiet'. This is not particularly new, either, for as Grace (1978, p. 30) indicates, a preoccupation with 'quiet orderliness' in the classroom has been evident since the times of the elementary schools in the last century. The question is, why does it persist in being a concern of teachers today despite a climate in schools that is seemingly more 'progressive' and certainly less authoritarian, cruel and repressive than it used to be? Why does 'keeping 'em quiet' continue to assume such significance in the work of teachers and why do teachers, even today, place so much emphasis on limiting noise during lessons? To this, there appear to be three broad answers.

In the first place, as members of society rather than members of the teaching profession, we should not be too much surprised if teachers exhibit a distaste for noise and a marked preference for a quiet working environment. It is not unreasonable to suppose that teachers might prefer quiet classrooms simply because quiet settings are seen as both more congenial and less fatiguing contexts than noisy ones in which to conduct the day's labours. Teachers, after all, are employees who suffer the same ill-effects of being subjected to noise over a period of time as those in other industries and by actively seeking a quiet environment their purpose could be simply to reduce one of the many tiring aspects of their job and create, in their eyes, a more pleasant climate for work.

At Ashton and Beechgrove, however, it was evident that the teachers' concern with noise was more complex and more far reaching than just the prevention of migraine. Quite apart from any personal preference for quiet orderliness in the classroom which they might have had, teachers at these schools suggested that their concern with levels of noise was inextricably bound-up with pedagogic considerations and that their attempts to limit the amount of noise during lessons reflected their efforts to create a classroom situation in which learning could occur most productively. At Beechgrove, the comments of an English teacher highlighted the reasoning more or less explicitly articulated in interviews with other staff at the schools. She said:

> I don't know how people can work with noise in their lessons. To me it seems unreasonable to expect the kids to work ... to really um ... concentrate and learn. And I know most of us who've been teaching here over a few years feel the same. You've got to get the classroom quiet before you can really teach ... and them learn. I mean ... I don't mean perfect silence but it's got to be pretty low so that you can talk and they can listen or they can get on with their own work without being disturbed.

Noise, in this case, posed a problem because it was regarded as interfering with the learning context. With only occasional reservations, the teachers argued that noise and learning were antithetical features of the classroom situation and that noise in classrooms only served to hinder communication and concentration.

This second facet of the practical problem of noise – what we might call the 'educational facet' – appeared to create particular problems where teachers were obliged to operate in circumstances in which interference from noise was effectively beyond their control and where, at least so far as noise was concerned, they were not masters of their own destiny. As the head of music at Ashton indicated, the circumstances could be bad enough to drive teachers to despair.

> We haven't any real music facilities here, you know, architecturally wise. Two of us, you know, including myself, are working in a canteen

... And it's the same at the lower school where the teacher there also works in a canteen. And it's even worse there because the canteen's smaller, therefore you've got all the noise of the dining room staff clanking and clinking. And you have PE and drama lesson in the hall which adjoins the canteens – so the noise problem is phenomenal. If you're trying to do music – which is essentially aural ... even if you're playing an instrument you're listening all the time to what you're playing and seeing if you're in tune, is it making some sort of sense ... and it's very difficult under those sort of conditions. So much so that that's why I've got a member of staff now leaving after one term's work. She can't stand it. She can't cope with the situation. And we've had six music teachers since I came here in three years in that building, and it's for that reason ... teachers have found that ... that it's an impossible situation.

Admittedly music was particularly susceptible to such interference because its instruction relied heavily on aural communication and attention to various intricacies of sound but, though it was specially prone to interference by noise impinging from external sources, other subjects were not immune. The head of music went on to recall, with some irony, how a move away from the canteen had proved impractical because the noise *generated* in music lessons interfered with lessons in adjacent classrooms.

We had a mobile hut built in the grounds, very close to the main building. And, everybody pointed out that the mobile hut ... it'd be a good idea to put it right away, far away from the building, so if music was going on it wouldn't disturb five classrooms – three lower and two upstairs – with the noise of instruments and singing and pianos and record players. But the Brent Borough refused because that meant the expense of building a concrete path leading to the hut, whereas if they placed it at the side of the main building the path was already there. And in the summer, because there's so much glass and everybody wants to open windows, I mean, the situation's impossible. They begged me not to teach music as such ... could I just talk to them. I mean this was the approach. I mean it is very, very difficult. And then the noise was so much there that then we were taken out of the hut and put back in the canteen. For a while, you see, we had a respite, you see, from the canteen, but we've been put back again because one music class was hitting five classrooms the way it was positioned ... as I say, three there and two upstairs. So it's really hell.

Interference by noise from adjacent classrooms, indeed, appeared to be a general problem experienced by teachers and one which existed, in this sense, irrespective of the type of noise or its causes. Problems could arise as much from Mozart as 'messers', as a languages teacher at Beechgrove indicated when arguing that he 'suffered' from the audio-visual employed in an adjacent room:

> I'm not saying [the other teacher] is wrong to use tapes and so on ... er, in fact they're good, I think. But it doesn't help me. Sometimes you can't hear yourself think and ... er, it's very difficult to teach the kids when everyone can hear what's going on next door.

Noise from outside the classroom was seen to hinder the learning process and interfere with the progress of instruction by interrupting pupils' concentration on work, and thus it constituted an aspect of the problem of noise which was specific to the situation of teaching, rather than a product of personal preference or predisposition. Yet, as the situation of music as Ashton served to illustrate, such a concern with the effects of noise on instruction was double-sided. Operating in settings which were not soundproofed, teachers were aware that their classes were far from isolated in terms of noise and that, as the head of music had noted, noise created within their own classroom would be audible to colleagues and could interfere with colleagues' lessons. The problem of noise, consequently, was not just one of interference from outside, but also entailed a concern by teachers to prevent noise in their own class from affecting adjacent rooms. Acknowledging that they occasionally suffered the adverse effects of noise created in colleagues' classrooms, it appeared that teachers sought to prevent the possibility that they would be responsible for a similar misdemeanour.

Without walls to separate the classes, this anxiety about the two-way effects of noise could only be increased. In the humanities lessons at Cedars, for example, when attempting to instruct subgroups within the open area there was the danger that either the teacher's instructions were audible to all the groups – in which case they could prove a disruptive influence – or the noise levels from the other groups could prevent the teacher from being heard by the group he/she was trying to instruct. So where instruction occurred in the discrete teacher–pupil units the level of noise emanating from the units needed to be finely attuned to the situation in adjacent groups and teachers frequently appealed to their own subgroup not to interfere with the others. It was common to hear them say things like, 'All right, cut the noise down a bit. Jim's trying to talk to his group and they can't hear him if you don't shut up a bit.'

The fact that noise in one subgroup could interrupt other subgroups in the open-plan area meant in practice that certain kinds of teaching were inhibited. The reading of plays or poetry aloud was mentioned in this context because it either involved the whole unit (which was seen as impractical) or constituted a disruptive influence on those not engaged in the reading. Pupils themselves suffered from the noise created by other groups and claimed that it interfered with their concentration on work. They indicated that there was more noise in the open-plan classrooms and, while many regarded it as just as incidental feature of the particular lesson, others regarded it as an indictment on the humanities situation:

> The open-plan classroom is quite good. I like it when we can all work together as one big group, but there can be quite a lot of noise.

> I think that the volume of noise should be kept lower, so that you can concentrate better. Thus your work will be better.

> In open classrooms there is more noise but in conventional classrooms you can concentrate because the teacher only has one class to keep quiet. But there is two other classes to keep quiet in open-plan classrooms.

> When you are listening to your teacher you can hear the other two still talking and it can put you off.

> In an open-plan classroom you get more noise which breaks your concentration and you lose where you are when people start talking to you.

So far as teachers in the *closed* classroom were concerned this interference had one immediate repercussion on their approach to the job. Accounting for their style of teaching, staff at Ashton and Beechgrove frequently made a distinction between what they would like to do under ideal circumstances and what it was feasible to do under real teaching conditions. In this connection, constraints of noise were a common theme. When teachers were asked why they opted for a particular arrangement of desks in class, for instance, a common reply was that, while recognizing the pedagogic implications of grouping desks or having desks facing into the centre of the classroom and while seeing advantages to this arrangement, it was not really practical *under the circumstances*. The time involved in rearranging desks proved largely prohibitive for those staff who did not operate in their own classroom and who needed to alter the setting at the start of the lesson and revert to the original arrangement at the finish, and noise generated by such manoeuvres simply served to exacerbate the problem and provide a formidable deterrent to such classroom innovations. The classroom furniture at Ashton and Beechgrove was heavy and wooden and, with no carpeting on the floors, the prospect of desk rearrangement unaccompanied by high levels of noise was remote. Given the proximity of classrooms and the lack of soundproofing between them, teachers recognized that desk rearrangement would almost certainly entail levels of noise which would impinge on and interfere with lessons going on in adjacent rooms and had to weigh this effect against the anticipated benefits for their own classroom situation. For practical purposes, that is, teachers did not regard themselves as free to operate according to their personal preference despite the setting of the closed classroom. Although they had individual responsibility for the classroom they were not entirely freed from the influence of external agencies and, in their conduct of the lesson, they exhibited a concern to prevent noise emanating from their classroom. This concern subsequently influenced their approach to classroom teaching by inhibiting methods that generated noise. Although the autonomy afforded by closed classrooms meant that teachers were ostensibly free to experiment and innovate according to their individual wishes, it was evident that they took into consideration the level of noise that would accompany any such innovation and that where they anticipated high levels of noise they were reluctant to use the approach even where they recognized potential pedagogic advantages.

Now, to indicate that noise is a problem for teachers because it interferes with the progress of lessons and that teachers generally make efforts to prevent noise in their classrooms from disturbing other lessons may appear to be banal. It tells teachers nothing they do not already know. It does, however, present the problem of noise as an educational issue and, when considering the problem of noise for the practical activity of teaching, it is worthy of note that the teachers' concern with noise was significantly affected by their appraisal of the impact of noise on the ability of pupils to concentrate on work. The analysis which follows is not intended to denigrate or deny this aspect of the problem but to offer an analytically distinct source of the problem of noise and a separate, if complementary, reason for 'Keeping 'em quiet'.

Noise and classroom control

The accounts given by staff at Ashton and Beechgrove revealed a further dimension to the problem of noise, a dimension which discriminated between different kinds of noise and which treated noise not as a problem in its own right but as an indicator of other things crucial to the social world of teachers. In a nutshell, it was clear that noise also posed a problem because it was easily interpreted as the end-product of poor classroom control.

The reasoning behind this was superficially quite straightforward. Since the general feeling of the teachers was that lessons had to be relatively quiet if learning was to occur, and since they saw their job as centred around the creation of a suitable learning environment to the classroom, a noisy classroom could not reasonably be seen as a product of choice on the part of the teacher in charge and must, instead, be viewed as an undesired state brought about by the particular teacher's inability to exercise control over the pupils. As a result, the competence of the teacher responsible for a noisy classroom could become suspect in the eyes, or should we say ears, of colleagues. But the significance of noise was more than this. As we have already seen in Chapter 3, most teachers work in closed classrooms and in this conventional set-up teachers tend to suffer a distinct lack of first-hand information about how colleagues operate. The result is that, as at Ashton and Beechgrove, they rely almost exclusively on bits of information which manage to transcend the physical and social isolation of the classroom and which can be used to *infer* what is going on behind the closed door. Because they rarely witness other teachers' lessons, what they know about the work of colleagues necessarily depends, if not exclusively at least quite heavily, on a kind of informed guesswork based on hints gleaned from sources of information which escape the prison of the classroom. Amongst these sources of information noise figures quite prominently. Teachers may not be able to *see* colleagues in action very often but, particularly in view of the close proximity of classrooms, they are certainly in a position to *hear* what is going on.

It is worth stressing, however, that when they use what they hear as a means for identifying poor classroom control, teachers do not seem to rely on decibel levels to provide a simple barometer of control. Far from it, the teachers at Ashton and Beechgrove, were not simplistic in their analysis of noise and were prepared to use a number of subtle variations according to their detailed knowledge of the situation in order to produce a fairly sophisticated appraisal of what significance could be attributed to the noise. They took into account 'allowably noisy' lessons such as PE, drama and music where it was recognized that the normal rules could not reasonably operate and where, within bounds, more noise could be tolerated without impugning the competence of the teacher in charge. Likewise, the nature of the pupils and the specific demands they placed on staff also led to an increased tolerance of noise. As all the teachers knew, some groups were especially difficult to subdue and any teacher could be excused for failing to keep them in check all the time. Different subjects, different pupils, different schools, all involved a separate set of expectations about noise levels and the problem for the teacher in charge of a class (and for those who interpreted the noise from outside the confines of the lesson) was not one of absolute decibel levels but one of the levels of noise acceptable under the circumstances. What was in question was the level of noise emanating from a classroom *relative to the norm* for the particular class, subject or school. What was not in question, however, was the idea that teachers who flouted the norm, intentionally or otherwise, ran the risk of being identified as teachers who could not, or would not, exercise classroom control.

Judgements about control also involved some idea of the *frequency* with which teachers had exceptionally noisy classes. Apart from taking into consideration the particular subject and class, any conclusions about the general ability of a teacher to control a class were arrived at usually after some time and after colleagues could identify some persistent level of noise outside the norm. For new teachers, of course, this history did not exist and for them noise took on additional significance in the sense that 'first impressions count'. For established staff, however, the occasional rumpus in class did not instantly challenge their image of competence. These were allowable aberrations suffered by just about everybody. It was the recurrent or persistent offender who actually stood to lose.

Finally, rather than attribute the same significance to all noise emanating from the classroom – whether it be from musical instruments, audio-visual aids or pupils running riot – teachers were clearly discerning about the source of the noise when treating it as a clue to what was happening behind the closed doors of a classroom. Specifically, when using noise as a measure of classroom control it was *pupil-initiated* noise, created by pupils and/or their teacher's responses, which was taken to be indicative of a lack of control in the classroom. Whereas the blaring of a tape recorder or the rasping noise of classroom furniture being scraped across the floor was a nuisance that interfered with adjacent lessons, such noise did not immediately signify poor control. The cacophony of talking pupils interspersed with the raised voice of a teacher, on the other hand, carried all the connotations of a control problem.

Against these criteria for interpreting noise it was possible for teachers to have 'lively' classes occasionally which would be interpreted outside the class as a sign of action and enthusiasm rather than apathy and poor control. At Cedars the point was made patently clear by a lead lesson conducted by Mr Wright. Mr Wright was well liked by the pupils and respected by colleagues as an enthusiastic and highly competent teacher. As a division head he held pastoral responsibilities that more or less demanded a good rapport with pupils and, significantly, a reputation for good control. The lesson, involving over sixty pupils, sought to show the effects of the division of labour on productivity and the extent of frustration that could be caused where opportunities to improve productivity were restricted. Mr Wright orchestrated proceedings, whipping up excitement and anger as groups and individuals tried to reach production targets and claim their reward in the form of Milky Ways and Mars Bars. The whole game was made more 'interesting' by the fact that some groups or individuals were given blunt scissors, others were kept waiting for fresh materials. In all, the lesson carried three features that could well have been attributed to poor control. Mr Wright was subjected to abusive comments and even physical threats by some to those pupils who found themselves on the losing end of the (heavily loaded) production game. Some pupils gave up in frustration and despair and refused point blank to take further part in the lesson. And the noise level was very high indeed. As an observer inside the classroom I watched a brilliantly planned and executed lesson that gave the pupils an emotionally charged experience of the inequities of the productive system. To the outsiders, it was a riotous, noisy lesson that interrupted adjacent classes. Yet the comments passed about the noise in the staffroom at lunchtime showed that no one doubted the competence of Mr Wright. Because it was *his* lesson, the many comments were either genuine inquiries about 'what *was* going on' or light-hearted banter about the effects of the disturbance. The noise and disturbance were treated as an acceptable aberration of the norm for the school purely on the basis of Mr Wright's personal reputation.

The strategy of 'keeping 'em quiet'

In contrast to Mr Wright at Cedars, at Ashton a chemistry teacher was the butt of a standing joke in the staffroom which went:

Teacher:	What are you doing, Nigel?
Nigel:	I'm — beating-up Eric
	I'm — cheating
	I'm — making explosives
	I'm — going to sleep
Teacher:	Well quietly, quietly, boy. Do it *quietly*.

The point of the joke will not be lost on practising teachers. It puts in comic relief the pressures and priorities they endure when operating at the chalk-face. From the teacher's point of view it is the noisiness of pupil behaviour which comes to serve as a guide to the severity of its disruptiveness and the urgency with which it needs to be remedied. As they recognize this, however, teachers are put under considerable pressure to keep pupils quiet – a pressure which stems not from their belief in the pedagogic advantages of quietness during lessons but from the expectations which colleagues hold about appropriate classroom conduct. In fact, in their efforts to keep noise levels to a minimum, teachers are frequently responding to peer-group pressure rather than exercising professional judgement on the necessary conditions for learning in class and thus end up relegating pedagogic considerations in favour of practical criteria for survival and acceptability amongst other teachers. Keeping 'em quiet becomes something of a strategy for survival – in this case survival in the community of teachers, not the pupils. *Keeping 'em quiet, as a strategy, protects the teacher against suggestions that their work might not be up to standard by eliminating the factor that colleagues might take to be symptomatic of a lack of control in the class, that is pupil-initiated noise.* It gives the outsider less opportunity to cast doubt on the (hidden) performance of the teacher in question and, if anything, only prompts the outsider to assume that the class is under control.

Awareness of the need to 'keep 'em quiet' is essential right from the start. As Leacock found from her research, 'a new teacher soon learns that it is her success in maintaining quiet and order, in the narrow sense, which is first noted and which is apt to be the school administrator's first measure of her performance' (Leacock, 1969, p. 87). Also McPherson (1972) gives a graphic description of how that early learning can occur. In her account of life at 'Adams' elementary school in the United States, she recalls how the 'Old Guard' of well-established teachers at the school socialized newcomers into their way of thinking:

> In the effort to let others observe that which was ordinarily hidden, the Adams teachers developed an 'open door' policy, a non-verbal series of cues that were never discussed but were tacitly understood by all. A teacher kept her classroom door open during the teaching day to show her control over her class. A good disciplinarian's door stood open; a poor one's door was frequently shut. Unless a teacher ... was going to have art (an allowably noisy subject) or do dramatics ... her closed door meant that her class was too noisy and she was afraid of being overheard.
>
> (McPherson, 1972, p. 32)

The strategic importance for teachers of 'keeping 'em quiet' is not lost on pupils. Teachers' efforts to control noise and thus protect the impression that there is control in the classroom opens up for pupils a whole array of *counter-strategies* which they can use to challenge the control of the teacher and assert their will on the progress of the lesson. Pupils, for their part, can use noise as part of a repertoire of strategies of resistance to teacher control of the situation. By generating noises which the teacher cannot locate or which the teacher cannot treat as intentionally contravening agreed conventions, pupils can signify resistance to a teacher-imposed requirement for quietness in the classroom and generally 'play up' the teacher. The twang of rulers that ghosts around the room, the exaggerated cough whose contagious powers seem powerful and immediate, the shuffling of feet and a host of other noises can be used to annoy teachers not only by challenging the teacher's command over the pupils but also by hitting at the very heart of what is used to *signify* control. In the struggle to limit or oppose the control exercised by the teacher, the poignancy of noise has been evident to generation upon generation of pupils whose teachers have sought to impose silence in class.

Against this background it is hardly surprising that teachers are very sensitive about the amount of pupil talk and pupil noise they allow during lessons, and they tend to regard pupil-initiated noise as an immediate signal for some sort of remedial action (Kounin, 1970). But we should remember that pupil-initiated noise is nothing more than a *socially constructed indicator* of control, and that, as such, it is both culturally specific and context specific. Its culturally specific nature is well illustrated by the research of Dumont and Wax (1969) at a Cherokee reservation school in north-eastern Oklahoma. Being rather 'culture bound' the teachers had come to assume that hostility and resistance to teacher authority would be manifest in terms of the pupils' open defiance, noisiness and general taunting of the teacher. What they failed to see was that, because Cherokee culture shuns overt conflict, the pupils' resistance to the non-Cherokee teachers was subtle and evident only to the other pupils. Because it did not threaten the quiet orderliness of the classroom, the teachers did not recognize the behaviour as a resistance to their control and were thus baffled by the absence of progress made by the pupils. For their part, though, the pupils' resistance was subtle enough to fool the teachers and complete enough to allow them to side-step the teaching they did not regard as legitimate.

Such findings are all too easily dismissed as anthropologically cute and their implications for the British classroom ignored. What it means in the British context, however, is that teachers might be deluded in this context too into thinking that those forms of pupil behaviour which are not noisy or overtly disruptive are 'under control' while, in fact, *quiet resistance* can go unnoticed and unattended to. Pupils who quietly daydream, who

quietly gaze out of the window, who quietly devote disproportionate
amounts of time to intricate drawings – any of those whose behaviour
poses no immediate problems for the teacher – can be actually resisting
control in a way that escapes the 'disorderly behaviour set' of teachers (cf.
Stebbins, 1970). It simply is not what teachers would ordinarily recognize
as disruptive behaviour. As Stebbins discovered from his observations in
classrooms, 'not paying attention' or 'being away' are the kinds of pupil
behaviour which do not normally trouble the teacher. Such quiet
behaviour 'although subverting his teaching aims, is a more palatable form
of disorderly behaviour for the teacher than almost any other' (Stebbins,
1970, p.229). A similar point emerges from the work of D. H. Hargreaves
et al. who quote from the notes of one of their field-workers:

> It seems obvious that anything the pupils do that does not make a noise
> is acceptable.
> Three or four pupils are obviously not paying attention to the reading
> but because they are quiet, their conduct is acceptable.
> (D. H. Hargreaves et al., 1975, p. 37)

As Spender (1982) amongst others has argued, the fact that quiet non-
learners do not cause the same sense of urgency as noisy ones means that
boys are usually more 'trouble' than girls. Because girls are expected to be
dependent and docile,

> their failure to co-operate can lead to withdrawal; to either 'getting on
> with the work' and not expecting it to be meaningful or interesting, or
> to quietly opting out in the corner. Either way, such behaviour of the
> girls is not likely to be seen as evidence that teachers cannot control
> their classes, for in most classrooms it is the noise level which is used as
> the criterion for teacher efficiency, and inside and outside education it is
> the male who makes more noise.
> (Spender, 1982, p. 59)

At Beechgrove this point was illustrated in a fourth-year social studies
group where the teacher's attention was constantly focused on four boys
who were 'cheeky', walked around the room, called to each other in loud
voices and exhibited a penchant for slamming desk lids. Three girls who
sat at the back of the class reading magazines or quietly talking to each
other about their social lives received far less attention and were cajoled to
get on with their work only on occasions when the four boys were settled.
Although the behaviour of neither group was conducive to a (curriculum)
learning situation, it was invariably the boys who were attended

to first. It was, it seemed, the noisiness of their non-learning behaviour which gave it overriding importance for the classroom teacher and which allowed the behaviour of the girls to be relegated in significance so far as control was concerned.

When interviewed, the teacher concerned openly acknowledged the extra attention she gave to the boys. She saw it as a fact of life that the noisiest pupils got the most time and attention and that these tended to be the boys. As she explained

> With this non-examination group it's hard enough to spark some enthusiasm, so at least the kids who are not creating havoc are some sort of blessing – and they tend to be the girls. The girls at this age just get all sulky and very conscious of not acting 'silly'. The trouble is that if you, as a teacher, really share out your time equally ... evenly, then the boys will run riot and people think you're a lousy teacher. The system kind of forces you to be sexist.

Reference to 'the system' in this teacher's account of her approach to the job was implicitly a reference to the closed classroom circumstances in which she operated and the way this forced her to focus on fragments of information like noise that transcended the insularity of the setting. The 'system' at Cedars, of course, offered an interesting contrast. In the humanities lessons at Cedars, the significance of any extra noise for the competence of staff was countered by the observability which accompanied team teaching in open-plan classrooms. Because teachers worked alongside each other, frequently entering and leaving areas used by colleagues, they had less need to worry about whether the amount of noise might be interpreted by 'outsiders' as indicative of a lack of control. People could see what was going on and did not need to resort to informed guesswork. The general level of noise in the open-plan units was higher than elsewhere and there was much better tolerance of noise. Radios were occasionally switched on during lessons and, though pupils were usually asked to switch them off, it brought no immediate caustic response from the staff. Though staff sometimes called for 'more work and less chat', pupils were not generally prohibited from talking to one another during the course of a lesson. The tolerance in itself, of course, can be attributed to three factors: the open classroom ethos accepted by the staff, the situation of team teaching in open-plan classrooms which largely negated the subtle implications of noise for teacher control, and the amount of inter-pupil contact and pupil movement around the room regarded as acceptable and/or necessary.

The results of this tolerance none the less proved to be quite interesting.

Effectively, the tolerance negated pupil counter-strategies based on noise. We have seen how strategies which teachers adopt in their attempts to control noise and thus protect the impression that there is control in the classroom have some special significance for pupils because they open up for pupils a whole array of counter-strategies which can be used to challenge the control of the teacher and assert pupil influence on the progress of the lesson. If, on the other hand, teachers like those in humanities showed less concern to prevent noise, the strategy could become irrelevant because it would not provide a challenge to anything relating to classroom control. No longer would whispered conversations be a source of annoyance to teachers. No longer could pupils hope to challenge the progress of the lesson by interrupting with coughs and sneezes of exaggerated proportion, or any other form of sudden or surreptitious noise. In fact in the case of humanities lessons, the relatively high tolerance of noise effectively cancelled out and rendered redundant pupil strategies for control which utilized forms of noise. Notably absent from the lessons were the tried and tested genre of pupil strategy based on creation of noise.

Conclusion

We have seen how teachers exhibit a marked sensitivity to noise in classrooms and how this sensitivity is not simply because noise interferes with good instruction. Teachers worry that noisy classrooms might be interpreted by colleagues (and pupils come to that) as a sign of poor classroom control and as the outcome of inadequate standards of teaching. Not surprisingly, therefore, efforts to minimize the levels of noise permeate the routine work of teachers. These efforts constitute something of a strategy on the part of teachers, a strategy which provides protection against the implications of teacher incompetence that are likely to accompany noise emanating from the room. It serves as a means of protection for the teacher – one which obviates any slur on their abilities or hints that they are not doing their job properly. Strategies, however, foster counter-strategies and pupils generally recognize that they can use noisy behaviour in class as a potent challenge to control by the teacher. When pupils are noisy, they threaten the basis of teacher competence by suggesting that the teacher cannot establish control over the class: they undermine the *image* of a controlled class.

The teacher strategy of 'keeping 'em quiet' and its pupil counterpart, as we have stressed throughout, though being normal features of the classroom, are not absolute laws or universal features of the classroom because they reflect the specific arrangements associated with the closed classroom. It is specifically under these circumstances that noise provides a valued channel of communication between classrooms that are otherwise physically and socially insular. It is specifically under these circumstances that noise provides a source of publicly available information about events behind the closed doors and acts as an evidential strategy for inferring classroom control. Other circumstances give rise to different problems and different pressures and this is why the open-plan classrooms of humanities lessons at Cedars offered a useful contrast. Here, while the absence of walls heightened the problem of interruptions caused by noise in adjacent units, the openness significantly reduced the role of noise as an arbiter of classroom control. Teachers could directly observe colleagues in action and therefore did not need to rely on the evidential strategy of noise, and the greater tolerance of noise in these lessons reduced the potency of pupil counter-strategies based on noise.

The example of teaching at Cedars reminds us of the inherent context-specificity of classroom strategies for control and, perhaps, has additional value in suggesting what alternative kinds of classrooms might offer in the way of solutions to the pressures and problems faced by those in the conventional classroom. But it cannot detract from the fact that the large majority of teachers and pupils, especially in secondary schools, continue to work in closed classrooms. For them, noise remains crucial in their quest for control. To say that noise is crucial, however, is not to say that it is the only factor taken into consideration and, in fact, research at Ashton and Beechgrove revealed one other vital concern in the quest for control. It became evident when studying the house systems at these two schools that teachers were expected by colleagues and pupils alike to fend for themselves on matters of classroom control and not to rely on outside help. It is to this second facet of control that we can now turn our attention.

6
Pastoral Guidance

At first glance, responsibility for pastoral care of pupils would seem quite separate from that part of a teacher's work concerned with discipline and classroom control. Pastoral care, after all, deals with the general welfare of the pupils and their integration into the school and the wider community. It deals with 'personal' problems which arise from the social background of the pupil or emotional difficulties experienced by the pupil at school. In practice, however, pastoral care almost inevitably includes some specific involvement with discipline and control problems as well. One reason for this is the fact that the kind of behaviour which is symptomatic of a personal or emotional problem is also the kind of behaviour that the classroom teacher tends to regard as a discipline problem. As Docking (1980) points out, pupils who seem unable to cope with 'stressful situations' and those who find it difficult to 'develop meaningful relationships with school staff' are not only a problem in terms of their own welfare and development but also likely to pose a problem in terms of orderly classroom behaviour and teacher control of the situation. Another reason, and one explored more fully in this chapter, is that the system of pastoral care officially established in a school can find its aims being adapted, it not perverted, to meet the demands created by staff who choose to use the pastoral system quite deliberately to deal with control problems. Because teachers evidently face a number of practical problems in their efforts to implement the pastoral care system in connection with long-term emotional problems and because the system can be used effectively to cope with difficult pupils, teachers can be encouraged to incorporate the pastoral care system in their efforts to maintain classroom control. Used in a particular way, in fact, the system would seem admirably suited to helping teachers' efforts to get a smooth, orderly classroom life and to their not unreasonable wish to minimize the fatigue, the time, the frustration and the risks of getting through a normal day's work.

Initially, therefore, we might be led to expect a fairly uninhibited use of the pastoral care system to back up classroom control. But one other factor needs to be taken into consideration in order to understand the relationship between efforts to maintain classrom control and the school's pastoral care system. Use of the pastoral care system to back up classroom control carries with it certain implicit dangers and subtle connotations that make it a hazardous exercise. In practice, the realization of this limits any wholesale dependence by teachers on the pastoral care system to deal with problems of classroom control and what distinguishes the 'experienced' teachers' use of the pastoral care system from allegedly excessive and inappropriate use of it by the 'inexperienced' teachers to back up control is the awareness of these hidden dangers. Indeed, on the basis of findings at Ashton and Beechgrove, it appeared to be this *understanding of the implications* , as much as any ability to achieve a state of classroom control *per se*, that was crucial to a teacher's reputation as being 'good at keeping control' or being 'poor at keeping control'.

The formal organization of pastoral care and guidance

Like most organizations, schools tend to adopt a more formalized structure as their size increases. Greater reliance is placed upon explicit and documented statements about the specialization of roles, the hierarchy of authority, the rules and regulations governing the conduct of members in their work, and the channels of communication through which information and directives are to be transmitted.

In the case of schools like Ashton and Beechgrove, each with over 1,200 pupils and 80 or more teachers, it was not surprising, therefore, to find that something like the pastoral care of the pupils had become the subject of formally designated responsibilities and procedures. A significant degree of specialization was evident in the fact that both Ashton and Beechgrove located responsibility for pastoral care within their house systems, and within these house systems it was clear that most of the power and the bulk of the duties rested on the shoulders of those teachers who were 'heads of house'. In fact, both in terms of their position in the *hierarchy of authority* and in terms of their *specialist duties*, the heads of house assumed a crucial role and were linchpins in the organization of pastoral care.

At Ashton, each building had a house representative – with heads of house being primarily responsible for dealing with extreme cases of disruptive behaviour, official records in connection with court cases, probation, and special attention to cases of emotional disturbance. However, some of the five 'senior teachers' also took an active interest in pupil welfare. The deputy head in charge of the two lower schools was officially responsible for co-ordinating house activities and the heads of building at the two respective lower sites also helped out with counselling and the administration of pupil welfare. The heads of house were none the less the most senior posts with *specialist* responsibility for pastoral matters and it was they, rather than the heads of building, who were actually in charge of the pastoral work. The heads of building took a supporting role and were called upon basically because the split-site lower school left each building with only two heads of house who, for practical reasons, sometimes needed another senior person to help them deal with 'crises' and other tasks demanding the immediate attention of house staff. At the upper site, of course, the four heads of house worked in the same building so there was no need for this supplementary role and, consequently, none of the senior teachers based on that site had any remit to be concerned with pastoral care (see Figure 6.1.). All teachers were allocated to a house, and school assemblies brought together pupils and teachers of the same house for religious instruction and the dissemination of general information. The house system was not, however, coupled to the administrative system in any direct way. Year-based form groups were used for registration and administration and these did not discriminate between pupils from different houses.

Pastoral care and guidance at Beechgrove combined a house system with tutor groups. Beechgrove, having all buildings on one site, did not face the problem of having heads of house widely dispersed and, like the upper site at Ashton, had no need to supplement numbers by incorporating senior teachers into house duties. It was left to eight heads of house, two for each of the four houses, to co-ordinate the pastoral care and guidance offered to the pupils in the house. The first year, however, was organized on a somewhat separate basis from the rest of the school and being under the overall auspices of a head of first year. This organization existed only for the first year and reflected an attempt to integrate the pupils gradually from relatively small primary schools into the large secondary school but it had the effect of reducing the first year pupils' involvement in house activities to that of sporting activities, charitable collections and so on rather than the tutor-group situation which started in the second year. In the second year, and subsequently until leaving school, pupils were put in house 'tutor groups', vertically arranged and each with about twenty-five pupils (see Figure 6.2).

Tutor groups at Beechgrove were an integral part of the house system and were a facet of the organization of pastoral care that contrasted with that of Ashton where the house staff operated through the medium of conventional form groups based on years. In terms of function, however, the form groups at Ashton were not far removed from the tutor groups.

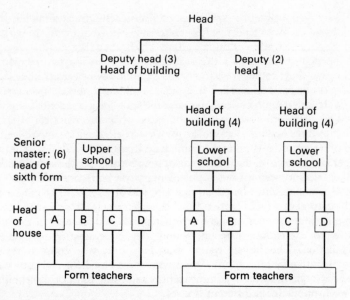

Note: The deputy head in charge of the lower site was second in command of the overall school. The other deputy head was third in the chain of command and was in charge of the upper site. His responsibilities were primarily for staff and school discipline. The three other senior teachers comprised a fourth level of command, two being in charge of respective buildings at the lower end of the site and the other being the senior master in charge of the sixth form building at the upper site.

Figure 6.1   *Organization of Pastoral Care at Ashton*

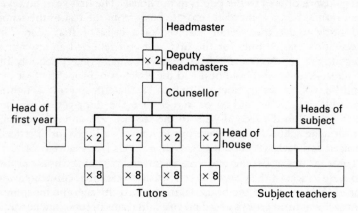

Figure 6.2 *Organization of Pastoral Care at Beechgrove.*

The official guidelines at Ashton made explicit reference to the duty of form teachers to liaise with heads of house and co-ordinate activities for the pastoral care of pupils and, essentially, the difference was only that Ashton's form teachers administered groups from the same year but belonging to different houses, while tutors at Beechgrove administered pupils from all years but belonging to the same house. So, *in both schools the heads of house stood in a similar strategic position for collecting information and taking action related to pastoral care.* In fact, even the presence of a 'school counsellor' at Beechgrove did little to detract from the crucial executive and administrative role of the heads of house. Technically the school counsellor had seniority over the heads of house and his official task was to take over those problems which were either too time consuming or too serious for the sole attention of the house staff. However, his role in the school, in practice, was specifically concerned with the longer-term problems which normally involved outside agencies. Those issues which were internal to the school were normally left to the heads of house.

The key position of the heads of house was not entirely the result of this formal responsibility. It was the nature of *communications* and the official *regulations* about pastoral matters which ensured and consolidated their pre-eminence in such matters. At both Ashton and Beechgrove they were put in a central position as far as the dissemination of information on pastoral matters was concerned – a point made quite explicit in the official guidelines at Ashton when it was stated that:

Any pupil who is persistently difficult or inadequate should be discussed with the Head of House so that the House if fully informed of the problem. Form teachers should acquaint House staff with any new information, cases of truancy, fresh incidents or change of attitude of any pupil in their form. Heads of House will have the records and other information about their pupils and will be able both to give advice and take suitable action. It is the responsibility of Heads of House to keep the teacher-in-charge of the building and Form teachers adequately informed of any pupils who require special attention and to discuss any cases they think necessary with the Headmaster or Deputy Heads.

The kind of communication envisaged in this extract was what can be termed the 'personal' mode of referral. Teachers might merely inform the head of house of events for future reference (which in connection with other contemporary and pertinent data could give rise for concern and subsequent action) or possibly request the head of house to take action.

Conversely the head of house might seek out teachers to inform them of action being taken at house level. In either case, the information was normally *verbal* and the communication *personal*. It was this personal mode of referral which was regarded officially as fundamental to the successful operation of pastoral care and, at both schools, it was promoted by the official guidelines as the most suitable basis for the system of pastoral care. It was not, however, the only officially approved way in which information could be passed on. At Ashton, for example, there was a 'demerit' system which provided, in effect, a way of referring pupils to the house system without any face to face contact between the referring teacher and the head of house. The 'demerit' system, as the official guidelines explained, acted as a formal notification to heads of house of a pupil's poor conduct.

> Teachers will make out demerit forms in cases where it is thought the behaviour is serious enough to be permanently recorded. Such demerit forms will be handed in by the teacher to the Heads of House rooms. Heads of House will keep a record of demerits received, and will take appropriate action to discuss cases at House assemblies, with form teachers or with the individual pupil and teacher concerned.

Using the 'demerit' system, there was no absolute necessity for personal contact because the information could be left on a desk or put in the internal mail and the heads of house could consequently have pupils brought to their attention through a process relying entirely on documents rather than word of mouth. In this sense the 'demerit' system constituted a 'documentary' mode of referral. The content of such documents, of course, was strictly 'for the record' – unlike the personal referrals which frequently involved informal bits of information just to keep people in the picture about events and developments concerning particular pupils. In this case, as a result of information received from a tutor or subject, a pupil might be put 'on report' by the head of house. This process required the offending pupil to get the teacher of each lesson to sign a report confirming the pupil's satisfactory conduct during that lesson. In effect it acted as a punishment for the pupil and a control mechanism deterring further bad behaviour but, from an organizational point of view, it had another interesting function. Although the process was a response to a personal referral by a tutor or subject teacher, it also involved an element of documentary communication between heads of house and subject teachers about the pupil. Subject teachers were inevitably made aware of the pupil's previous misdemeanours by the request to sign the report – and such reports consequently added another dimension to channels of communication about pastoral matters.

The absence of personal contact between subject teachers and heads of house was not, in practice, confined to the documentary mode of referral. It was a particular characteristic of a third mode of referral evident in the official guidelines and prominent in use in the schools – what can be termed the *'direct' mode of referral*. Where a pupil was sent directly from the classroom during the course of a lesson to see the head of house, or where a head of house was requested to come to the classroom to deal with a pupil, the contact between the pupil and the head of house was direct, without the mediation of reports, demerits or detailed personal consultation between the teachers.

It was recognized in the official guidelines that under certain circumstances the extremity of the disruptive behaviour might warrant the expulsion of a pupil in the classroom. It was in this instance that the direct mode of referral was officially approved because, as the official guidelines of the schools indicted, it was not sufficient merely to remove the offending pupil from the classroom since he/she might persist in being disruptive in the corridor. Rather, under these conditions, the pupil was to be referred direct to a relevant member of staff:

> Isolated cases of anti-social behaviour may occasionally blow up in the classroom and threaten to disrupt a lesson. If an emotional outburst seems imminent, it may be advisable to remove the pupil from the classroom.

This mode of referral, however, though it was recognized as occasionally necessary, was generally discouraged. The official guidelines at both schools charged individual teachers with responsibility for control during their own lessons and discouraged direct referrals as a method of coping with uncooperative pupils because referrals of this kind could undermine the teacher's authority. As the point was made at Beechgrove:

> Discipline within the classroom is the responsibility of the individual teacher but Heads of Department and Heads of Houses are always ready and willing to support members of staff. However, it should be realised that in the end no useful and lasting purpose is served if too many problems arising within the classroom are referred to higher authority. This practice only serves to weaken the authority of the individual teacher in the eyes of the children.
>
> (Official guidelines: Beechgrove)

So, though the personal, documentary and direct modes of referral were each acknowledged by the official guidelines, it was clear that the personal, and to some lesser extent the documentary, modes of referral were seen as the proper methods of getting information to and from the heads of house, while the direct model of referral was officially viewed with some anxiety. The official stance was clear: the direct mode of referral was to be used rarely and in extreme circumstances, and never as a substitute for classroom control. Classroom control was the province of the teacher in the classroom, not the house system, and teachers were clearly reminded in the official guidelines of both schools that control was not to be abdicated by relying on direct referrals to the heads of house.

Practical problems of referral: communications and effectiveness

Such unequivocal statements should have left the teachers in little doubt about the formal distinction between the pastoral responsibilities of house staff and their own role as managers of the classroom. Yet in practice the house systems had become heavily involved in problems of classroom control. Although proscribed by the official guidelines and deplored by the heads of house, it was acknowledged by house staff and classroom teachers alike that the heads of house were developing a 'discipline specialist' function.

The heads of house for their part argued that they were being obliged to adopt this function as a result of the nature of referrals. They maintained that pupils brought to their attention were all too often the wrong kind and reflected short-term problems of discipline and classroom control rather than the longer-term emotional problems. In terms of the school organization, of course, this implied that the channels of communication were not providing the heads of house with the appropriate and necessary information and that the pressure to adopt the discipline specialist role arose as a consequence of the informal organization of communications. It meant that, for whatever reason, teachers were deviating from the proscribed procedure and using the system in a way never intended by the official guidelines.

Any difference between the official procedures and the actual use of the house system, however, could not be explained simply in terms of ignorance about preferred procedures. Because files containing an outline of the formal structure of the school and the preferred modes of procedure were given to members of the permanent staff when they joined the school, only the recent arrivals and temporary staff such as supply teachers were left without some clear statement about the formal organization of pastoral care in the schools. For the rest, though, 'proper' use of the house system was unlikely to be hindered by ignorance of formal procedures as such. Much more important for them were the practical problems they faced when trying to implement procedures.

At Ashton and Beechgrove one obvious problem facing the teachers was that of *'naming the pupil'*. Before any action could be taken teachers had to know the name of the pupil but, because they did not necessarily know all the pupils in the school by name, this meant that it was difficult to instigate 'personal' or 'documentary' referrals to the house system. One category of teachers faced particular problems of this nature. New teachers – probationers, supply teachers and teachers recently arrived at the school – faced special practical difficulties in their attempts to invoke the system because they were less likely than others to be familiar with the names of pupils.

Knowledge of pupils' names, although it posed problems for these teachers to an extent greater than for others, could also affect established teachers in schools – particularly where there were 1,200 or more pupils such as Ashton and Beechgrove. In large schools, even the established staff might not know the names of the pupils with whom they had no direct teaching contact. In the corridor or playground, incidents which a teacher might otherwise have referred to the house staff could get ignored because the teacher was unable to identify the pupil. Or again when called upon to cover a lesson for an absent colleague, the established teacher could face the same problem. During fieldwork at a staffroom at Beechgrove a situation occurred which encapsulated the significance for the teacher of 'naming the pupil'. In the third period of the morning the door of the staffroom was flung open and a boy momentarily stood in the doorway, shouted some abuse, and ran off down the stairs. The two teachers in the staffroom did not give chase nor did they seem particularly anxious to apprehend the offender. One of them explained that since he did not know the pupil's name it was a fruitless and frustrating exercise to attempt to find the pupil, let alone gain a confession of guilt or take any further action. It was clear that the teachers' lack of effort in apprehending the perpetrators of 'bad' behaviour did not stem from a condonement of the act but was a result of their inability to 'name the pupil' and hence to secure any kind of official follow-up. In such situations they had to rely on the immediate apprehension of the culprit and on the qualities of teacher personality and pupil deference to teacher authority in order to secure any type of remedial action.

The influence of practical factors on the teachers' use of the house system was also evident in the 'problems of time' experienced by classroom teachers. Teachers argued that there was insufficient time in which to implement the proper procedures and that invoking the system required the use of non-classroom time – time such as morning and afternoon break, lunchtime and after school. The personal mode of referral was the most time consuming for the teacher in this sense because, in order to communicate the relevant information to the appropriate head of house, the teacher needed to search out the house staff perhaps during breaks or at the end of the day. Particularly in such large schools with separate buildings, the communication of relevant facts could require a prohibitively large amount of time – if not in the actual transmission of the facts in the location of the person to whom the information should be transmitted. The situation at Beechgrove, with three staffrooms in different buildings, meant that in order to contact a specific member of staff it might be necessary to conduct a lengthy tour of the buildings and, although house rooms existed at both Ashton and Beechgrove, a teacher had no guarantee that the head of house would be in the room at the time he or she went to the room because house staff themselves needed to contact people at times such as breaks, just when other staff might be looking for them. In effect this meant that communication took place on a rather *ad hoc* basis and that the information received by the heads of house was selective. The information did not necessarily reflect the actual state of affairs in the classroom because the classroom teachers did not have the time to communicate with the house staff on every occasion and in connection with each incident, with the result that the picture of events built up by the house staff was partial and incomplete.

In practice, then, the amount of time involved in the personal mode of referral acted as an effective deterrent to the use of such referrals as envisaged in the official guidelines. The documentary mode of referral, on the other hand, had the advantage that it did not require a great deal of the teacher's time to implement. Inspection of the school records could be arranged to suit the particular teacher and was neither a lengthy nor involved process. Similarly, neither the processes of putting a pupil 'on report' nor giving him/her a 'demerit' entailed the amount of time-consuming activity which was associated with the personal mode of referral. Because it was literally documented, the necessity for searching out a particular member of staff was alleviated, along with the practical problems it entailed.

The direct mode of referral had similar advantages over the personal mode. It was even less time consuming for the classroom teacher, requiring little more than the instantaneous command to see the appropriate head of house (whether immediately or at a later date), and was normally executed during classroom time (and in relation to a classroom event) thus not encroaching upon other times in the teacher's day.

For their part, the heads of house faced difficulties as well in feeding back information to the relevant members of staff. It was clear to the heads of house that, unless they were to let the referring teachers know of the action which had been taken, the referring teachers might tend to assume that no action had been taken and thus feel that referring pupils was a fruitless process. This was a particular problem, elaborated upon by one of the heads of house at Beechgrove, where the action they took was not of a kind that was immediately recognizable to the teacher in the classroom situation:

We write to parents, we keep them fully informed. We ask parents to come up to school a lot and we have ... um ... pretty good contact with them in certain circumstances. We see social workers and all the other outside agencies. We refer kids to ... um ... you know, for help of one sort and another ... and so-on-and-so-forth. So one of the dangers is that people say there's nothing being done. But in the old days if you had a kid and you gave him a walloping well it was, you know, the kid said, 'I had the stick' or 'I got walloped for it' and something seemed to be done. But now ... um ... it's not so obvious, you know, when you do anything to a kid.

We had a situation not so long ago, when people got very uptight about a fifth-year boy in my House who had been doing a lot of leaping about in the building over there and generally being obnoxious. He's a very big, hefty lad, taller than almost anybody in the school, staff included. I don't know why ... he's got a very loud mouth and he's very silly and although he's got a body of a man he's got a mind of, you know, a 12 year old. And he lumbers about and he bashed on doors and swears at people. He makes everybody's life a misery. I have been to see his parents, his father had been to see the Head and he had been excluded from school for a couple of weeks but, you know, it's not possible to inform every member of the staff what's happening about every kid, unless of course somebody comes and say, 'Look, I'm a bit bothered about this kid, he's giving me hell', and I will say, 'Well, I'm doing this, that and the other with him, and you know, it would perhaps help if you could do this and let me know if he doesn't do any work', and, you know, we will work closely together. And I think for the kid ... for his own sake more than anyone else, one doesn't publicise ... um ... things generally about him. One would only repeat to people who would need to know it, and in that situation you get people feeling that ... um ... you know, things aren't being done, where in fact they are being done behind the scenes.

For the heads of house, then, communication of their responses to referrals was considered essential in avoiding the impression that no action had been taken but in doing this, they confronted practical difficulties of contacting the relevant staff and of keeping enough people informed without 'broadcasting' the problems and treatment of particular pupils. Such communication and the associated problems arose, though, only because the nature of that action was not immediately apparent to the referring teacher: it occurred behind the scenes and was not self-evident in the classroom situation.

Intertwined with the whole problem of communication, and evident to some extent in the anxiety expressed by heads of house about the feed-back of information to subject teachers, was another practical problem experienced in connection with the operation of the house systems – the *problem of the effectiveness of referrals*. Teachers who referred pupils to the house system often felt that there was little positive action taken as a result of their referral and that referrals were unlikely to have any immediate effect on the classroom situation. As a French teacher as Beechgrove expressed her misgivings about the system:

> I don't know whether it is because it's a large school but if you do not try and get a head of house to do something about somebody in your house, you wait months and months and there is somebody who's disrupting the whole class who doesn't do the work and this has been going on for a time. Well, there's one boy in particular, about 3 months you know, and every time I see the, you know, the particular staff member involved, he's going to do something, he's going to set up a course of action; we have got a letter dated months ago you know and this boy is still exactly the same.

The problem, it seemed, was that the house system could do little to help the teacher because the time lapse between noting an event, it being referred, and effective action being taken by the house staff meant that referrals were of little consequence for the immediate classroom situation. In expressing such reservations, however, it was apparent, first, that the teachers' notion of 'effective' action referred primarily to the 'disruption' of pupils rather than any 'emotional' problem *pe se* and that the problem of time delay arose in the context of attempts to secure remedial action on 'disruptive' pupils rather than a clear-cut concern for the pastoral care of the pupils. Second, it was the personal mode of referral which fared worst in this respect because its reliance on personal contact precluded any immediacy of effect in the classroom situation (although, of course, according to the official guidelines it was not the function of the house system to deal with classroom 'problems', these being the responsibility of the subject teacher).

Teachers regarded the effective feed-back from documentary modes of referral, on the other hand, with a bit more optimism, particularly the demerit and report systems. These documentary modes of referral were acknowledged as being a deterrent to bad behaviour and had the advantage over the personal mode of referral that their effect was of immediate help in the control of the classroom. Staff were not in agreement as to whether the demerits and reports *should* be used in this fashion but they generally acknowledged the reality that they were used in this manner by some members of staff. Interestingly the members of staff who tended to use demerits and reports were often cited as being the young or the inexperienced teachers for whom they provided a back-up for discipline in the absence of any more material deterrent to bad behaviour,

You will find that the more experienced teacher very seldom gives a demerit because they don't need to, but the younger ones have got no other weapon really ... I mean they aren't allowed to smack. Some children run riot, so they get a demerit.

(Deputy head of maths: Ashton)

So, to this extent, the documentary mode of referral was bound up with matters of classroom control and its particular benefit for the classroom teacher stemmed from the fact that documentary referrals were more immediately and observably effective on matters of classroom control than the personal mode of referral.

In its immediacy and observability the *direct mode of referral* was even more effective. Direct referrals had an instantaneous and self-evident effect on the classroom situation by alleviating the source of the problem. More than with documentary referrals, and particularly more than with personal referrals, the product of direct referral to the house system was immediately apparent to the referring teacher in terms of classroom control and did not depend on protracted communication and negotiation with heads of house. For the teachers, this posed something of a dilemma. The direct mode of referral, it should be remembered, was officially discouraged at both Ashton and Beechgrove. Teachers were regarded as responsible for the establishment of discipline and control in their own classroom and the house system was intended to offer pastoral care for those pupils with emotional problems. It was acknowledged by the official guidelines and house staff alike that, on occasion, a situation might arise in which it was appropriate to call upon the assistance of the house staff through the direct mode of referral but such situations were limited to *emotional* problems which might flare up in the classroom situation and perhaps to those occasions where the teacher would otherwise lose his/her temper with the pupil in question. As a head of house at Beechgrove put the point:

> We don't encourage staff to send kids out of the classroom unless they really feel they can't cope. They're advised *not* to send kids out. Obviously, if the kid is just so impossible that they just can't cope, then they do.

The same applied at Ashton where, in the words of a head of house,

> If someone gets to the stage where they send a child out, it's really for an immediate relief of the situation in the classroom, isn't it?

Direct referral provided an immediate tension release mechanism, then, which was regarded officially as a last resort to be employed rarely and with reluctance by the classroom teacher. But from the stance of the classroom teacher, it was less time consuming and was more immediate and recognizable in its influence on the classroom situation than documentary or personal referrals. And this was the quandary facing classroom teachers in their use of the house system. The officially favoured procedure, the personal mode of referral, was not regarded as very practicable because, even when the teachers could identify the pupil by name, they still had to contend with the time consumed by putting the system into operation, the time delay in action that was taken by the house staff after the event or the first referral and the (perceived) lack of effective action by house staff in relation to the classroom situation. The documentary and particularly the direct modes of referral, on the other hand, were considered by the classroom teachers to be more efficient in terms of time and more effective in terms of immediate control problems in the classroom yet, in the case of the direct referrals, were officially frowned upon.

The role of heads of house as 'discipline specialists'

As a result of the type of referral they receive, the heads of house argued that their role was less involved with the pastoral care and guidance of (all) the pupils in their house, or even those with particular emotional problems and was, instead, being pushed towards a 'discipline specialist' or 'trouble-shooter' role – precisely the kind of back-up to control problems deplored in the official guidelines.

Too much of my time and too much of the house staff's time I think is taken up with the ... um ... day-to-day ritual type school problems of an institutional nature, rather than long term emotional ones. I certainly spend far too much time on that type of problem as opposed to the serious ones.

(head of house: W: Ashton)

One reason for this was that they had to rely on information which resulted from informally organized channels of communication. In practice this had the effect, noted with some dissatisfaction by all the house staff, that the pupils with whom they had contact (in pastoral terms) were but a small minority of the pupils in the school. There existed no positive organizational provision for the heads of house to come into contact with *all* the pupils in their house:

There is no formal ... um ... procedure ... as there is no definite time when every pupil in a house sees the house teacher. Um ... some pupils will get *very* well known by the house teacher because they have a particular problem while they are at school or because they are in a number of discipline problems and get referred to the house teacher. Other pupils may get to know the house teacher for quite the opposite reason, because they're a very good participant in sporting activities or house activities of some kind, or very good academically and get gossiped about in the staffroom for this reason. And house teachers get to know them that way. And, in between, there are a vast number of pupils who are neither very bad nor are they very good in any way you like to specify – and hardly get known at all. In fact, it's certainly true that ... er ... in the house which I run, there must be a large number of pupils which I hardly know. In fact, I'd have to look them up in the records to find out if they're in my house or not.

(head of house: H: Ashton)

In the absence of any formal contact with all the pupils in their house, then, the small minority of pupils who were brought to their attention for 'pastoral treatment' were those identified primarily through particularly poor behaviour and, though the heads of house did not regard discipline as their proper concern, they acknowledged that a state of affairs existed in their school which obliged them to deal with such matters to an increasing degree (cf. Guthrie, 1979). Indeed, the pressure of work stemming from the discipline side prompted one of them to comment:

I suppose I'll go for weeks and it will only be discipline problems really because, in my opinion, [the house] room is being used wrongly – as a discipline room.

(head of house: D: Ashton)

So much had this become a feature of the head of house role that the ability of teachers in matters of discipline was seen to affect their prospects of selection to pastoral posts in the schools. Heads of house were not teachers who had problems of control in the classroom and as one of them indicated:

Usually, House teachers appear to be appointed on a discipline bases. If they can keep good discipline, then they'll become a house teacher.

Discipline duties, none the less, posed some special problems for the house staff. It puts them in something of a dilemma in terms of their relationships with pupils because they were called on to adopt a 'Jekyll and Hyde'personality where, in one instance, they could be required to 'discipline' a pupil and thus invoke an authoritarian distinction between the position of 'teacher' and 'pupil', while in the next they might need to break down such barriers in order to provide an effective counselling service:

We have all applied for these jobs as house teachers and the house teacher's job originally was to be a counsellor, plus discipline. Which means one has to have a Jekyll and Hyde personality really, 'cos ... um ... at one moment you are trying to discipline pupils ... er ... actually for other people, not always for yourself ... very rarely for yourself because you have usually got quite a good relationship with your own house. And one of the great problems is, you get sent people to the house room with behaviour problems within the classroom.

You have to deal with those behaviour problems and then say a week after, they may be coming to you, or ought to come to you, for some advice – they might have got themselves into some sort of trouble outside and you have this strange ... er ... thing where you have got some ... one moment you're sort of telling them off and trying to put ... er ... trying to sort of put them on the straight and narrow and the next moment you are trying to get their confidence because they might be depressed over something.

(head of house: D: Ashton)

The house staff at both schools were in general agreement that their pastoral role called for a degree of sympathy and understanding with the pupils and that this required an attempt to break through any authoritarian relationship which might characterize a normal teacher/ pupil relationship but that where the house staff were called upon regularly to deal with discipline problems it became progressively more difficult to establish the necessary rapport. The strain between the two aspects of the house teachers' everyday duties existed in any case because they ordinarily had to conduct classroom lessons and thus maintain their own control of the classroom as well as provide pastoral care and guidance for pupils who might happen by coincidence to be members of their class. As a head of house explained:

> When you are in the classroom you expect the kind of relationship where you are trying to help someone to solve a problem. Um ... it's difficult I think because it's two different roles – two different images – and ... er ... I find it difficult and I think the children find it difficult as well. Where do you stop being an authoritarian and where do you start being someone who can offer help?
>
> (head of house: W : Ashton)

The house staff recognized this and accepted it as part of the job but what they objected to was the additional strain imposed through having to deal with direct referrals which they considered as dealing with 'other people's' problems and constituting an inappropriate use of the house system. The abundance of 'inappropriate' referrals with which they had to deal put under more pressure their already ambivalent relationship with the pupils.

Direct referrals also posed problems for house staff in terms of their availability to deal with the instant demands of such referrals and the sometimes conflicting requirements of pastoral and classroom duties. House staff at both schools saw limitations being imposed by the fact that they received only 5 – 6 extra 'free' periods, over and above the normal allocation, in which to execute their duties as heads of house. As a head of house at Ashton put it:

> The house teacher has a certain amount of free periods a week, ... er ... normally about 5 or 6 extra – which doesn't seem enough – um ... during which he's supposed to get to know the pupils in his house well enough to write a report at the end of the course – at the end of each year – on the pupil, which is quite a difficult thing to do in fact with 200 pupils.
>
> (head of house: H : Ashton)

The insufficient amount of extra 'free' periods available meant that the house staff operated under very considerable pressures of time. This lack of time specifically allocated to house duties led one of the house teachers at Beechgrove to suggest that the house duties were more or less performed on top of teaching duties:

> We only have ten periods considered to be for house work. So we're almost, you know, teachers ... full time teachers anyway.
>
> (head of house: M : Beechgrove)

There was a further diminution of this time through the fact that much of it was specifically put aside for meetings. At Beechgrove a head of house indicated that, of the periods allocated for house duties, at least five every week were taken up with prearranged meetings concerned with careers guidance, welfare agencies and the headmaster. It was, then, perhaps a misnomer to call these periods 'free' since many of them were taken up with predictable meetings which prevented the house teachers from being available at these times to deal with day-to-day problems. Patently these free periods did not provide sufficient time to cover the extra duties and the heads of house argued that the only way in which they could cope was to draw on other times in the day – lunchtime, morning and afternoon break, and even the time officially allocated for academic work.

> Sometimes lessons have to go by the board. Um ... a parent arrives and says,'I want to see Mr W., such-and-such's happened', you know. Mr W is actually teaching, then someone has to come and sit in the lesson while I come and interview the parent, and see what all the problem's about.
>
> (head of house: W : Ashton)

The problems of time allocation faced by the house teachers were exacerbated where the nature of the calls on their time were immediate and unpredictable. It was not the long-term counselling of pupils (which could be arranged for specific times) that posed problems for the house teachers so much as those duties which arose without forewarning and without prior notice. House staff were regularly called upon to deal with what they called 'crisis' events – such as dealing with a truculent pupil who had been sent from the classroom or having to go to a classroom to sort out problems arising in that setting. In such cases it could not automatically be assumed that the (relevant) members of the house staff were not themselves committed to classroom teaching. In the event of a 'crisis' house staff might have to leave their own classroom in order to deal with a problem arising elsewhere. The practical problems facing a house teacher in such a situation were identified by a head of house at Beechgrove who said that:

> You have to choose your priority at that moment. Very often the classroom teaching goes because there's an irate parent or a distressed child or whatever. And you have to, at that time, make your priority. It's a choice the whole time. I'm lucky in that one of the subjects I teach is typing which is very easy to leave for a little while because when the kids are doing something they can get on with it. The other subject I teach, which is community services, I rarely leave unless it really is an absolute 'crisis', because the class needs teaching the whole time and I'm actually involved every minute in the lesson with all of the kids in the class.
>
> (head of house: M: Beechgrove)

Because a house teacher was also a subject teacher, the operation of house duties had to take into account the practical problems which arose from the house teacher's classroom commitment as well as the straightforward commitment to duties as head of house, so when 'crises' occurred they could be put in a position of weighing one against the other in deciding upon the course of action to be taken. As a result, these heads of house felt that they were often put in the undesirable position of having to make a choice between their commitment to house duties and their commitment to class teaching – a kind of strain that could be reduced only where there was less use of the direct mode of referral.

> I have been trying to cut down on the amount of time on this, I feel quite strongly that it ought to be a ... um... prior arrangement whereby the teacher will say to me, 'I've got such-and-such a class, so-and-so'causing a problem, can I send him to you?', and I might say, 'Well, hang on ... um ... he'll come to the lesson – if you are having problems, send for me.' I would prefer to do it that way rather than him say, 'Mr W's in Room 8, he'll come at a moment's notice.'
>
> (head of house: W : Ashton)

The practical problem with 'coming at a moment's notice' was that it involved leaving a classroom unattended if the house teacher happened to be teaching and this put the house teacher in something of a dilemma.

> There are some groups I'd be very reluctant to leave to be ... um ... to be honest about it. I'd hate to have to leave them alone and it's not only

the remedials but there are some groups you can't afford to leave on their own. You know, you might have to say to the secretary, 'Would you ask so-and-so to wait for 10 minutes and I'll be down as soon as I can', and ... um ... there's that problem, you know. Just because you are house staff or you're in charge of this building shall we say, it doesn't mean to say that your pupils are just going to sort of obey your authority – I don't think that works at all.

(head of house: W : Ashton)

In an attempt to offset these strains on their commitment, the house staff at both schools had adopted an informal arrangement in which one of the heads of house would be in the house at most times to deal with the direct referrals.

It's interesting that at Ashton there's now a system by which a house teacher is on duty continuously every lesson of the day ... and always in the house room. So that a teacher during any time of the day, can send a pupil to the house room where a house teacher will be found. It could be any house teacher, not necessarily the house teacher of the pupil concerned. In fact the house teachers operate very much on a group basis and it doesn't really matter whether the pupil who arrives is in your house or not, unless it's a particular problem which is undoubtedly going to involve a great deal of counselling. When it comes to ... um ... disciplining of a ... a particular problem within a class, who's really talking or throwing things around, or ... or fighting or something of this kind, where it appears a quick solution may be found – the house teacher in charge will just deal with it, and that'll be it.

(head of house: H : Ashton)

This was not an officially recognized arrangement but one that the house staff had developed to cope specifically with the conflict of commitments which might arise through direct referrals or when they were asked to deal with an immediate 'crisis' event. By informally arranging that at least one of them should be in the house room at most times of the school day there were the practical advantages of providing classroom teachers with a place and person upon which they could call for aid at any time, and of allowing house teachers to continue their lessons with less chance of interruption or conflicting claims on their time. This system did not operate to perfection because of timetabling limitations, staff absenteeism, and so on. Further the lower schools at Ashton had the difficulty that there were only two heads of house in each building. They did, however, draw on support of the head of the building in this respect. The increasing discipline specialism of the house staff was, none the less, enhanced by this informal organization. Though the longer-term emotional disturbance problems were still dealt with in terms of house membership, the heads of house acted in a positional capacity qua 'head of house' rather than head of any particular house when called upon to deal with immediate 'crisis' problems.

> If it's ... er ... a crisis thing and the kid's having hysterics or the teacher's having hysterics, then any of the house staff will deal with it, anybody that's here. Or if ... or, what happens quite often ... a message comes down and says could somebody come up and help with so-and-so, whoever's in there – regardless of who the kid is – will go up and deal with it temporarily, but won't make any long-term arrangements. You ... you'll deal with it at the moment and then pass it on to the appropriate head of house.
>
> (head of house: M : Beechgrove)

The head of house on duty in the house room, then, could be called upon to deal with problems which did not arise from pupils in their house and they acknowledged an obligation to deal with all situations of a particularly disruptive nature irrespective of the house of the offending pupil. But by accepting the arrangement of having one member of the house staff available at most times to deal with immediate problems, the house staff involved themselves with the task of control (in addition to the counselling which they regarded as their proper task) and further, did so at a generalized level. The way in which they were involved in control situations did not reflect any expertise which resulted from a significant knowledge of the personal problems of the pupil because in many instances they were called to cope with situations where their particular knowledge of the pupil was no greater than that of other teachers.

The implications of 'direct referrals' for teacher competence.

Their 'discipline specialism' as the heads of house saw it, was the outcome of an 'excessive and inappropriate' use of direct referrals to the system which they associated not with classroom teachers in general but with a particular kind of teacher:

> As far as discipline is concerned ... um ... usually the house teacher's function is to help the discipline of new members of staff who are ... who have problems with discipline, for one reason or another, and who will send pupils to a house teacher if they have problems with them.
>
> (head of house: H : Ashton)

It was specifically the new teachers, the young, probationary, inex-perienced and new arrivals who were considered to be the ones who would use the system in this 'inappropriate' manner. One explanation for this, frequently proffered by experienced members of staff, was that new teachers sometimes failed to realize that the most important aspect of being a successful teacher was to establish control of the class *before* any attempt at teaching could really be made. The colleges of education were regarded as not equipping teachers with the kinds of expectations which were relevant to real teaching situations and generally underplaying the practical necessities of establishing control in the classroom. The colleges of education were accused of providing the schools with teachers who were not willing enough to impose their authority and control on the classroom situation and who were, in consequence, all too willing to fall back on to the services of the house staff to back up their control of the classroom instead of coping with the problems themselves.

> Now, it may not be a criticism of teachers – it might be a criticism of the system that trains them – but many teachers coming into the schools now, I feel, aren't willing to fight hard enough to get control. [The house system] is providing a feather bedding for people who aren't willing to try to win within the classroom situation. So, I get kids sent down here for various ... for very small things.
> There are people in this school who will, at the slightest little thing, send a kid down here. Now you see I'm not marvellous, I have my discipline problems that I have to cope with in all the ways that I know, but sometimes people send a kid down here for chewing or not doing his work or things like that. Now I maintain that if that happens in your class, you ought to be able to solve these problems.
>
> (head of house: D : Ashton)

Such understanding of 'excessive and inappropriate' direct referrals coloured the way in which the house staff dealt with the referrals. The house staff, in practice, regarded many of the referrals as problems of teacher control rather than problems of the particular pupil and there was no automatic assumption that pupils who were referred required some counselling in order to find the cause of their disruptive behaviour because the cause of that behaviour was often attributed to the classroom control of the teacher. As a house teacher at Ashton put it:

> It's my experience that house teachers spend a lot of their time dealing with high-spiritedness which the ... er ... the particular class teacher had been unable to cope with and for which there's no real need for

counselling. And … um … it's due to a *lack of experience* on the side of the particular class teacher in charge.

(head of house : H : Ashton)

The problem in other words, was seen as the teacher not the pupil. As a head of house at Beechgrove pointed out, 'They'll often come into teacher "A" or teacher "B" [heads of house] very often *with problems created by colleagues and not of their own making.*

Numerous instances were observed in the house room where direct referrals were greeted with a casual and light-hearted air which was ostensibly inappropriate. The heads of house appeared little concerned to conduct counselling or dispense punishment. An example, characteristic of such occasions, was afforded at Ashton when a 'regular' referral arrived at the room. Head of house (H), laughing, asked 'And what have we been doing today?' The boy shrugged his shoulders and another member of the house staff (D) in the room joined in the laughter. No detailed account of his referral was sought and the boy was told to sit and read for the rest of the period. The reaction was explained by the head of house:

> "He's a regular. He's O.K., … just a bit cranky. But some of the staff can't cope with him and he plays them up and gets sent down here. It's not his fault."

The response of the teacher appeared to stem from the view that the disruption exhibited in the classroom by the pupil need not be purely the product of the pupil. The 'problem' associated with a referral was sometimes interpreted as a result of the interaction of the teacher with the pupil and not necessarily a result of a problem with either the pupil or the teacher.

> I get on well with John and when I teach John in the class everything's fine. But someone else, for a reason which might be John's fault or it might be the teacher's fault, doesn't get on well with John. And therefore if John is causing trouble with another teacher and is sent to me I therefore, try to get John to fit into that situation and if necessary to get the teacher to fit into the situation.

(head of house: I : Ashton)

When teaching a direct referral, then, the heads of house bore in mind the fact that the disruptive behaviour which gave rise to the referral might not necessarily reflect a problem of the pupil but might be an indication of a particular teacher's inability to control the classroom generally or a problem of control which arose between the teacher and the pupil as a personal factor. In other words they recognized that the referral could result from personal rather than personality factors, from situational rather than emotional problems. And where they considered that this was the case the house teacher role could not be directed purely at the pupil but had to take account of the teacher as well. Under such circumstances they suggested that their role was rather one of 'mediating' between the protagonists in a situation.

> Well, very often we are mediators in an offence. It sounds very grand but that is clearly what we are doing. And quite often we talk to children and we talk to staff, and then we will ask the staff if they would like to talk to the child again, and sometimes this works very well.
>
> (head of house: U : Ashton)

The discretion with which house teachers acted not only reflected their understanding of the causes of the problem but also provided a possible source of conflict between the referring teacher and the house teacher. Referring teachers sometimes felt that the pupil being referred should receive some form of punishment from the house staff while, on the basis of their experience and pastoral expertise, the house staff considered that to punish the child would be inappropriate. The house teachers felt that, once it had been referred to them, the problem would be dealt with by them and in the manner which they saw fit. In other words they reserved the right to treat referrals according to their own interpretation of the problem.

> You see we don't have the cane now ... but I know the situations when we did, where somebody would come in and say, 'Would you please cane this child because they've done that', and I think that is ludicrous. If they're passing over the problem for you to deal with then they've got to expect that you'll deal with it in your own way. As long as you deal with it, I mean, I always tell staff what I've done, but what I do is my decision. If they're asking me to do it, I'm not necessarily going to do the heavy-handed bit – or maybe I am because maybe that colleague thought it was a very light thing – but I know that that kid has been terrible all week and this is just the last straw as far as I'm concerned.
>
> (head of house: M : Beechgrove)

For their part, the classroom teachers were not always enthusiastic about this discretion. Their dissatisfaction was particularly noticeable in relation to referrals for disruptive behaviour where they tended to express the opinion that the house staff were too lenient with the pupils and were not willing enough to punish them.

> Look, for instance, a child gets a demerit for being cheeky or something, all right, gets a demerit and then goes to the house teacher. The house teacher calls the child and gives him or her a talking-to, but more whether they have done it in school and why they have done it, what their home background is, and they try to solve it psychologically. And then perhaps after a week or so they call them back again, 'Have you been now a bit better?', but it doesn't really sink in that it's a really dreadful thing.
>
> (Maths teacher: Ashton)

Certainly subject teachers were conscious that the treatment of referrals was dependent more on the disposition of the house teacher than on their perception of the nature of the classroom event provoking the referral. Above all else, however, when making direct referrals classroom teachers had to consider that the action which followed the referral was out of their hands.

Autonomy, experience and 'direct' referrals

Given the discretion open to the heads of house in the way they dealt with the pupils referred to them, direct referrals had but one positive and self-evident effect on the pupil's behaviour in the classroom – to eliminate it from the classroom setting. In the terms of classroom control this had particular advantages in the immediacy of its impact on disruptive behaviour. Teachers did not have to wait for a chance to pass on messages about a problem pupil and continue to suffer while counselling work by the heads of house filtered down into improved classroom behaviour. They could expect instantaneous beneficial results. At first glance, therefore, direct referral to the house system would seem to be an enticing strategy for classroom control and it would seem reasonable to expect to see it as part of the standard repertoire of methods used by teachers for this vital part of their work. But, in practice, it was evident that the established teachers showed a marked disinclination to send troublesome pupils to the house room and, as the heads of house said with a certain unanimity, it was the young and inexperienced staff who were the major users of referrals.

This reticence of the experienced teachers, it seemed, owed much to their unwillingness to hand over *their* problems to someone else. They were very cautious about sending pupils down to the house room or calling a member of the house staff to deal with a pupil in their classroom because to do so might imply that they could not cope with the problem alone – and this was a dangerous implication. Calling on someone else to help in the routine control of a class suggested, to colleagues and pupils alike, that the teacher was unable to deal with matters 'autonomously' and was thus failing in a vital aspect of the job.

The heads of house themselves were quite sensitive to this point. Because they, like the other 'experienced' teachers, felt that subject teachers should normally be able to control their own classes, they tended to regard regular calls for assistance through direct referrals as an indictment on the competence of the referring teacher. Because of this, any intervention by the heads of house by their own admission needed very delicate handling. As a head of house at Ashton put the point:

> Teachers generally would feel ... I myself as a teacher would feel ... um ... rather than as a house teacher ... that it is important that a class teacher is able to keep control of his own class, because no matter how carefully a house teacher puts himself in a position of walking into someone else's class or being sent someone else's problem, ... um ... however carefully he may attempt to approach the subject of why the particular teacher had to send the pupil to the house teacher, he needs to avoid the impression of ... of failure by the class teacher to discipline the child himself.
>
> It's very difficult to escape from the fact that this is rather the impression the pupils get. They're certainly aware that some teachers send pupils to house teachers and others do not. For example, they are themselves taught by people who are house teachers, and they are aware that house teachers don't send pupils to other house teachers. They are also aware that ... er ... many of the senior members of staff would not operate discipline in this way.
>
> I think the pupils are aware that it's um ... that um ... that teachers send them to house teachers because they themselves can't cope. It's often been the case that pupils have in fact refused to leave the room, and the teacher's had to send for a house teacher to come and take them out. There's never any trouble. As soon as house teacher arrives the pupil's perfectly willing to go .. in my experience. I think that the pupils feel that it's a shortcoming of the teacher in charge.
>
> (head of house: H : Ashton)

On this kind of occasion the relationship between the house teacher and the classroom teacher became very delicate. Whether or not the house teachers felt they were impugning the authority of the classroom teacher, they were at pains to give the impression that this was not in fact the case. The house staff felt that in these situations it was important not to exacerbate the impression which pupils may already have been fostering that the teacher had been unable to cope and had therefore to call for assistance from the head of house and, as part of professional etiquette, the heads of house attempted to disguise the purpose and implications of their presence in order to prevent the possibility of the teacher's 'losing face' in front of the pupils.

> I think teachers appreciate from time to time if you *do* go into a classroom where there is noise, and the younger member of staff's definitely having difficulties ... um ... go in for any particular reason and fetch a book or something or ask for a chalk. Um ... the class, you know, being particularly difficult ... um ... it does have some effect on the way they behave.
> Interviewer: You use this sort of tactic then, go in under a pretence?
> W: Yes, I prefer that rather than ... um ... I think there is a professional thing here, although some people say they don't mind, and obviously in this little box system, where you close the door the teacher is in the room and ... um ... I would argue in control of that particular group for a particular period of time. Um ... and really if a teacher's, for instance, having difficulty, sends for me and the pupils then immediately come under control, they more-or-less say to the teacher, 'Well, we'll behave for him but we won't behave for you!' You know ... um ... I don't think this a good tactic and it's ... um ... or if I went into the lesson and took over, it would place that teacher in a very difficult position ... because the pupils are there obviously and can see what's happening.
> (head of house: W : Ashton)

The risk of 'losing face' was heightened, of course, where the house teacher was less than delicate in his/her treatment of the problem. An episode at Ashton served to illustrate the point. I had been observing a supply teacher at one of the lower school sites and conducted an interview with her. The methods of teaching she adopted were in her own words 'authoritarian', because as a supply teacher she felt this to be the best method of gaining immediate impact and control in new situations. As a rule she would not attempt to use the house system because of practical difficulties like those we have already noted. Not long after the interview she rushed into the staffroom, in the middle of the teaching period, bursting into tears and exclaiming, 'I've never been so humiliated in all my life!', a phrase she repeated time and again in the course of accounting for what had happened. The source of this humiliation and embarrassment was explained thus: that a particular class (acknowledged by her colleagues to be 'difficult') had been noisy and inattentive and responded to none of her pleas for order or threats of detention. In desperation, and against her normal practice, she had sought the aid of a head of house. The head of building, who was deputizing for a head of house at the time, had been unable to come immediately and the teacher had returned to the classroom. She imposed a detention and managed to start the lesson. To her satisfaction, that is, she had gained control of the class and no longer needed the support she had sought. Five minutes later the head of building was alleged to have stormed into the classroom and taken a seat with the pupils. In doing so, she was effectively undermining the authority and status of the teacher by implying, in front of the pupils, that the fault lay with the teacher, not with the pupils. In the dumbfoundment that followed, the supply teacher hesitated and faltered, in response to which the head of building grabbed the lesson notes and chalk and literally proceeded to take over the lesson. Not only was it the supply teacher who was embarrassed. She emphasized later in accounting for what happened that the pupils too were very embarrassed. Pupils were so acutely conscious of the situation that those nearby apparently whispered things to the effect, 'I wouldn't stand for it, Miss. I'd walk out if I was you.' She did in fact leave the room, retaining the anguish of such utter humiliation until reaching the sanctuary of the staffroom where she burst into tears.

This event illustrated the possibility, which could not have escaped the notice of the other members of staff, that to call upon another teacher for help was to run the risk of publicly 'losing face'. Despite this, though, the insensitive action of the head of building in this case was seen to be wholly unacceptable and petitions to that effect were immediately set in motion. It was an example (and in its extremity rare example) of the risks involved for staff when seeking aid for situations in 'their' classrooms from other members of staff. The head of building in this instance had caused humiliation for the classroom teacher, a near outrage from other members of staff who became aware of the event, by showing disregard for two sensitive areas of teaching. She had covertly challenged the competence of the teacher and she had violated the privacy of the teaching context. But the important point to note is that both aspects were opened for violation only because of the initial request for help in controlling a class.

Summary and conclusion

At both Ashton and Beechgrove, as we have seen, the house system was used not just in connection with the long-term pastoral welfare of the pupils but also as an aid to control in the classroom. Despite the reluctance of the heads of house, the house systems had become bound up with the routine maintenance of control and had developed informal arrangements to cope with the practical difficulties posed by this unofficial function. A rota system had been adopted so that a head of house would be on duty in the house room to receive, or attend to, any direct referrals that arose during lesson times.

This pressure to deal with direct referrals stemmed from two main sources. First, there were the *organizational factors of time and communications* which heightened the prospects of referrals being instigated to backup control rather than to inform the heads of house about emerging emotional or welfare problems experienced by a pupil. Classroom teachers and tutors suffered constraints of time which militated against the use of the personal mode of referral and the heads of house likewise suffered a lack of time to investigate and discover appropriate problems for themselves. These practical constraints of time had a bearing on communications with the result that heads of house were made aware of only a small minority of pupils in their houses warranting remedial attention and these were predominantly the pupils exhibiting disruptive behaviour in class.

The second source of pressure to deal with direct referrals came from the *'new'* or *'inexperienced' members of staff* who allegedly used direct referrals in an excessive and inappropriate manner. They were seen as the main users of the house system as a means for bolstering classroom control because, for reasons of choice or necessity, they were prepared to involve colleagues in 'their own' control problems. Use of direct referrals to aid classroom control, though, was a precarious practice and its advantages needed to be weighed against its potential drawbacks. It was, after all, a practice frowned upon by the heads of house and explicitly discouraged by the official guidelines because it inevitably posed a threat to the residual position of authority vested in the classroom teacher. A direct referral either involved 'passing the buck' by sending a troublesome pupil out of the classroom or, if it meant the house teacher coming to the classroom to deal with a pupil, it became all the more problematic because it involved trespass on the privacy of the classroom with its additional implications for residual control of the teacher, and took place in front of the pupils who were far from unaware of the connotations of the presence of the head of house. In either case, use of the direct referral ran the risk of giving the impression to colleagues and pupils alike that the referring teacher was unable or unwilling *to maintain control without outside help*. It could imply, in other words, a dual failing in the teacher: to control the class and to operate autonomously.

Teachers generally value autonomy (Grace, 1972; Jackson, 1968; McPherson, 1972) but direct referrals potentially threaten this autonomy. Direct referrals not only threatened the *isolation* of the closed classroom by providing a publicly available indicator of classroom control but also threatened the *autonomy* of the teacher by possibly constituting an invitation to another teacher to enter the classroom and engage in the running of that classroom. When a house teacher was called to a classroom to deal with a truculent pupil there were implications of failure – failure of the classroom teacher to achieve the necessary control *on his/her own* – and this was likely to entail a loss of face and embarrassment for the teacher which was evident to both colleagues and pupils.

This would explain the reluctance of experienced staff to draw on the services of the house system. Experienced teachers were wary of using the house system because their 'experience' allowed them to recognize the implicit failure entailed. They appreciated that it could be seen as indicative of the teacher's inability to control the classroom – a 'publicly available' indicator of (lack of) classroom control. Direct referrals, in effect, provided a gauge of the situation which existed behind the closed doors of the classroom; an alternative to noise for assessing the extent of control in the closed classroom. And experienced teachers, cognisant of this implication, were reluctant to engage in such referrals.

7
Conclusion

The sociological perspective on classroom control adopted in this book has been based on the sociology of work and organizations and, as we noted in the Introduction, this perspective has an inherent tendency to focus on classroom control as a feature of the teacher's world of work in terms of teacher's perceptions of their job. The result of this is that, while pupils' attitudes and behaviour have been examined as a crucial part of the phenomenon – inexorably bound up with teachers' efforts to get control – the conclusions tend to dwell on the implications of the findings for teachers more than pupils. This emphasis on teachers is justifiable to the extent that teachers are the instigators and proponents of classroom control. As we saw in Chapter 1, the evidence leaves little doubt that responsibility for classroom control is a basic feature of the work of the schoolteacher. It is embedded in society's delegation of rights and duties to the teacher, the school organization's allocation of responsibilities and the expectations held by both teachers and pupils about the competent teacher. But pupils can never be eliminated from the scene because it is only through interaction with pupils that it is sensible to think of successful or unsuccessful attempts to establish control. Classroom control without the class is nonsense.

This element of interaction is apparent when we consider the qualities of the 'good' teacher. In view of the importance attached to control as part of the work of the teacher it would be easy to assume that being good at control is enough to qualify a teacher as 'good'. However, not only does the 'good' teacher have to have some other attributes and skills relating to the learning element of the job, but also proficiency at teaching requires the ability to achieve good personal relationships with the pupils, a point indicated recently by both Docking (1980) and Saunders (1979) in their separate reviews of research findings concerned with the characteristics of 'good' teaching. Empathy and respect for the pupils, along with predictability, compassion, firmness, a sense of humour, impartiality and, of course, an ability to put over the subject, all seem vital to this broader concept of the 'good' teacher. Having made this point, it is also true that there are many situations where these other attributes will be held in relatively low esteem. In schools with a 'low achievement orientation', as we saw in Chapters 2 – 4, the control element of the job can take on mammoth proportions and can dictate the major requirements for success as a teacher. Obviously, under extremely adverse conditions a teacher who is good at control but no good at the other skills associated with teaching, might, in fact, survive quite well and be regarded as competent on the basis of the control factor alone. Fewer demands would be placed on the teacher in terms of proficiency at a specialist subject or developing pastoral relationships with the pupils. But this will depend on the extent to which the particular school or the particular class exhibits a low achievement orientation, and it needs to be recognized that in most cases competent teaching requires more than just the ability to control a class. It requires a teacher to be able to gain control *and* in addition to develop the academic and pastoral sides of the work.

It would be wrong, though, to believe that classroom control is simply one amongst many of the skills needed for competent teaching. According to the teachers, especially at Ashton and Beechgrove, the ability to get control is a fundamental prerequisite for competent teaching and one that cannot be compensated for by particular strengths in other areas. So far as they were concerned, no matter how skilled a teacher might be in a specialist subject area, there could be little, if any, chance of being regarded as competent if the teacher failed in terms of classroom control. This leads us to the conclusion that from the teachers' point of view *classroom control is a necessary though not sufficient condition for teacher competence* – an absolutely fundamental part of teaching which, even if it does not ensure competence, certainly precludes competence if it is not there.

But what constitutes classroom control? This, as we have stressed, depends on the social circumstances surrounding the classroom. The nature of classroom control is context specific and the whole question of what control is, how it is recognized, how it is achieved and how it is challenged cannot be divorced from an examination of the social context of the classroom.

The closed classroom tends to be prevalent particularly in secondary schooling and, though it is not the only contemporary context, it can be regarded as the conventional classroom situation. The closed classroom carries with it a characteristic set of social and physical arrangements that have considerable bearing on what passes for classroom control. The social and physical arrangements foster and re-inforce the idea of classrooms as insular units and the idea of the teacher's job as primarily to keep them that way (that is, an ethos of privacy). This means that despite the importance given to classroom control, teachers are in a rather bad position to assess the competence of their colleagues in this respect. There are, it is true, a number of ways in which information about other aspects of the classroom performance of a teacher can be gathered. *Examination passes*, for instance, allow colleagues to make some pretty well-founded judgements about how good a teacher has been at putting over the specialist subject, particularly in the light of any knowledge they have about the ability and motivation of the group of pupils involved. Or lower down the school, at the start of a new school year when teachers take over a new class, the *work of the previous teacher* will become apparent in terms of what material the pupils have covered and how well they have covered it. But as it was argued in Chapter 3, the nature of teachers' work and the organizational set-up in which it occurs do not lend themselves to strict accountability and, though teachers might be held to account in a rather loose way on the academic part of their work, there is, at least officially, no counterpart upon which the control side of teachers' work can be judged. Teachers are consequently faced with a dearth of formal information about this side of the job.

There are, by contrast, *in*formal ways and means of assessing how well a teacher is coping in terms of control. Watching how a teacher deals with events outside the classroom is one such means. Over a period of time teachers will have witnessed others coping with difficult pupils in the more public areas of the school – the corridors, playground, outside the staffroom – and will be able to draw certain conclusions from these observations about the teacher's ability to control pupils. Alternatively *gossip* provides a major source of information about how good teachers are and it acts as an important form of informal communication in schools. Pupils pass on observations in class about other teachers, anecdotes get told in the staffroom, and reputations get established all as part of normal school life. Such gossip, naturally enough, covers classroom control as well as a teacher's strengths or weaknesses at putting over their subject or being a likeable person. But when it comes to *first-hand* knowledge about other teachers' abilities to establish control during lessons there is an acute shortage of information. In fact, under typical teaching conditions, when it comes to first-hand information about how good a teacher is at getting classroom control pupils would seem to be in a better position than teachers because, during the course of a normal week, they see a variety of teachers in operation and have a chance to compare the performances. Teachers do not normally have this opportunity. To assess whether or not a particular teacher has got control of the class they cannot directly observe events because the lessons tend to be hidden from view by the four walls and closed door that isolates the separate classes so, instead, they have to interpret any hints about the situation which manage to transcend the isolation of the classroom. The staff almost inevitably rely on what we can call 'publicly available indicators' of control since they are not in the position to see for themselves what is going on. As we noted in Chapters 5 and 6, there are two such sources of information which provide vital clues about a teacher's ability to control the class:

1   noise emanating from classrooms,
2   excessive use of outside help to get classroom control.

The point about these two sources of publicly available information is that, by transcending the isolation of the classroom, they provide information that is in one sense more direct than gossip or inferences made on the basis of a teacher's efforts in the corridor, playground, and so on. Because they provide clues about a teacher's performance that have not been filtered through gossip and because they are a direct product of the teacher's classroom performance, they offer some firm evidence about classroom control.

The significance of these channels of publicly available information is not simply that noise and outside help might indicate control problems. As well as this they go against the idea of privacy and, from what was established in Chapters 5 and 6, privacy would seem to be a vital part of successful teaching in conventional circumstances. It is part and parcel of the radical individualism that permeates teaching and which fosters teachers' claims to both autonomy over classroom decisions and claims to professional status (see Chapter 3). Practices which jeopardize this privacy by providing publicly available information about what is happening behind the closed doors of the classroom, therefore, cut deep at the heart of teaching. It is this fact, as well as the more immediate implications for the appearance of control in the classroom, which explains the dire consequences of ignoring the informal code of conduct amongst staff in respect of noise levels and the use of outside help to help establish control. The implications need to be seen, in other words, not simply in terms of any particular individual's ability to get classroom control but in terms of a set of wider beliefs about the work of teachers captured in *the culture of privacy*.

The aims of control *strategies* are, logically to protect the privacy of the classroom by protecting the impression of control to outsiders. The absence of noise and requests for help tend to lead to the conclusion that all must be well in terms of classroom control. But the strategies, themselves, need to conform to the culture of privacy. Methods for achieving control under these circumstances tend to be:

(1) *individualized*, in the sense that responsibility rests with the individual classroom teacher rather than discipline specialists or dependence on help from other classroom teachers and

(2) *Personalized*, in the sense that classroom teachers cannot depend on either official authority or technical aids in their efforts to establish control. The circumstances dictate that teachers rely on charisma, or a repertoire of control strategies that effectively routinize the charisma, and that control is negotiated between the pupils and teacher at a personal rather than official or technical level.

It is new and inexperienced teachers who tend to be accused of lacking classroom control. From what we have argued, any failing in this vital sphere of teaching might be because they are less likely than experienced teachers to appreciate the significance that can be attached to factors which transcend the isolation of the classroom but, perhaps, more likely, it may be because they have yet to master the strategies for dealing with the threats and thus managing to actually protect the desired privacy. In Chapter 2 we noted that most newcomers were clued in to the fundamental requirements of the work as a result of their experiences as pupils in class, so it is likely that for most newcomers the problem of classroom control is not one of recognizing that 'noise' or 'outside help' pose problems, it is getting to grips with the strategies that eliminate or at least satisfactorily cope with the amount of noise and the need to call on colleagues for help in the first place. They are, as it was explained in Chapter 2, usually familiar with the Hidden Pedagogy and what they lack, if anything, is expertise at the strategies to implement it.

Teacher perceptions of classroom control

The consequence of all this is that teachers' understanding of classroom control generally involves an amalgam of five related ideas:

(1) Classroom control exists when a teacher can, to his/her satisfaction, direct events during a lesson without calling on colleagues for help. Preferably this involves the teacher, working as an individual, managing to obviate any challenges to his/her right to direct events; realistically it means coping with,

containing and quashing efforts by pupils to move from the path set by the teacher. This applies to progressive approaches which try to minimize the teacher's directoral role as well as to more traditional approaches.

(2)   Classroom control depends not so much on an absolute state of affairs in class so much as the absence or presence of certain *indicators* of control. Pupil-initiated noise is crucial in this context. Such noise is generally regarded as antithetical to a learning context and, on the assumption that a teacher's job is to create a learning context, it is taken to be indicative of a failing on the part of the teacher to direct events appropriately. Pupil-initiated noise, therefore, comes to imply poor classroom control.

(3)   In terms of classroom control, it is not the 'cause' of pupil behaviour which troubles the teacher, but its effect on the appearance of control in class. 'Disruptive behaviour', then, gets gauged according to its actual or potential impact on indicators of classroom control – which explains why noisy behaviour, or behaviour which requires the class teacher to call on other teachers for assistance, pose major problems for the teacher. Such behaviour is likely to produce what colleagues might take to be evidence of poor control in the class and suggests to all involved that the teacher is failing on this vital aspect of the job.

(4)   Threats to control cut deep at the heart of the teacher's classroom credibility. There are situations in the work of teaching where teachers feel they can hope to do little more than exercise control over their pupils. In these circumstances, the task of teaching is likely to involve little more than an effort to 'keep 'em quiet' for the duration of the lesson, and to do so without calling for assistance from colleagues. This is a minimum survival situation that calls for nothing more than a holding operation on the part of the teacher. In most cases, however, such an effort to obtain quiet orderliness is seen as a means to an end rather than an end in itself. It is seen as an essential prerequisite without which teaching proper cannot proceed – a foundation upon which the teacher can build a method for teaching the subject of the lesson. For this reason, a challenge to control is a challenge to the fundamental part of a teacher's skill and a competence at the job.

(5)   Control relies on a constant negotiation between teacher and pupils about the extent of conformity, involvement and effort pupils are to give. Teachers are in the stronger bargaining position but, none the less, they see classroom control as

something that needs to be nurtured and reinforced as a frequent and routine part of the job.

This reprise of points raised in earlier chapters serves two purposes. First, it shows clear links between the analysis of *teacher training* (with the notion of the Hidden Pedagogy), *school organization* (with its emphasis on the closed classroom and individual responsibility for control) and *classroom strategies* (which, among other things, go some way to protecting the privacy of the teaching situation). It demonstrates the pervasive nature of classroom control for the work of teachers and emphasizes the convention that control is accomplished alone. It also raises some further points about classroom control, more or less implicit in the preceding analysis which deserve consideration as a conclusion to the sociological perspective adopted on classroom control.

Classroom control is a socially constructed phenomenon

From what we have seen about teachers' understanding of classroom control it is obviously unacceptable to treat classroom control simply as a state of affairs in a classroom. What is actually happening in class is certainly relevant but, whether control is deemed to exist in a particular class is dependent not just on an absolute state of affairs in class but also on the extent to which outsiders are to infer that control, or lack of control, exists in the class. This in turn depends on the extent to which those outside the classroom are made aware of events behind the closed door and the extent to which activities in class come to threaten the privacy of the setting (by generating noise or, perhaps, inviting the need for outside help to quell behaviour). This is not to suggest that *only* those behaviours which jeopardize classroom privacy will be deemed control problems, but it does suggest that these will receive priority treatment by teachers in recognition of the rather nasty repercussions they can have on the teacher's reputation outside the particular lesson. As we saw in Chapter 5, quiet recalcitrance, like reading a comic at the back of the class, is certainly seen as a problem in most lessons but it is far less urgent or threatening than noisy behaviour in class – possibly even noisy behaviour linked with the aims of the lesson itself. The problem of control, from the teacher's point of view, is first and foremost dictated by the need for privacy and only secondly by the desire to instigate learning in class. In answer to the question, 'What is control?', then, we are led to conclude that teachers themselves would take 'quiet orderliness' as the baseline for recognizing whether or not it exists because quiet orderliness serves to create the *impression* of control by preserving the privacy of the classroom situation. Pupil-initiated noise, in contrast, tends to symbolize the absence of control and it is noisy pupil behaviour which creates the most urgent control problems during lessons.

Teacher competence is dependent on informal modes of understanding and action
Teacher competence, it has been evident, is largely bound up with informal practices, informal interpretations of events and a general understanding of the situation which comes from the community of teachers. Competence, therefore, depends on becoming part of a culture. Competence as a teacher quite clearly does not come automatically as a result of the official mandate from society (Chapter 1) or official authority within the school organization (Chapter 2). Though both stress the responsibility of the teacher to control the class and delegate certain rights and duties in this respect, they provide no guarantee that a teacher will, in fact, be able to exercise control. In reality, *competence is to be found in action not in status.* Control, a prerequisiste to competence, demands a set of practices that need to be learnt and administered in accord with the situation and neither an official mandate nor teaching qualifications for that matter act as the basis for this (Denscombe, 1980c).

The question is, where do teachers learn the kind of interpretation and action that allows them to be competent? The answer, arrived at in Chapters 1, 2 and 3, is that it is not to be found in the official kinds of directives about teacher behaviour because, at best, these provided only scant outlines covering broad objectives and, at worst, they could prove hopelessly irrelevant or inadequate for the urgent needs of the teacher in the classroom. The law, local authority regulations and school rules give teachers certain rights and duties, and they dictate some of the methods available to the teacher in the classroom but, in practice, no teacher could succeed through relying on these skeleton rules. It is no use either, as we saw in Chapter 2, expecting pedagogies to provide the answer because, here again, the suggestions for actions are geared to broad parameters of action and based on ideal principles rather than the complex and harsh realities of the classroom situation. What teachers need in order to survive and emerge as 'competent' are detailed grounds for acting in the classroom – something that will cover the routine, practical, day-to-day problems that arise in class. They need something geared to the real world of the classroom with its intricate and complicated social relationships and something geared to the demands they meet during lessons for immediate decisions on a host of simultaneous things.

Where, then, do the rules for action come from? They come, in the first place, from the community of teachers who, to some extent, share a culture. They share certain beliefs about the job that do not arise from official rules and policies but which are generated and perpetuated nformally by social contact in school. There is, as in most occupations, an nformal culture amongst teachers and it is this culture that goes a long way to providing the entrant to the profession with a way of seeing events and making decisions in a 'competent' fashion. There is, as we suggested in Chapter 2, a *Hidden Pedagogy* contained in the culture of teaching which provides guidelines for teacher activity and which is the basis for teacher competence. In every sense the Hidden Pedagogy is an *informal* phenomenon. It is, none the less a powerful and pervasive feature of the world of teaching and one that new entrants to the profession are generally primed to accept. Their willingness to embrace the Hidden Pedagogy, as Chapter 2 indicated, comes from their classroom experience as pupils in which, having observed teachers at work over a long period of time, they developed a shrewd picture of what competence as a teacher required. This picture seems to become deep-set enough to resist the principles of pedagogy espoused during training and emerge relatively unscathed soon after the newcomer enters the classroom as a teacher. There is, in other words, a rather fundamental continuity in the world of teaching based on classroom experience, first as a pupil and later as a teacher, and this perpetuates the Hidden Pedagogy. Clasroom control, of course, figures highly in this and, for those who embrace this Hidden Pedagogy, there are implicit guidelines for action which govern what they interpret as disruptive behaviour, what they should treat as a control problem and what priority should be given to remedy different sorts of behaviour.

The Hidden Pedagogy can be a subtle source of resistance to innovation
Any innovation which is to be effective has to be accepted and implemented by those who work at the chalk-face – the teachers. From what we know about teachers' understanding of their situation, however, there are some things which are likely to prove unacceptable. The reason for this, following the notion of the Hidden Pedagogy, is that classroom experience presents itself to teachers as a reality that dictates which practices are reasonable and which are not. Classroom experience, in effect, renders some kind of alternative practices completely unthinkable. This does not mean that the alternatives are incomprehensible – certainly just about all aspects of, for instance, liberal, progressive pedagogy make sense to teachers in as much as the ideas and ambitions can be grasped. What it means is that some of the ideas linked with such pedagogies are regarded as unfeasible and, in this sense, unrealistic. In a manner of speaking, then, classroom experience has a hegemonic influence by controlling the range of alternatives that can be considered as real possibilities and, more to the point, by excluding others.

Teachers, of course, are aware that decisions about staffing, material resources and classroom design are essentially political decisions and that, ultimately, these can be swayed by political means. Yet at the same time as acknowledging the politically inspired source of their predicament, teachers tend to gear their working lives towards coping with existing circumstances rather than striving to change these by political action. The classroom arena and the political arena are seen, for the most part, as quite distinct arenas of activity with the kind of activity appropriate for the classroom having to accept rather than negotiate the circumstances found to exist. The resources, clientele and classrooms are things that teachers, as individuals, can do little to alter in the short run and the dilemma facing them is that, while they might not support the policy decisions which create the classroom circumstances and might even be politically active in fighting those policies, in the classroom they can hardly ignore the prevailing conditions.

The constraints experienced as a result of these 'prevailing conditions' act as the basis for a conservatism in the practice of teaching. They persuade teachers to avoid certain kinds of innovatory practice. In particular, as we can see from Chapters 5 and 6, those innovations that threaten the privacy of the classroom by undermining the autonomy of the teacher or by generating increased (pupil-initiated) noise are the kind that create anxiety amongst experienced staff because, however innocuous such innovations might appear at first glance, they are extremely radical and fly in the face of both tradition and, possibly more important, the prevailing classroom conditions.

The material circumstances that shape classroom experience, then, would seem to provide the basis for a deep-rooted conservatism of practice amongst teachers. The circumstances foster an emphasis on the autonomy and control of teachers as individuals over both the conduct of pupils and the content of the syllabus and this effectively complements the hidden curriculum of schooling by encouraging the teachers to approach their job in such a way that generation after generation of pupils experience a socialization that stresses the need to acquiesce to official authority, to tolerate boredom and to accept the right of specific individuals to be the final arbiters of knowledge, truth and fairness. More than this the prevailing circumstances explain how and why these facets of the dominant ideology continue to be transmitted via schooling despite liberal pedagogies espoused in training establishments and despite personal pedagogic preferences on the part of individual teachers in schools.

Classroom control is context specific
Throughout this book we have stressed the need to recognize classroom control as a context-specific phenomenon. From a sociological perspective

t is absurd to treat classroom control in absolute terms as consisting of an objective set of criteria. Answering the question, 'What is classroom control?', we have seen that it depends on the circumstances, and what we have done is to explore the way the prevailing circumstances of the closed classroom moulds teachers' and pupils' understandings about classroom control. The contrast with Cedars served to emphasize the point that what passes for control depends on the situation at hand. The same applies, of course, in terms of the differing demands imposed by 'low achievement oriented' schools when compared with more academically oriented schools. Though classroom control remains fundamental to teacher competence in either instance, its importance as an indicator of successful teaching, will obviously be far greater in the former type of school. Again, we have to see how the nature of classroom control varies according to the particular time. Different times of the day, week or term, and even different phases during a lesson, carry with them implications for classroom control in the sense that they each invoke different standards by which to judge whether behaviour is 'out of control'.

Diagnosis to prognosis: recommendations concerning classroom control

The purpose of this book has been first and foremost to describe and analyse the reality of classroom control as perceived by those involved. There has been no attempt to suggest how things *ought* to be, and not too much emphasis on how things *might* be other than in the comparison of the open classrooms at Cedars with the closed classrooms of Ashton and Beechgrove. Having now reflected on the participants' experience of the phenomenon of classroom control, the concluding chapter would not be complete without some brief comment in the form of recommendations based on the description and analysis.

Such recommendations will be necessarily limited in their scope and attention because there are aspects of the phenomenon of classroom control which are so fundamentally interwoven with current conceptions of schooling that certain possible recommendations for change get ruled out of order. Consider, for instance, compulsory attendance at school. It gives rise to a level of resentment and hostility by pupils irrespective of the skills of particular teachers or the specific ethos of the school. Resistance and opposition are, for all intents and purposes, made inevitable by compulsory attendance at schools whose organization rests heavily on disparities of authority between teachers and pupils, rigid and heavy workloads determined by the curriculum, and spatial boundaries dictated by the closed classroom. Obliged to attend, pupils are also obliged to sit through lessons and follow a pattern of learning more or less set in the subject syllabus. They are obliged to conform to timetables, standards of dress and hierarchies of authority that might lead a visiting alien to wonder why the body of pupils are so passive. A stranger might be forgiven for asking why there is so little retaliation by pupils in a setting that is blatantly hostile to their personal liberties and identity. Indeed, in view of their experience of schooling, the outsider would seem justified in posing the curious sounding question: 'Why is there not more conflict, disruption and violence in today's schools?'

Herded like sheep and denied basic rights, a conflict of interests is more or less built into conventional schooling in a way that only massive moves in the direction of deschooling seem likely to cure. For most of the public, most of the politicians and most of the educationalists, however, deschooling measures appear to seem unpalatable, unrealistic or futuristic, and for them the whole issue of control is limited in scope to suggestions that can be contained within the contemporary, conventional notion of schooling. The question becomes how to minimize and/or resolve control problems within the context of compulsory attendance at formally organized schools. And here attention must get focused on changes that can be made to the motivation of the pupils, or the skills of the teachers, or the organizational context within which lessons occur. Clearly any recommendations to emerge from this study will concern the last of these – the organizational context.

An obvious example of how this sociological account of classroom control suggests changes in school organization arises in connection with the noise in classrooms. In Chapter 5, noise was shown to pose a very significant problem for teachers because, if it impinged on adjacent classes, it could both interrupt the lessons and signify a lack of control. Measures to reduce the prospects of noise impinging on adjacent classes would presumably have an influence on the social constraints governing teaching, relaxing the social pressures for quietness and first allowing experimental, innovative approaches whose noisiness might otherwise inhibit their introduction and second, reducing teacher sensitivity to noisy pupil (mis)behaviour at the expense of devoting attention to the quiet resisters. In the context of the closed classroom such measures would involve relatively inexpensive action towards soundproofing rooms. Walls, floors and furniture could be designed with the understanding that by soundproofing classrooms basic social pressure on teachers entailed in the Hidden Pedagogy can be reduced or possibly removed.

Attention to soundproofing will enhance the isolation of lessons and, in this way, reinforce the emphasis of closed classrooms on privacy. But, as the example of humanities teaching Cedars suggested, control problems can be eased for teachers where they work in teams in open plan classrooms. The research on these contexts revealed grounds for suggesting that architectural and organizational changes that actually *reduce* privacy and teacher autonomy might have benefits in the way they would allow teachers mutual support in their efforts to establish control. This, in turn, would reduce control anxiety (particularly amongst newcomers) and aid the professional induction of trainee and probationary teachers. Organizational moves to open up the closed classroom would go some way towards breaking the traditional Hidden Pedagogy of teaching in the closed classroom with its (context specific, social construction of) control based on privacy.

Such recommendations clearly use the ethnographic material on classroom control as a way of bolstering teachers' efforts to impose control and improve standards of teacher competence. They also expose the value-laden nature of recommendations that assume the status quo as their basis and then propose remedies for existing 'problems' – a point raised right at the start of this book. They beg the question: 'Why should we want to help teachers impose classroom control in the first place?' An immediately appealing answer to the question lies with the so-called 'crisis' of control in today's schools. But as we saw in Chapter 1, without adopting a complacent attitude towards the issue of control, it seems that such a 'crisis' might owe more to a figment of media sensationalism and political rhetoric than a genuine, proven breakdown in the fabric of authority in schools. It became apparent from the discussions of Chapter 1 that, despite social, political and educational importance attached to standards of control in schools, there was surprisingly little hard data on which to assess the situation. The research that *has* been conducted, however, reveals a situation where control problems are generally more along the lines of disruption than violence. To the extent that violence against teachers in schools gets reported and recorded, it appears to be relatively rare – although violence against pupils committed by other pupils, or by teachers in the form of corporal punishment, is another matter.

In the event, the resistance that does occur would seem to be fairly muted. Certainly physical violence perpetrated by pupils against teachers, other pupils or property is a reality of school life. But it is nothing new and it is not rampant. So far as those in the front line are concerned it is the frequency and level of disruptive behaviour, disorderly conduct, cheekiness, indiscipline, laziness, uncooperativeness and verbal abuse which are the most fundamental aspects of the control problem and these are something to be dealt with by the professional capacities of normal teachers. This does not deny the value of educational psychologists, remedial education or the broader notion of special education needs involving a minority of pupils who have difficulty in adjusting to the impositions and demands of school life. It does, on the other hand, make the point that the main problem of classroom control today is one of disruptive behaviour rather than violent behaviour and that, at the present time in Britain, the profession of teachers is not clamouring for assistance from external agencies whether in the form of security patrols or the wholesale segregation of troublesome pupils.

In parts of New York City and other notorious areas in the U.S.A. the same does not apply. Nor need it continue to apply in places like Britain, Australia, Canada and so on. In view of the appalling levels of youth unemployment in the Western industrialized world – especially amongst minority groups – we have to ask whether the period leading up to the year 2000 will not witness a marked increase in school violence and indiscipline if, and when, the social conflict and tensions existing outside the school gates become more of a feature of social relations in school and if, and when, the utter despair and frustration of those who face a lifetime on the (un)employment scrapheap spills over into open resentment against the pointless hoops and hurdles their school life entails. In Britain in 1985, it is difficult to foresee anything other than increased youth unemployment staved off temporarily by special employment schemes for school-leavers. Whether this is a portent of wholesale violence in tomorrow's schools is less easy to foretell. In the 1960s and 1970s who would have envisaged 4 million people unemployed in Britain without also foreseeing riots and rebellion on the streets? Yet this has not come about in anything other than sporadic and relatively isolated incidents. Perhaps schools will manage to cope with the situation in a way that avoids widening violence. If they do, it will probably be because they have moved with the social tide and not stood firm on antiquated values and standards. A particular strength of David Hargreave's *The Challenge for the Comprehensive School* (1982) was the plea he makes for increased respect for the dignity of pupils. To allow that dignity where it matters, the ethos of schools will have to change with the realities of society. Viable schooling will demand increasing sensitivity to issues such as women's rights and ethnic minority rights. If the identity and dignity of such groups are not catered for the band of disaffected pupils will increase and the basic acquiescence on which school order exists will become more fragile than ever.

Attempts to reinstate Victorian values will provide only a recipe for resistance and rebellion by pupils for whom such values are irrelevant and repressive. What is needed instead is a relaxation of the three Rs of control – rules, rituals and regimentation – to allow a more informal, less authoritarian basis on which to conduct daily life in schools. By loosening the reins there is the hope of avoiding the indignation and resentment that repressive control measures will bottle up, releasing the pressure rather than waiting for a mighty explosion. In the light of pupils' views on control, in the light of teachers' attitudes towards control, and on the basis of the sociological analysis conducted in this book, it seems clear that attempts to repress the opposition to authority and to impose a work ethic would fly in the face of recent developments in schools and would certainly go against the tide of social history. The attempts would be, in every sense of the word, unrealistic. So in nutshell the prognosis is this: with traditional deference to teacher authority diminishing (along with traditional authority in society), with heightened awareness of their separate identity by large sections of the pupil population, and with diminishing prospects of relying on appeals to the work ethic or the need for educational qualifications, the possibility of classroom control will rest on the ability of schools to adapt and reflect the social changes rather than try to hold fast on outdated domination strategies for control.

References

Acton, T. A. (1980), 'Educational criteria of success', *Educational Research*, vol. 22, no. 5, pp. 163–73.

Adams, R. S. and Biddle, B. J. (1970), *Realities of Teaching* (New York: Holt, Rinehart & Winston).

Althusser, L. (1971), 'Ideology and ideological state apparatuses', in L. Althusser, *Lenin and Philosophy and other essays* (London: New Left Books).

Anderson, J. G. (1968), *Bureaucracy in Education* (Baltimore, Md: Johns Hopkins Press).

Anyon, J. (1981), 'Social class and school knowledge', *Curriculum Inquiry*, vol. II, no. 1.

Apple, M. W. (1982) *Education and Power* (London: Routledge & Kegan Paul).

Association of Education Committees (1975), *Survey of Violence, Indiscipline and Vandalism in Schools* (London: Department of Education and Science).

Bagley, C. (1975), 'The background of deviance in black children in London', in Bagley, C. and Verma, G. (eds) *Race and Education Across Cultures* (London: Heinemann).

Bagley, C. (1976), 'Behavioural deviance in ethnic minority children: a review of published studies', *New Community*, vol. 5, no. 3, pp. 230–8.

Bagley, C. (1979), 'A comparative perspective on the education of black children in Britain', *Comparative Education*, vol. 15, no. 1, pp. 63–81.

Bagley C., Mallick, K. and Verma, G. (1978), 'Pupil self-esteem: a comparison of black and white teenagers in British schools', in Bagley, C. and Verma, G. (eds) *Race, Education and Identity* (London: Macmillan).

Ball, S. J. (1980), 'Mixed ability teaching: the worksheet method', *Brit. J. Educational Technology*, vol. 11, no, 1, pp. 36–48.

Ball, S. J. (1981), *Beachside Comprehensive* (Cambridge: Cambridge University Press).

Banks, O. (1976), *The Sociology of Education* (3rd edn) (London: Batsford).

Barrell, G. (1975), *Teachers and the Law* (4th edn) (London: Methuen).

Bennett, B. and Martin, K. (1980), *The Practice of Teaching* (London: Harper & Row.

Bennett, N. (1976), *Teaching Styles and Pupil Progress* (London: Open Books).

Bernbaum, G. (1972), 'At the school level', in *Case Studies of Educational Innovation* (Paris: OECD).

Bernstein, B. (1977), 'Class and pedagogies: visible and invisible', in J. Karabel and A. H. Halsey (eds), *Power and Ideology In Education* (New York: Oxford University Press).

Bidwell, G. E. (1965), 'The school as a formal organization', in J. March (ed.), *Handbook of Organization* (Chicago: Rand McNally).

Bird, C. (1980), 'Deviant labelling in school, the pupils' perspective' in P. Woods, (ed.), *Pupil Strategies* (London: Croom-Helm).

Blackham, G. J. (1967), *The Deviant Child in the Classroom* (Belmont, Ca: Wadsworth).

Bossert, S. T. (1979), *Tasks and Social Relationships in the Classroom* (Cambridge: Cambridge University Press).

Bourdieu, P. (1977), 'Cultural reproduction and social reproduction', in J. Karabel and A. H. Halsey (eds), *Power and Ideology in Education* (New York: Oxford University Press).

Bowles, S. and Gintis, H. (1976), *Schooling in Capitalist America* (London: Routledge & Kegan Paul).

Breed, G. and Colaiuta, V. (1974), 'Looking, blinking and sitting: non-verbal dynamics in the classroom', *J. Communication*, vol. 24, no. 2, pp. 75–81.

Burgess, R. G. (1983), *Experiencing Comprehensive Education* (London: Methuen).

Butcher, H. J. (1965), 'The attitudes of student teachers to education', *Brit. J. Social and Clinical Psychology*, vol. 4, no. 1, pp. 17–24.

Carrington, B. (1983), 'Sport as a side-track', in L. Barton and S. Walker (eds) *Race, Class and Education* (London: Hutchinson).

Centre for Contemporary Cultural Studies (1981), *Unpopular Education: Schooling and Social Democracy in England since 1944* (London: Hutchinson).

Chamberlain, L. J. (1969), *Team Teaching: Organization and Administration* (Columbus, Ohio: Merrill).

Cicourel, A. V. and Kitsuse, J. I. (1963), *The Educational Decision-Makers* (New: York: Bobbs-Merrill).

Cicourel, A. V. and Kitsuse, J. I. (1968), 'The social organization of the high school and deviant adolescent careers',in E. Rubington and M. S. Weinberg (eds), *Deviance: The Interactionist Perspective* (Toronto: Collier Macmillan).

Clarricoates, K. (1978), '"Dinosaurs in the classroom" – a re-examination of some aspects of the "hidden" curriculum in primary schools', *Women's Studies International Quarterly*, vol. 1, pp. 353–64.

Coard, B. (1971) *How the West Indian child is made educationally sub-normal in the British school system* (London: New Beacon).

Cochrane, R. (1979) 'Psychological and behavioural disturbances in West Indians, Indians and Pakistanis in Britain', *Brit. J. Psychiatry*, vo. 134, pp. 201–10.

Cohen, L. and Manion, L. (1981), *Perspective on Classrooms and Schools* (London: Holt, Rinehart & Winston).

Coleman, J. S. (1961), *The Adolescent Society* (New York: Free Press).

Comber, L. C. and Whitfield, R. C. (1979), *Action on Indiscipline: a Practical Guide for Teachers* (Hemel Hempstead: NAS/UWT.).

Corbishley, P. *et al.* (1981), 'Teacher strategies and pupil identities in mixed ability curricula', in L. Barton and S. Walker (eds) *Schools, Teachers and Teaching* (Lewes: Falmer).

Corrigan, P. (1979), *Schooling the Smash Street Kids* (London: Macmillan).

Coulter, F. and Taft, R. (1973), 'The professional socialization of school teachers as social assimilation', *Human Relations*, vol. 26, no. 6, pp. 681–94.

Cox, C. B. and Boyson, R. (eds) (1975), *Black Papers 1975: the Fight for Education* (London: Dent).

Cox, C. B. and Boyson, R. (eds) (1977), *Black Paper 1977* (London: Temple Smith).

Cox, C. B. and Dyson, A. E. (eds) (1969–70), *Black Papers I–III* (London: Critical Quarterly Society).

Curwin, R. L. and Mendler, A. N. (1980), *The Discipline Book: a Complete Guide to School and Classroom Management* (Reston, Va: Reston).

Davies, L. (1978), 'The view from the girls', *Educational Review*, vol. 30, no. 2, pp. 103–9.

Davies, L (1979), 'Deadlier than the male? Girls' conformity and deviance in school', in L. Barton and R. Meighan (eds) *Schools, Pupils and Deviance* (Driffield: Nafferton).

Davis, H. (1966), *How to Organize an Effective Team Teaching Program* (Englewood Cliffs, NJ: Prentice Hall).

Davis, K. and Moore, W. E. (1945), 'Some principles of stratification', *American Sociological Review*, vol. 10, no. 2, pp. 242–9.

Dawson, R. L. (1980), *Special Provisions for Disturbed Pupils: a Survey* (London: Macmillan/Schools Council).

Deem, R. (1978), *Women and Schooling* (London: Routledge & Kegan Paul).

Delamont, S. (1980), *Sex Roles and the School* (London: Methuen).

Delamont, S. (1983), *Interaction in the Classroom*, second edition (London: Methuen).

Denscombe, M. (1977), *The Social Organization of Teaching* (unpublished Ph.D. thesis: University of Leicester).

Denscombe, M. (1980a), 'Keeping 'em quiet: the significance of noise for the practical activity of teaching', in P. Woods (ed.), *Teacher Strategies* (London: Croom-Helm).

Denscombe, M. (1980b), 'Pupil strategies and the open classroom', in P. Woods (ed.), *Pupil Strategies* (London: Croom-Helm).

Denscombe, M. (1980c), 'The work context of teaching: an analytic framework for the study of teaching', *Brit. J. Sociology of Education*, vol. 1, no. 3, pp. 279–92.

Denscombe, M. (1981), 'Organization and innovation in schools: a case study of team teaching', *School Organization*, vol. 1, no. 3, pp. 195–210.

Denscombe, M. (1982), 'The "Hidden Pedagogy" and its implications for teacher training', *Brit. J. Sociology of Education*, vol. 3, no. 3, pp. 249–65.

Denscombe, M. (1983), 'Interviews, accounts and ethnographic research on teachers', in M. Hammersley (ed.), *Ethnography of Schooling* (Driffield: Nafferton).

Department of Education and Science (1981), *Interim Report of the Committee of Inquiry into the Education of Children from Ethnic Minority Groups: West Indian Children in Our Schools* ('The Rampton Report') (London: HMSO).

Dierenfield, R. (1982), 'All you need to know about disruption', *Times Educational Supplement*, 29 January, 1982.

Docking, J. W. (1980), *Control and Discipline in Schools* (London: Harper & Row).

Dreeben, R. (1970), *The Nature of Teaching* (Glenview, Ill.: Scott Foresman).

Dreeben, R. (1973), 'The school as a workplace', in R. M. W. Travers (ed.), *Second Handbook of Research on Teaching* (Chicago: Rand McNally).

Dumont, R. V. and Wax, M. L. (1969), 'Cherokee school society and the intercultural classroom', *Human Organization*, vol. 28, no. 3, pp. 217–26.

Durkheim, E. (1925) *Moral Education* (New York: Free Press).

Durkheim, E. (1956), *Education and Sociology* (New York: Free Press).

Edgar, D. E. (ed.) (1974), *The Competent Teacher* (Sydney: Angus & Robertson).

Eggen, P. D. *et al.* (1979), *Strategies for Teachers* (Englewood Cliffs, NJ: Prentice Hall).

Eggleston, J. (ed.) (1979), *Teacher Decision-Making in the Classroom* (London: Routledge & Kegan Paul).

Evans, J. (1982), *Teacher Strategies and Pupil Identities in Mixed Ability Curricula: a Case Study* (unpublished Ph.D. thesis: University of London, Chelsea College).

Forward, R. W. (1971), *Teaching Together* (Themes in Education, no. 27) (University of Exeter, Institute of Education).

Francis, P. (1975), *Beyond Control? A Study of Discipline in the Comprehensive School* (London: George Allen & Unwin).

Freeman, J. (1969), *Team Teaching in Britain* (London: Ward Lock Educational).

Fuller, M. (1980), 'Black girls in a London comprehensive school', in R. Deem (ed.), *Schooling for Women's Work* (London: Routledge & Kegan Paul).

Fuller, M. (1982), 'Young, female and black', in E. Cashmore and B. Troyna (eds), *Black Youth in Crisis* (London: George Allen & Unwin).

Fuller, M. (1983), 'Qualified criticism, critical qualifications', in L. Barton and S. Walker (eds), *Race, Class and Education* (London: Croom-Helm).

Furlong, V. J. (1976), 'Interaction sets in the classroom', in M. Hammersley and P. Woods (eds), *The Process of Schooling* (London: Routledge & Kegan Paul).

Galloway, D. *et al.* (1982), *Schools and Disruptive Pupils* (London: Longman).

Galton, M. *et al.* (1980), *Progress and Performance in the Primary Classroom* (London: Routledge & Kegan Paul).

Gannaway, H. (1976), 'Making sense of school', in M. Stubbs and S. Delamont (eds), *Explorations in Classroom Observation* (London: Wiley).

Gillham, B. (ed.) (1981), *Problem Behaviour in the Secondary School* (London: Croom-Helm).

Giroux, H. A. (1981), *Ideology, Culture and the Process of Schooling* (London: Falmer).

Glaser, B. G. and Strauss, A. L. (1967), *The Discovery of Grounded Theory* (London: Weidenfeld & Nicolson).

Gnagey, W. J. (1975), *Maintaining Discipline in Classroom Instruction* (New York: Macmillan).

Gnagey, W. J. (1981), *Motivating Classroom Discipline* (New York: Macmillan).

Goffman, E. (1968), *Asylums* (Harmondsworth: Penguin).

Grace, G. (1972), *Role Conflict and the Teacher* (London: Routledge & Kegan Paul).

Grace, G. (1978), *Teachers, Ideology and Control: a Study in Urban Education* (London: Routledge & Kegan Paul).

Gramsci, A. (1971), *Selections from the Prison Notebooks* (London: Lawrence & Wishart).

Gray, H. L. (1979), *The School as an Organization* (Driffield: Nafferton).

Guthrie, I. D. (1979), *The Sociology of Pastoral Care in an Urban School* (unpublished MA dissertation: University of London, King's College).

Haigh, G. (ed.) (1979), *On Our Side: Order, Authority and Interaction in School* (London: Maurice Temple Smith).

Hammersley, M. (1974), 'The organization of pupil participation', *Sociological Review*, vol. 22, no. 3, pp. 355–68.

Hammersley, M. (1976), 'The mobilisation of pupil attention', in M. Hammersley and P. Woods (eds), *The Process of Schooling* (London: Routledge & Kegan Paul).

Hammersley, M. (1980), 'Classroom ethnography', *Educational Analysis*, vol. 2, no. 2, pp. 47–74.

Hammersley, M. (ed.) (1983), *Ethnography of Schooling* (Driffield: Nafferton).

Hannan, A. W. (1978), *Problems, Conflicts and School Policy: a Case Study of an Innovative Comprehensive School* (unpublished Ph.D. thesis: University of Leicester).

Hanson, D. (1975), 'The reality of classroom life', *New Society*, 4 September.

Hanson, D. and Herrington, M. (1976), *From College to Classroom* (London: Routledge & Kegan Paul).

Hargreaves, A. (1977), 'Progressivism and pupil autonomy', *Sociological Review*, vol. 25, no. 3, pp. 585–621.

Hargreaves, A. (1978), 'The significance of classroom coping strategies' in L. Barton and R. Meighan (eds), *Sociological Interpretations of Schooling and Classrooms* (Driffield: Nafferton).

Hargreaves, A. (1979), 'Strategies, decisions and control: interaction in a middle school classroom', in J. Eggleston (ed.), *Teacher Decision-Making in the Classroom* (London: Routledge & Kegan Paul).

Hargreaves, A. (1982), 'Resistance and relative autonomy theories: problems of distortion and incoherence in recent Marxist analyses of education', *Brit. J. Sociology of Education*, vol. 3, no. 2, pp. 107–26.

Hargreaves, D. H. (1967), *Social Relations in a Secondary School* (London: Routledge & Kegan Paul).

Hargreaves, D. H. *et al.* (1975), *Deviance in Classrooms* (London: Routledge & Kegan Paul).

Hargreaves, D. H. (1981), 'Schooling for delinquency', in L. Barton and S. Walker (eds), *Schools, Teachers and Teaching* (Lewes: Falmer).

Hargreaves, D. H. (1982), *The Challenge for the Comprehensive School* (London: Routledge & Kegan Paul).

Harris, K. (1982), *Teachers and Classes: a Marxist Analysis* (London: Routledge & Kegan Paul).

Haynes, J. (1971), *Educational Assessment of Immigrant Pupils* (Slough: NFER).

Her Majesty's Inspectorate of Schools (1978), *Behavioural Units: a Survey of Special Units for Pupils with Behavioural Problems* (London: HMSO).

Her Majesty's Inspectorate of Schools (1979), *Aspects of Secondary Education in England* (London: HMSO).

Her Majesty's Inspectorate of Schools (1982a), *Content of Initial Teacher Training Courses for Teachers* (London: HMSO).

Her Majesty's Inspectorate of Schools (1982b), *The New Teacher in the School* (London: HMSO).

Herman, D. (1972), 'Asian girls are the best behaved', *Times Educational Supplement*, 5 May.

Hoetker, J. and Ahlbrand, W. (1969), 'The persistence of the recitation', *American Educational Research Journal*, vol. 6, no. 2, pp. 145–67.

Hoy, W. K. (1967), 'Organizational socialization: the student teacher and pupil control ideology', *Educational Research*, vol. 61, no. 4, pp. 153–5.

Hoy, W. K. (1968), 'The influence of experience on the beginning teacher', *School Review*, vol. 76, pp. 312–23.

Hoy, W. K. (1969), 'Pupil control ideology and organizational socialization', *School Review*, vol. 77, pp. 257–65.

Hoy, W. K. (1974), 'Pupil control ideologies', in D. E. Edgar (ed.), *The Competent Teacher* (Sydney: Angus & Robertson).

Hoy, W. K. and Rees, R. (1977), 'The bureaucratic socialization of student teachers', *J. Teacher Education*, vol. 28, no. 1, pp. 23–6.

Humphries, S. (1981), *Hooligans or Rebels? An Oral History of Working Class Childhood and Youth 1889–1939* (Oxford: Blackwell).

Hunter, C. (1980), 'The politics of participation', in P. Woods (ed.), *Teacher Strategies* (London: Croom-Helm).

Jackson, P. W. (1968), *Life in Classrooms* (New York: Holt, Rinehart & Winston).

Jeffcoate, R. (1984), *Ethnic Minorities and Education* (London: Harper & Row).

Jones-Davies, C. and Cave, R. G. (eds) (1976), *The Disruptive Pupil in the Secondary School* (London: Ward Lock).

Keddie, N. (1971), 'Classroom knowledge', in M. F. D. Young (ed.), *Knowledge and Control* (London: Collier Macmillan).

Kelly, A. V. (1974), *Teaching Mixed-Ability Classes* (London: Harper & Row).

King, R. (1983), *The Sociology of School Organization* (London: Methuen).

Kohl, H. R. (1970), *The Open Classroom* (London: Methuen).

Kounin, J. (1970), *Discipline and Group Management in Classrooms* (New York: Holt, Rinehart & Winston).

Kuhlman, E. L. and Hoy, W. K. (1974), 'The socialization of professionals into bureaucracies: the beginning teacher in the school', *J. Educational Administration*, vol. 12, no. 2, pp. 18–27.

Lacey, C. (1970), *Hightown Grammar* (Manchester: University of Manchester Press).

Lacey, C. (1977), *The Socialization of Teachers* (London: Methuen).

Lambart, R. (1966), 'The public schools: a sociological introduction', in G. Kalton (ed.), *The Public Schools: a Factual Survey* (London: Longman).

Lambart, R. and Millham, S. (1968), *The Hothouse Society* (London: Weidenfeld & Nicolson).

Lambart, R. *et al.* (1970), *A Manual to the Sociology of the School* (London: Weidenfeld & Nicolson).

Lambart, R. *et al.* (1975), *The Chance of a Lifetime?* (London: Weidenfeld & Nicolson).

Laslett, R. (1977a), 'Disruptive and violent pupils: the facts and the fallacies', *Educational Review*, vol. 29, no. 3, pp. 152–62.

Laslett, R. (1977b), *Educating Maladjusted Children* (London: Crosby, Lockwood, Staples).

Lawrence, J. et al. (1977), *Disruptive Behaviour in a Secondary School* (London: Goldsmiths' College, University of London).

Lawrence, J. et al. (1983), 'Monitoring teachers' reports of incidents of disruptive behaviour in two secondary schools', *Educational Studies*, vol. 9, no. 2, pp. 81–91.

Leacock, E. B. (1969), *Teaching and Learning in City Schools* (New York: Basic Books).

Linton, T. E. (1966), *Social and Cultural Factors in Deviant Classroom Behavior* (Ottawa: Canada's Mental Health Supplement CMH no. 52).

Lomax, P. (1978), 'The attitudes of girls with varying degrees of school adjustment to different aspects of their school experience', *Educational Review*, vol. 30, no. 2, pp. 117–24.

Lortie, D. C. (1964), 'The teacher and team teaching: suggestions for long-range research', in J. T. Shaplin and H. F. Olds, jun. (eds), *Teach Teaching* (New York: Harper & Row).

Lortie, D. C. (1968), 'Shared ordeal and induction to work', in H. S. Becker et al. (eds) *Institutions and the Person* (Chicago: Aldine).

Lortie, D. C. (1969), 'The balance of control and autonomy in elementary school teaching', in A. Etzioni (ed.), *The Semi-Professions and their Organization* (New York: Free Press).

Lortie, D. C. (1973), 'Observations on teaching as work', in R. M. W. Travers (ed.), *Second Handbook of Research on Teaching* (Chicago: Rand McNally).

Lortie, D. C. (1975), *Schoolteacher: a Sociological Study* (Chicago: University of Chicago Press).

Lovell, K. (1967), *Team Teaching* (University of Leeds: Institutes of Education, Occasional Paper no. 5).

Lowenstein, L. (1972), *Violence in School: and its Treatment* (Hemel Hempstead: National Association of Schoolmasters).

Lowenstein, L. (1975), *Disruptive Behaviour in Schools* (Hemel Hempstead: National Association of Schoolmasters).

McIntyre, D. and Morrison, A. (1967), 'The educational opinions of teachers in training', *Brit. J. Social and Clinical Psychology*, vol. 6, no. 1, pp. 32–7.

McPherson, G. (1972), *Small Town Teacher* (Cambridge, Mass.: Harvard University Press).

Maddox, H. (1968), 'A descriptive study of teaching practice', *Educational Review*, vol. 20, no. 3, pp. 177–90.

Mardle, G. and Walker, M. (1979), 'Autonomy and organization: a theoretical perspective on teacher decisions', in J. Eggleston (ed.), *Teacher Decision-Making in the Classroom* (London: Routledge & Kegan Paul).

Mardle, G. and Walker, M. (1980), 'Strategies and structure: some critical notes on teacher socialization', in P. Woods (ed.), *Teacher Strategies* (London: Croom-Helm).

Marland, M. (1975), *The Craft of the Classroom* (London: Heinemann).

Marsh, P. et al. (1978), *The Rules of Disorder* (London: Routledge & Kegan Paul).

Martin, W. B. W. (1975), 'The negotiated order of teachers in team teaching situations', *Sociology of Education*, vol. 48, no. 2, pp. 202–22.

Metz, M. (1978), *Classrooms and Corridors: the Crisis of Authority in Desegregated Secondary Schools* (Los Angeles, Ca: University of California Press).

Meyenn, R. J. (1980), 'School girls peer groups', in P. Woods (ed.), *Pupil Strategies* (London: Croom-Helm).

Miller, G. (1970), *Educational Opportunity and the Home* (London: Longman).

Millman, H. L. et al. (1981), *Therapies for School Behavior Problems* (Hollywood, Ca: Jossey-Bass).

Mills, W. C. P. (1976), *The Seriously Disruptive Behaviour of Pupils in Secondary Schools in One Local Education Authority* (unpublished M.Ed. thesis: University of Birmingham).

Morrison, A. and McIntyre, D. (1967), 'Changes in opinions about education during the first year of teaching', *Brit. J. Social and Clinical Psychology*, vol. 6, no. 3, pp. 161-3.

Morrison, A. and McIntyre, D. (1969), *Teachers and Teaching* (Harmondsworth: Penguin).

Nash, R. (1976), 'Pupils' expectations of their teachers', in M. Stubbs and S. Delamont (eds) *Explorations in Classroom Behaviour* (London: Wiley).

O'Leary, K. D. and O'Leary, S. G. (1977), *Classroom Management: the Successful Use of Behavior Modification* (2nd edn) (Oxford: Pergamon).

Pack Report (1977), *Truancy and Indiscipline in Schools in Scotland* (Edinburgh: Scottish Education Department).

Paisey, A. (1981), *Organization and Management in Schools* (London: Longman).

Parsons, T. (1959), 'The school class as a social system', *Harvard Educational Review*, vol. 29, no. 4.

Payne, G. and Hustler, D. (1980), 'Teaching the class: the practical management of a cohort', *Brit. J. Sociology of Education*, vol. 1, no. 1, pp. 49-66.

Petty, M. F. and Hogben, D. (1980), 'Explorations of semantic space with beginning teachers: a study of socialization into teaching', *Brit. J. Teacher Education*, vol. 6, no. 1, pp. 51-61.

Pollard, A. (1982), 'A model of classroom coping strategies', *Brit. J. Sociology of Education*, vol. 3, no. 1, pp. 19-37.

Polos, N. C. (1965), *The Dynamics of Team Teaching* (Dubuque, Iowa: Brown).

Reid, M. I. et al. (1981), *Mixed Ability Teaching: Problems and Possibilities* (Windsor: NFER/Nelson).

Reynolds, D. and Sullivan, M. (1979), 'Bringing schools back in', in L. Barton and R. Meighan (eds), *Schools, Pupils and Deviance* (Driffield: Nafferton).

Robertson, J. (1981), *Effective Classroom Control* (London: Hodder & Stoughton).

Rogers, T. (1971), 'Looking to the future', in T. Rogers (ed.), *School for the Community* (London: Routledge & Kegan Paul).

Rutter, M. et al. (1974), 'Children of West Indian immigrants: rates of behavioural deviance and of psychiatric disorder', *J. Child Psychology and Psychiatry*, vol. 15, pp. 241-62.

Rutter, M. et al. (1979), *Fifteen Thousand Hours: Secondary Schools and their Effects on Children* (London: Open Books).

Saunders, M. (1979), *Class Control and Behaviour Problems* (London: McGraw-Hill).

Selznick, P. (1966), *TVA and the Grass Roots: a Study in the Sociology of Formal*

Organization (New York: Harper & Row).

Shaplin, J. (1964), 'Description and definition of team teaching', in J. Shaplin and H.F. Olds, jnr (eds) *Team Teaching* (New York: Harper & Row).

Sharp, R. and Green, A. (1975), *Education and Social Control* (London: Routledge & Kegan Paul).

Shipman, M. D. (1966), 'The assessment of teaching practice', *Education for Teaching*, vol. 70, no. 1, pp. 28–31.

Shipman, M. D. (1967), 'Theory and practice in the education of teachers', *Educational Research*, vol. 9, no. 2. pp. 208–12.

Sinclair, J. M. and Coulthard, R. M. (1975), *Towards an Analysis of Discourse: the English Used by Teachers and Pupils* (Oxford: Oxford University Press).

Sloane, H. N. (1976), *Classroom Management: Remediation and Prevention* (New York: Wiley).

Smith, L. M. and Geoffrey, W. (1968), *The Complexities of an Urban Classroom* (New York: Holt, Rinehart & Winston).

Snyder, B. R. (1971), *The Hidden Curriculum* (Cambridge, Mass.: MIT Press).

Sommer, R. (1967), 'Classroom ecology', *J. Applied Behavioral Science*, vol. 3, no. 4, pp. 489–503.

Spender, D. (1982), *Invisible Women: the Schooling Scandal* (London: Writers & Readers).

Stanworth, M. (1983), *Gender and Schooling* (London: Hutchinson).

Stebbins, R. (1970), 'The meaning of disorderly behavior', *Sociology of Education*, vol. 44, spring, pp. 217–36.

Stebbins, R. (1973), 'Physical context influences on behavior: the case of classroom disorderliness', *Environment and Behaviour*, vol. 5, no. 3, pp. 291–314.

Stebbins, R. (1980), 'The use of humour in teaching', P. Woods (ed.), *Teacher Strategies* (London: Croom-Helm).

Stenhouse, L. (ed.) (1967), *Discipline in Schools* (London: Pergamon).

Stewart, G. (1972), 'Crisis in the comprehensives', *Daily Mail*, 15 March.

Sugarman, B. (1967), 'Involvement in youth culture, academic achievement and conformity in schools', *Brit. J. of Sociology*, vol. 18, no. 2, pp. 151–64.

Swidler, A. (1979), *Organization without Authority* (Cambridge, Mass.: Harvard University Press).

Swift, D. W. (1971), *Ideology and Change in the Public Schools* (Columbus, Ohio: Merrill).

Tattum, D. (1982), *Disruptive Pupils in Schools and Units* (Chichester: Wiley).

Taylor, J. K. and Dale, I. R. (1971), *A Survey of Teachers in their First Year of Teaching* (Bristol: Bristol University Press).

Taylor, M. J. (1981), *Caught Between – a Review of Research into the Education of Pupils of West Indian Origin* (Slough: NFER).

Tomlinson, S. (1983), *Ethnic Minorities in British Schools – a Review of the Literature 1960–82* (London: Policy Studies Institute/Heinemann).

Torode, B. (1976), 'Teachers' talk and classroom discipline', in M. Stubbs and S. Delamont (eds), *Explorations in Classroom Observation* (London: Wiley).

Townsend, H. E. R. and Brittan, E. (1972), *Organization in Multiracial Schools*

(Slough: NFER).

Troyna, B. (1984), 'Fact or artefact? The "educational underachievement" of black pupils', *Brit. J. Sociology of Education*, vol. 5, no. 2, pp. 153–66.

Troyna, B. and Smith, D. (eds) (1983), *Racism, School and the Labour Market* (Leicester: National Youth Bureau).

Turner, R. H. (1971), 'Sponsored and contest mobility and the school system', in E. Hopper (ed.), *Readings in the Theory of Educational Systems* (London: Hutchinson).

Walberg, H. J. (1969), 'Physical and psychological distance in the classroom', *School Review*, vol. 77, no. 1, pp. 64–70.

Walker, R. and Adelman, C. (1976), 'Strawberries', in M. Stubbs and S. Delamont (eds), *Explorations in Classroom Observation* (London: Wiley).

Walker, R. and Goodson, I. (1977), 'Humour in the classroom', in P. Woods and M. Hammersley (eds), *School Experience* (London: Croom-Helm).

Walker, R. et al. (1973), *Teaching That's a Joke* (Norwich: CARE, University of East Anglia).

Waller, W. (1932), *The Sociology of Teaching* (New York: Wiley).

Warnes, T. (1975), 'French' in R. P. Davies (ed.), *Mixed-Ability Grouping* (London: Temple Smith).

Warren, R. L. (1973), 'The classroom as a sanctuary for teachers', *American Anthropologist*, vol. 75, no. 1, pp. 280–91.

Webb, J. (1962), 'The sociology of the school', *Brit. J. Sociology*, vol. 13, no. 3, pp. 264–72.

Westbury, I. (1973), 'Conventional classrooms, "open" classrooms and the technology of teaching', *J. Curriculum Studies*, vol. 5, no. 2, pp. 91–121.

White, M. A. and Charry, J. (1966), *School Disorder, Intelligence and Social Class* (New York: Columbia University Press).

Wilensky, H. R. (1964), 'The professionalization of everyone?', *American J. Sociology*, vol. 70, no. 2, pp. 137–58.

Williams, R. H. (1963), 'Professional studies in teacher training', *Education for Teaching*, vol. 61, no. 1, pp. 29–33.

Willis, P. (1977), *Learning to Labour* (London: Saxon House).

Willower, D. J. (1969), 'The teacher subculture and rites of passage', *Urban Education*, vol. 4, no. 2, pp. 103–14.

Willower, D. J. et al. (1973), *The School and Pupil Control Ideology* (1st edn 1967) (Pennsylvania: Pennsylvania State University Studies, no. 24).

Wilson, J. (1981), *Discipline and Moral Education: a Survey of Public Opinion and Understanding* (Windsor: NFER/Nelson).

Wiseman, S. and Start, K. B. (1965), 'A follow-up of teachers five years after completing their training', *Brit. J. Educational Psychology*, vol. 35, no. 3, pp. 342–61.

Woods, P. (1975), ' "Showing them up" in secondary school', in G. Chanan and S. Delamont (eds), *Frontiers of Classroom Research* (Slough: NFER).

Woods. P. (1976a), 'Having a laugh: an antidote to schooling', in M. Hammersley and P. Woods (eds), *The Process of Schooling* (London: Routledge & Kegan Paul).

Woods, P. (1976b), 'Pupils' views of school', *Educational Review*, vol. 28, no. 2, pp. 126–37.

Woods, P. (1977), 'Teaching for survival', in P. Woods and M. Hammersley (eds), *School Experience* (London: Croom-Helm).

Woods, P. (1978a), 'Relating to schoolwork: some pupil perceptions', *Educational Review*, vol. 30, no. 2, pp. 167–77.

Woods, P. (1978b), 'Negotiating the demands of schoolwork', *J. Curriculum Studies*, vol. 10, no. 4, pp. 309–29.

Woods, P. (1979), *The Divided School* (London: Routledge & Kegan Paul).

Woods, P. (1980a), *Teacher Strategies* (London: Croom-Helm).

Woods, P. (1980b), *Pupil Strategies* (London: Croom-Helm).

Woods, P. (1983), 'Coping at school through humour', *Brit. J. Sociology of Education*, (vol. 4, no. 2, pp. 111–24).

Young, M. F. D. (ed.) (1971), Knowledge and Control (London: Collier-Macmillan).

Author Index

Subject Index